Reason, Truth and Self

'*Reason, Truth and Self* is an honest and spritely attempt to counter the corrosive relativism of postmodernism. Far from old-fashioned, the author offers a sterling defence of Enlightenment virtues, including reason and truth. Highly recommended.'

Michael Ruse, *University of Guelph*

'Luntley's vivid delineation of the postmodern and its ancestry will be invaluable to all who seek structure in this area, and his balanced case for the reminting of our notions of reason, truth and self must be welcomed as a rare opportunity for fruitful controversy.'

Alistair Hannay, *University of Oslo*

Postmodernism has had a significant and divisive impact on late twentieth-century thought. Proponents of the postmodernist critique of absolute knowledge have felt it necessary to jettison the Enlightenment concepts of truth, reason and the self. Opponents of postmodernism have seized on this abandonment of rational standards to ignore the very real problems raised by the postmodernists. Michael Luntley provides a lively introduction to the debate and offers a clear and careful exposition of how rational standards can survive even if the main postmodernist critique of the Enlightenment is accepted.

Offering a philosophy of postmodernism that shows it is possible to have rational enquiry in our postmodern age, Michael Luntley's book is ideal for introductory courses in philosophy and the social sciences.

Michael Luntley is Senior Lecturer in Philosophy at the University of Warwick. He is the author of *Language, Logic and Experience* (1988) and *The Meaning of Socialism* (1989). He also plays the tenor sax.

Reason, Truth and Self

the postmodern reconditioned

Michael Luntley

London and New York

First published 1995
by Routledge
11 New Fetter Lane, London EC4P 4EE

Simultaneously published in the USA and Canada
by Routledge
29 West 35th Street, New York, NY 10001

Phototypeset in Times by Intype, London
Printed and bound in Great Britain by
Clays Ltd, St Ives PLC

British Library Cataloguing in Publication Data
A catalogue record for this book is available from the British Library

Library of Congress Cataloguing in Publication Data
Luntley, Michael, 1953–
    Reason, truth, and self : the postmodern reconditioned/Michael
    Luntley.
    p.   cm.
    Includes bibliographical references and index.
    1. Postmodernism – Controversial literature.   2. Philosophy.
    3. Relativity.   4. Reason.   5. Truth.   6. Self.   I. Title.
    B831.2.L86   1995
    149–dc20   95–14748

ISBN 0–415–11852–2 (hbk)
ISBN 0–415–11853–0 (pbk)

for
Chris, Sam and Nicky

Contents

Preface

This is a picture book. Its aim is to provide a picture of how we can continue to think about ourselves and our world as subject to the demands of truth and rationality while acknowledging the critique of those concepts that passes under the label 'postmodernism'. The book provides a picture of how this can be achieved. It does not seek to argue definitively for the truth of the picture. The picture is a comprehensive picture, but taken from a considerable distance in order to fit so much within the viewfinder. In order to argue satisfactorily to the truth of the position described one would need to look in much greater detail at everything that lies within the conceptual landscape I survey. But it has not been my purpose to convince you of the truth of the position described. My main purpose has been simply to exhibit the fact that a picture such as the one presented is so much as possible and makes a coherent whole.

The concepts of reason, truth and self have been central to the search for knowledge ever since the Enlightenment. They have been the motors for our achievements in science, history, art and literature. According to a growing number of contemporary thinkers these engines of enquiry are now thoroughly clapped out. Students in all faculties in our universities are familiar with the banner proclamations of the postmodernist loss of rational standards of belief. This supposed loss is regularly reported in the mass media.

The picture that I offer shows that much of the fuss about postmodernism is misconceived. It shows that, if you take the time to think through the detail of the criticisms levelled against the Enlightenment concepts of reason, truth and self, you will find that these concepts survive postmodernist critique and, appropriately refashioned, can continue to shape our sense of cognitive purpose. The picture I sketch is then offered to anyone who has wondered how to meet the designer despairs of postmodernist fashion. The picture is a philosophical picture, although it is of relevance to any student, especially of the arts and social sciences, with a concern for the foundations of their discipline.

The book is intended to be introductory; it might serve on a number of introductory courses in philosophy and sociology. It is not introductory in the sense that it offers a detailed introduction to all the topics covered, for, as noted, its chief aim is to provide a picture. However, it is intended to be introductory in the sense of offering a wide-ranging invitation to engage in the rescue of significant notions of truth, knowledge and reason from a set of premises from which too many claim that irrationalism is the only option.

This book grew out of work that I did on a series of programmes called 'The Real Thing' made by London Weekend Television for Channel Four and transmitted in August 1992. Philosophy does not often make for exciting television. The medium is predominantly visual and although philosophers are rarely short of things to say, the quality of their visual sense is generally inversely proportional to their ability to discourse. Accordingly, most television philosophy tends to be a radio discussion format with cameras rolling. However, in 'The Real Thing' Nick Metcalfe made the boldest attempt so far to think through the issue of how to make maximum use of the medium in constructing a televisual essay in philosophy. Audio and visual signals were filled with sounds and images in the effort to communicate some of the issues that surround postmodernism. The widespread communication of ideas is intrinsically subversive and 'The Real Thing' was mainline subversion.

Nick produced and directed the series. It was a pleasure to work with him and I am proud to have been associated with the result. Thanks Nick. Thanks also to Tom Boyd, Nick's research assistant, who first suggested to Nick that I should help relieve their conceptual headaches.

At one point I was going to write this book to accompany the television series, but various delays in scheduling and other production concerns meant that, in the end, there was too little time to get a manuscript completed before transmission. Instead I wrote a pamphlet, *The Real Thing*, that Channel Four published at transmission and I shelved the book that I had started. Two years on, the book has changed in tone. It resolves issues where the television programmes were content simply to raise them. It covers much greater ground than the programmes ever dared.

We had hoped that the television series would cover issues of agency, morals and politics. However, the need to work to the constraints of the medium meant that there simply was not the time available in the slots provided to cover as much as we had initially hoped. This book not only offers a picture of how to resolve the core issues about truth and knowledge raised by postmodernism, but also fills in the gaps on the nature of the self and its knowledge of morals and politics.

The last three chapters covering the self are much more exploratory than the rest of the book. The closing chapters are promissory notes towards further research. If there is anything original in what follows other than in the arrangement and order of presentation, it lies in the ideas about how to think through the contingency of the self. As noted, the aim of the book is to show the possibility of reconditioning reason, truth and self in the light of postmodernism. It is the reconditioning of the self that stands most in need of more detailed fine tuning. What I offer in the closing chapters is only a start in that direction.

At Warwick, Peter Poellner and Martin Warner have regularly helped me think through some of the issues that follow; thanks to them and to Steven Lukes whose seminar in Florence assisted in the exploration of early versions of some of the ideas that have now found their way into the chapters on the self. Thanks also to my doctoral students, who keep me on my toes, and especially to Eric Newbigging and Paul Sturdee, whose own projects I can locate in the genealogy of some of the ideas contained herein.

Dee provided the sanity and much else besides, and Chris, Sam and Nicky the immediate reason for caring about the sort of future we create.

Introduction

THE THREAT OF ANARCHY

Once upon a time the answer to the question 'What should I believe?' was relatively easy. You believed what your elders and betters told you. However, as a way of finding out the truth, this was not altogether reliable. Too many elders were mistaken about too many things. In early modern Europe, the idea gained ground that there was a method to employ in answering this question. It was the method of reason and experiment. It was the method exemplified in the new sciences. It was, in principle, a method available to anyone. The answer to the question 'What should I believe?' became 'Believe in the results of science.' Such faith in the methods and results of science has served us well. But the idea that scientific method is a reliable way of finding out the truth is now being undermined. It has become fashionable to question whether human reason conforms to any objective standards of belief. It has become fashionable to question whether there is such a thing as human reason at all.

The fashion to deny any objective standards of belief is sometimes called 'postmodernism'. That is not a particularly useful label. It has many connotations that obscure rather than assist discussion. Like any label it is not worth fighting over. Nevertheless, there are profound and important philosophical issues that underpin this fashion. This book is an exploration of those issues.

The central issue concerns whether or not there is a legitimate notion of what we ought to believe. This is a general question. It is the question about whether or not there is a legitimate concept of objective truth. We can ask this question with regard to different areas of enquiry. For example, we can ask: is there such a thing as what we ought to believe with regard to the natural world? Is there such a thing as what we ought to believe about the rules of conduct? Is there such a thing as what we ought to believe about art and literature? Asking these questions amounts to asking whether a concept of objective truth can be applied to our discourses about the natural world, about morality or aesthetics.

Most interesting of all, we can raise the question whether there is such a thing as what we ought to believe about ourselves. Does a concept of objective truth apply to our conception of ourselves and, if so, what kind of conception of self is available to form our self-understanding? What kind of creature are we? In the first instance, we can raise and attempt to settle the general philosophical issue about whether any concept of objective truth is available to us regardless of the area in which we want to apply truth.

It is the general critique of any notion of objective truth that underlies the contemporary fashion for thinking that there are no objective standards of belief. This fashion is most apparent in the field of morals and in the arts. It has also entered the arena of current affairs. By what standards, if any, are we to judge the *fatwa* which condemned Salman Rushdie to death – or, for that matter, to judge him for publishing a novel which blasphemes Islam? The apparent lack of standards for our beliefs is no idle academic affair.

The idea that there are no objective standards of belief is an idea that comes from many sources. In 1887 Nietzsche said that 'The greatest recent event – that "God is dead", that the belief in the Christian God has ceased to be believable – is even now beginning to cast its first shadows over Europe.'[1] With less melodramatic flourish but with greater influence, Darwin's discoveries also challenged the need to see a divine design in the natural world. In our own century the Holocaust, two world wars, the enormous growth in knowledge of other cultures and ensuing acceptance of cultural diversity, not to mention countless post-imperialist conflicts, have shaken the common confidence with which people had once thought they knew what they ought to believe about how the world worked, what our place was in the world, and what kinds of conduct were acceptable and what were not.

In 1776 Mozart wrote, 'We live in this world to compel ourselves industriously to enlighten one another by means of reasoning and to apply ourselves always to carrying forward the sciences and the arts' (W. A. Mozart to Padre Martini: letter of 4 December 1776).[2] The sureness of vision and purpose that we find in Mozart now seems alien to the modern mind. Our uncertainty in comparison to Mozart has doubtless been brought about by the buffeting and bruising from the historical and social forces unleashed from Nietzsche and Darwin onwards. How could anyone feel sure of the objectivity of moral values in a century which has seen the technology of mass destruction applied repeatedly with such clinical ease? But underlying the social and historical causes of our current uncertainties about what we should believe, there lie deep philosophical problems about the legitimation of belief.

It is one thing to note that the confidence of earlier worldviews has been shaken by various historical developments. The philosophical issue concerns whether, despite all that, it is still legitimate to work with a notion of what we ought to believe. That is to say, despite the obvious pressures that have caused despair where Mozart enjoyed certainty, can we still hold on to the idea that in many different areas of human enquiry, whether in science, art, morality or religion, there is such a thing as truth? That is the question I shall answer in this book. The answer that I defend is that the concept of truth and the possibility of objective knowledge survives the current fashion for anarchy. In the rest of this introduction I want to sketch some of the ideas and issues that will be raised in the rest of the book.

RATIONALITY AND HISTORY

To say that something is true is to hold that it is true independently of what we may hope, wish, believe, etc. Truth is independent of us. That is why one can say that despite the social and historical causes of our current uncertainties, we can still ask whether there is such a thing as truth for morals and politics. Whatever we may be caused to believe by various social pressures, we can still ask the question about what we ought to believe. We need to distinguish between truth – that which we ought to believe – and those beliefs which we hold due to all manner of causes many of which may be irrelevant to, if not in opposition to, the truth.

This distinction is between the normative issue of what we

ought to believe and the descriptive issue of what we actually believe and have been caused to believe. Descriptively, it might be correct that certain social forces have caused people to entertain certain beliefs. For example, a train of theorists from Hume through Marx to Durkheim have hypothesised that religious beliefs have been held because of the social role they perform. If correct, that is a descriptive point. It is separate from the normative issue of whether such beliefs should be entertained. The general validity of the distinction between the descriptive account of the causes of belief and the normative truth of belief can be seen with a simple example.

It seems plausible to think that the preponderance of 'green' beliefs in contemporary society is, in part, caused by the following fact: the 'greenness' of a product is a valuable means by which a product can achieve a distinct position in the market. That is to say, many of us have been brought to consider 'green' issues because advertisers hit on the idea that 'greenness' provided a way of carving a distinct niche for the products they were promoting. 'Greenness' provides product differentiation. This is a causal claim. Suppose that it is true. Nevertheless, if true it does not follow that 'green' beliefs are unworthy, or false. If this causal claim were true it might give us reason to examine a little more carefully the warrant with which we adopt 'green' beliefs. But it can do no more than induce such caution. Of itself, the causal claim shows nothing about the truth or falsity of 'green' beliefs.

Of course, when advertisers try to cause us to entertain beliefs they are perhaps uninterested in the truth of the beliefs. Their interest extends no further than the utility of the beliefs with regard to the increased sale of the products in question. But if it is true that advertisers have no interest in the truth or falsity of the beliefs they try to instil in us, that still means that the issue of how they cause us to entertain beliefs is independent of the issue of whether they are beliefs that we ought to entertain.

Similarly, it seems right to distinguish our rationality from our historically and socially conditioned habits of belief. We are prone to think of rationality as a neutral ahistorical faculty. It is the faculty by which we employ our reason and the evidence gathered by our senses to arrive at the truth. The operation of rationality is, so the common picture goes, distinct from the operation of those methods of belief formation that are embedded in concrete historical and social settings. Some people believe things because authority figures tell them to. Some people believe things because advertisers induce them to do so. These are some of the ways in which people are caused to believe things. They are distinct from the rational normative method: the disinterested pursuit of truth which, in principle, accepts no authorities.

What is true is not necessarily the same as what we are caused to believe by our history and by our culture. The rational method for acquiring beliefs is distinct from the blind acceptance of historical and cultural traditions. Whether or not a belief is rational is distinct from the issue of how it came about. The genealogy of a belief does not determine its truth.

However, to proclaim the above stark distinction between rationality and history is already to have missed what I shall take as a central claim of postmodernist philosophy. This is the claim that rationality itself is historically and contingently conditioned. In particular, it is the claim that the idea of pure reason, the idea of a faculty unaffected by historical, cultural and other contingent conditions, is an illusion. Furthermore, if rationality is historically conditioned, then different historical settings may produce different notions of rationality. Rationality itself would become fragmented; so too would truth.

On the face of it, the thesis that rationality is historically conditioned runs into a number of obvious difficulties, difficulties that make it easy to refute. There are two familiar ways of understanding the thesis that rationality is historically conditioned that need to be mentioned now in order to clear the ground for a proper evaluation of the thesis.

First, the idea of different concepts of rationality appears to endorse relativism. Relativism is the thesis that what is true is relative to different traditions, cultures, epochs, etc. But relativism is self-defeating, for if the relativist does not endorse some notion of objective truth, why should we believe in relativism? And anyway, if relativism were true then different societies and cultures could not find themselves in opposition, for they would be operating by different standards. That conflicts with what is most apparent in our world, namely, the extent to which different societies and cultures are in opposition.

Second, the idea that rationality is historically conditioned looks like a blurring of the normative/descriptive distinction already noted. Such a blurring is familiar in much sociology. Some sociologists have attempted to give a sociological reduction of

the concepts of belief and truth. That is to say, they offer a
sociological causal theory to replace the normative account of
belief formation. A classic example of this is Marx's claim that
morality is ideological. This is an example of a descriptive claim
which appears to undermine the normative character of morality.
It is a claim that says that what we take as reasons for what we
ought to do are no more than rationalisations that serve the
function of protecting our economic class within the political
status quo.[3]

I believe that there are many cases in contemporary life in
which it is fruitful to consider the Marxist analysis and ask questions such as: what function, economic or otherwise, does the
promulgation of such-and-such beliefs serve in our society? Very
often, raising such a question is the first step to a critique of
those beliefs. What is misleading about the general 'Morality is
ideological' claim is its very generality. The fact that some beliefs
may serve certain functions in a society does not show that all
such beliefs serve that function. The thirst for a general theory
which accounts for, say, all moral beliefs in exactly the same
way is unmotivated. And, once again, such claims do nothing to
undermine the idea that a causal explanation of a belief has
nothing to do with the normative assessment of the belief as true
or false.

Of course, it has to be admitted that it is difficult not to
be impressed by the diversity of options currently available for
conceptualising our social and political life. Should we be liberals?
Islamic fundamentalists? Democratic socialists? Free-market
conservatives? These choices take on a very different flavour
when viewed from the array of perspectives from which people
currently try to make sense of their lives. In a Poland recently
released from the state capitalism of Stalinism the swing to
embrace a Catholic state seems almost inevitable at just the same
time that Ireland struggles to shake off the very same option. In
a climate of such diversity and seemingly interminable conflict
the idea can take hold that perhaps there are no rational choices
to be made about such matters. The worry prompted by relativism
and sociological reductionism is that in the face of such diversity
our choices are more a function of how our history pushes us
than a matter of our making rational decisions.

However, despite the variety of moral and political systems
around the globe, to despair at this and conclude that rationality

cannot guide us in politics is to give in to a glib generalising sociology that sees all belief formation as a function of social and historical forces. The apparent lack of rational criteria of selection between fundamentalism and liberalism, between socialism and conservatism, may be more a function of our ignorance than of the impossibility of rationality taking hold here. The fact that we are currently having a hard time making sensible selections about how to order our politics does not show that no sensible selections can be made. It simply suggests that if such selections can be made, we are not very good at it yet.

To the idea that rationality itself might be fragmented and historically conditioned there is then a simple response. It is to say that the complexity of the historical, social and cultural influences upon our beliefs does not force us to give up on the idea that truth and rationality apply in these areas. That such forces act upon our beliefs and our belief formation does not entail relativism or sociological reductionism. However, to make this simple conceptual point and say no more is to miss the opportunity to uncover the real philosophical issues underlying the apparent fragmentation of truth and rationality. For to respond with the correct conceptual claim that a genealogy of belief does not entail anything about the truth of a belief is to indulge in a complacent appeal to concepts of truth and rationality which stand in need of legitimation.

What I take as distinctive of philosophical postmodernism is the critique of a model of truth and rationality that arose from the eighteenth-century Enlightenment and which saw rationality as a neutral ahistorical tool. It was seen as a tool of pure reason. The paradigm of rationality became the abstract manipulation of symbols as found in the natural sciences, mathematics and logic. On this model, rationality was most clearly evidenced in our linguistic dealings, our ability to handle symbolic operations in ways that could be discussed in isolation from their historical context. Meaning itself was thought of and theorised in a way independent of context. The phenomenon of meaning came to be theorised as a function of symbol manipulation. No wonder then that a train of philosophers from Leibniz to Fodor should postulate variations on the idea of a pure language of thought – a symbolic system in which our very thought processes and rationality would be laid bare for what they were: sentence juggling.

In contrast to this, theorists of this century have repeatedly emphasised the contextual character of meaning, of language and of its understanding. They have emphasised how meaning can only be understood in real historical contexts, not borne by sentences construed simply as abstract strings of symbols. According to some interpreters, Wittgenstein derived the most intoxicating paradoxes from the insight of the essentially contextual character of meaning. His rule-following arguments are held to show that no determinate meanings can be tracked down for our sentences. For any given sentence, an infinite sequence of interpretations is always possible. No one interpretation is ever fixed. Derrida has similar thoughts when he speaks of the unending 'deferring' of meaning, as interpretations of a text are replaced with other interpretations and further ones still, so that the idea of a real meaning is always deferred.[4]

Wittgenstein, I am sure, peddled no such paradoxes, and the jury is still out on Derrida. Nevertheless, in an intellectual climate that has been so unsure about the robustness and context independence of meaning, it is perhaps no surprise that rationality and truth should be thought to succumb to contextualisation. It is this contextualisation which provides what I am taking as postmodernism's central challenge. It is a challenge that fragments the ahistorical character of reason as conceived by the Enlightenment. Reason is just one of the 'Big Ideas' that the Enlightenment bequeathed us and that helped shape the modern world.

The 'Big Ideas' were truth, rationality and the self. The idea that these concepts picked out universal timeless notions that would shape all human knowledge is the key to the Enlightenment project. These central concepts constitute what have been called the 'meta-narratives' of modernity; they are central concepts that have shaped our modern world. It is the fragmentation of these 'Big Ideas' into a jigsaw of contextualised accounts of them that I take as the definitive claim of philosophical postmodernism. On this account, postmodernism challenges the very distinction between rationality and history with which I opened this section. This is not necessarily to endorse relativism. It is not necessarily to endorse a general sociological reduction of truth and rationality. However, it is to expose real philosophical difficulties with the idea that these 'Big Ideas' can be understood in a timeless ahistorical manner. As such, it is a challenge that needs to be examined. If there is any truth in it, and I think there is, it is a challenge that requires us to offer a legitimation of the way we now proceed with these central ideas.

Postmodernism provides a challenge and an invitation to legitimise our concepts of reason, truth and self from a contextualised and historically embedded point of view. It is not enough to respond to postmodernism with the simple conceptual claim that the historical forces that shape belief do not show that belief to be true or false. We must provide an account of truth, rationality and selfhood that shows that it is legitimate to continue using these ideas, even if they have to be cut down to size a bit. We need to give an account of these concepts that proves why they are still in working order. That is the job of legitimation. That is what is required. That is what this book will attempt.

The challenge of philosophical postmodernism is then twofold. First, it comprises a critique of the idea that the central concepts of truth, rationality and self could be understood in an abstract way, abstracted from real historical contexts. Modernity's ideal was to disinherit our real historical human perspectives and achieve a transparent direct contact with reality. In the first instance, postmodernism criticises the idea of our experience, meaning, truth and rationality being treated as other than inheritances, embedded in real historical traditions. The challenge here is to see in what sense this critique is right. Second, the task this critique presents us is to legitimise the concepts of truth and rationality in a way that acknowledges the real historical contexts which shape them. Having done that, the job is to give an account of the self which is also embedded within real history but yet still rational and subject to the normative demands of truth and rationality.

What labels we employ here is, to an extent, a matter of choice. The critical point of postmodernism is an attack on the idea that reason, truth and self can be understood abstracted from history. This is an idea that originates in the Enlightenment. There is also considerable currency to the description of the idea that these concepts have no history as the hallmark of modernity.[5] In art and literature modernism is more often seen as a late nineteenth-century reaction to this conception of ahistorical reason than as an identification with it.[6] Still, reaction or identification, there is a common thread through these usages.

It is probably not possible to employ a usage that is coherent with all previous usages. But as long as it is clear how the label is used, that is all that can be required. I shall use 'modernity' as a label for the thesis of the ahistorical character of the concepts of reason, truth and self. This use is particularly relevant, for I want to discuss the philosophical problems that arise when modernity is criticised in the context of a particular model for the ahistorical treatment of these concepts. It is a model that grew out of the Enlightenment, but is a later development. It is the scientific model. This gives further reason for the label 'modernity' as the kernel of ideas to set postmodernism against. It also connects with the critiques of the dominance of scientific models of knowledge found in the works of the leading postmodernist philosopher, Rorty.[7]

In legitimising truth and rationality I shall be defending a position I shall call 'cognitivism'. I could call it a form of 'realism', but that word gets used for so many different things in philosophy that we would be in danger of being led up too many blind alleys. 'Cognitivism' is a useful label because it highlights the point that the use of reason in belief formation is to gain knowledge. When we gain knowledge we are in possession of truth. When we gain knowledge our beliefs are those that we ought to believe, they match an ideal notion of those beliefs we ought to hold if we want the truth. As a label 'cognitivism' is useful, for although it carries few of the suspect connotations of 'realism', like the latter label it applies easily to different fields of enquiry. So we can speak of a cognitivism about morals, a cognitivism about religion, a cognitivism about the human mind and self, etc. In each case, these are labels for positions that admit that there is such a thing as the truth, that which we ought to believe if we want to gain knowledge.

THE DEATH OF GOD AND THE END OF META-NARRATIVES

In order to legitimise the concepts of truth, rationality and self, we need to show how they can be employed in a contextualised way that is sensitive to their historical character. We need to show that there are ways of thinking of these concepts that do not require the 'Big Ideas', the meta-narratives of the Enlightenment.

In order to see how these ideas are problematic, I shall trace their role in the biggest meta-narrative of all, the idea of a grand narrative that is a complete and exhaustive account of the world that captures everything that needs to be said. This idea of a grand narrative is the idea not just of the truth, but of the whole truth. To employ another metaphor, it is the idea of the God's-eye view of the world; the account of the world that God would give from a vantage point that saw and comprehended everything. If the self, truth and rationality could be conceptualised in a thoroughly ahistorical manner, then these concepts would provide the framework for this absolute God's-eye view of the world. The true self would be the self stripped bare of its history, culture, gender, race and social class. It would be the self that disinherited its history and stood naked, beheld by the eye of God. Truth would then be what God thinks; rationality would be identified with God's way of thinking. Of course, these are mere metaphors, but they capture real and powerful ideas that have done much to shape our modern world.

Once again, this idea of a God's-eye view of the world can be traced to the Enlightenment. However, it is a more modern secular version of it that I shall be concerned with. The Enlightenment was a period during which our confidence in our cognitive abilities reached a peak at which it seemed, to those of religious faith, that mankind was learning to read the mind of God. Our understanding of the natural world developed rapidly during this period. With the achievements of Newton's general theory of mechanics it seemed that we were finally learning the secrets of the universe. The human mind was unravelling the way the world worked. We were unpicking the world's secrets, a world that was, to most Enlightenment thinkers, an object of divine creation. By learning to read the workings of the world, we were learning to read the mind of God. In the light of this success, not only did it seem that knowledge was possible, but also that we were on the point of achieving an almost divine state of revelation about the workings of the universe. For the Enlightenment thinker, truth was available. Human reason was the tool by which this knowledge had been achieved and, by the further application of human reason, one day the whole truth would be available to the human mind.

The Enlightenment project was an attempt to complete the task of acquiring the whole truth about creation. It was the project to attain absolute truth, the truth that transcends local points of view. It was the project to attain the truth that is available from the God's-eye point of view, the truth that makes up the grand narrative about the whole of creation.

The idea of this grand narrative has acquired a number of labels over the years. Sometimes it is called the 'absolute conception' of the world. A more extreme version of this idea has the label of the 'view from nowhere'. Whatever label is employed, what is at issue here is the idea that in seeking truth we are seeking an account of the world that gives a complete unified account of everything. It is tempting to employ deistic metaphors when trying to articulate this idea; hence, 'the God's-eye view'. A secular version of that label might be 'the world's own story'. That is the term I shall employ from now on. I shall use 'the world's own story' and 'absolute conception' or 'absolute truth' as interchangeable.

The Enlightenment then was a time when philosophers believed that there was such a thing as the world's own story. It was a religious story. They thought we were beginning to learn what this story was. Modernity proper, I take as the view that the world's own story can be told in a thoroughly ahistorical manner, abstracted from traditional beliefs. For modernists, the world's own story can be put together from first principles by pure reason and experience alone. That means it must be a secularised story, for the traditions of religion will, like all traditional beliefs, have to be disinherited. That such a thing is possible is what Rorty denies. It is what Lyotard denies when he says that there are no more meta-narratives.[8]

Writers such as Rorty and Lyotard, in arguing that there is no such thing as the world's own story, are arguing that the only accounts that we can give of the world are local human accounts. There is no such thing as the world's own story, but only varied and conflicting human stories about the world. This is the fragmentation of truth and rationality that is distinctive of postmodernism.

These postmodernist philosophers are not making a sceptical point about the unavailability of knowledge. They are not saying that knowledge is impossible to get. Rather, they are saying that the idea of the world's own story, the unified picture of reality, is an illusion. There is no such thing as the whole truth. The only stories to be told about the world are local stories and there is no presumption that such stories will have anything in common. The styles of narrative, the very kinds of things talked about in local human stories, may present no more than a patchwork of different approaches that resists unification. With regard to the self, the postmodernist says that there is no such thing as the real self abstracted from history. Abstracting from your history, society, culture, gender, race and class does not reveal to you your true self – it reveals an abyss. A nothingness is left when all the historical detail is peeled away. That is why feminism has become so important for many postmodernist thinkers. Feminist thought draws upon the idea that there are accounts of self-identity which are historically situated. Clearly, if there are distinct gender-specific concepts of self, these provide clear examples of concepts of the self which are contextualised.

The connection between postmodernism in philosophy and the use of the label in art and architecture can now be noted. In art, the modernist movement was a reaction against the ahistorical pursuit of reason and science. Nevertheless, it was a movement that saw the purpose of art as being to investigate and make apparent the underlying reality of human experience. Modernist art reached beyond the level of mere appearances to represent the truth underlying the human condition. Of course, in art as elsewhere 'modernism' is no more a precise label than 'postmodernism' and not too much should rest on the name-calling. Nevertheless, the key idea that there is a reality for art to probe, an objectivity to literary work, is central to most artists bearing the label 'modernist'.[9]

In contrast, postmodernism in art, architecture and literature emphasises the lack of any unifying form or method in art. Postmodernist architecture gaily employs a variety of styles. It juxtaposes styles and approaches, media and materials in an almost anarchic sense of playfulness, for there is, according to the postmodern artist, no such thing as the truth of the human condition. Postmodernist art revels in the fragmentation of artistic standards. A modernist novel, such as Joyce's *Ulysses*, uses a variety of devices and styles in order to plumb the nature of human experience. A postmodernist novel, such as Eco's *Foucault's Pendulum*, uses a variety of styles and devices not to plumb the truth, for there is none. It plays with styles and approaches in order to entertain and perhaps liberate. It does not aim to teach, for there is no objective truth to be imparted. For postmodernists there appear to be no standards.

In a climate in which embracing a label is more a function of fashion than clear thinking, any use of the labels 'modernism' and 'postmodernism' is in danger of appearing eccentric. I have now marked the connections between the usage I have said I am adopting and some current usages. That will have to suffice.

THE WORLD'S OWN STORY AND THE WORLD OF SCIENCE

If postmodernism attacks the idea of the world's own story, it clearly must take issue with the view that science is an attempt to piece together the world's own story. This brings out another respect in which the challenge with which I am concerned in this book is postmodernist and not just anti-Enlightenment.

The scientists of the Enlightenment, such as Newton, believed in the truth of religion. That is why I said that, for them, learning to read the workings of the world amounted to learning to read the mind of God. For Newton, the activity of science was an activity of pious devotion. Since the time of Newton, however, we have become familiar with the idea that the advance of science has signalled the demise of religion. The more that science has offered detailed explanations of how the world works, the less need there has seemed for religious accounts of the world. The transition from the Enlightenment belief in the power of human reason to deliver the whole truth about the world to the modernist vision of that truth being supplied by a disinterested and ahistorical science amounts to just this: the idea of reaching for the truth is the idea that we need to look behind the mere appearances of what is going on in the world to uncover the hidden mechanisms and forces that determine the way the world appears. Science is merely the tool that has, to date, dominated this activity of uncovering the way the world works. Science has become the dominant model for uncovering the world's own story.

The Enlightenment believed in the idea of the world's own story, but it also thought that this story was a divine one. The thoroughly modern outlook came about when the idea of the world's own story was secularised into the scientific story of the world. The idea that there is such a thing as the world's own story and that it is the story that is told in the language of the natural sciences is, perhaps, the dominant metaphysics in the world today. Postmodernism challenges the idea of the world's own story and also, therefore, the modern version of that idea that identifies the world's own story with the scientific image.

It is via a critique of the limitations of the scientific version of the world's own story that I shall develop the general critique of the very idea of absolute truth. The simplest way of seeing the force of the postmodernist challenge that truth and reason have become fragmented is to see that challenge in the guise of a critique of the limitations of the scientific version of the world's own story.

FOUR BASIC PROBLEMS?

So far, I have stated some of the ideas and positions that I shall be investigating in this book. I have not provided any arguments in support of them. Before we begin to examine the arguments that generate these ideas, I want to state the four basic claims that underpin the postmodernist challenge. The remainder of this book will then be an examination of whether we should accept these claims and, if so, whether they signal the fragmentation of the concepts of truth, reason and self that postmodernists claim.

The first claim is:

I All experience is based on interpretation.

This means that there is no neutral account of experience that is innocent of theoretical presuppositions. There is no account of experience that can be employed as a neutral arbitration point between different theories and worldviews. What we report on the basis of our experience is always, in part, a function of what beliefs and theories we already hold.

The second claim is:

II There are no secure foundations for knowledge.

This follows directly from Thesis I. If all experience is based on interpretation, then there is no neutral starting point on which to build our knowledge. The knowledge we claim about the world will depend on what reports about the world we take as basic. But there are no reports about the world which can be taken as universally basic, so there is no neutral starting point or foundations. Knowledge, if it exists at all, has no secure foundations.

The third claim is:

III There is no single language suitable for reporting all the things we want to say about the world.

This says that there is a plurality of languages for describing the world, no one of which has priority. This thesis does not follow directly from Theses I and II, although it is closely connected. If it is true that all experience is based on prior interpretation and theory and that therefore knowledge has no secure foundations, this is still compatible with the idea that, nevertheless, there is only one way of describing the truth. Theses I and II merely show that, if there is only one way of describing the truth, we can have no sure means of detecting it or discovering the truths expressible in it.

However, although Thesis III does not follow from I and II, it is still compatible with the idea of the world's own story; it merely requires that the world's own story be, as it were, a work of many tongues. The idea of the world's own story is finally challenged when we reach Thesis IV, which is:

IV All languages are local, perspectival human languages.

It is this thesis that challenges the idea of the grand narrative of the world's own story. Thesis IV states that our ways of describing the world are essentially ours: we cannot transcend, or break free from, our local human points of view. If Thesis IV is correct, then we cannot aspire to the absolute truth, the final definitive account of the world's own story. In rejecting this notion of the absolute conception of the world's own story, Thesis IV claims that all our descriptions of the world are perspectival.

In what follows I shall make use of the distinction between a perspectival and an absolute account of the world. The distinction lies at the heart of Thesis IV. It is a distinction between accounts of the world from a human perspective and accounts of the world that attempt to transcend the human point of view and tell the world's own story, the absolute truth. One thing that is distinctive of much recent philosophy is the belief that science offers us a non-perspectival account of the world. This is the modernist view that science offers an account that describes the world not from the point of view of one particular species of intelligent life with a very local history and set of preoccupations, ideologies, morals and religious dogmas; rather science tries to transcend all that and offer a non-perspectival account of world. Science tries to see the world as it is in itself. Science offers the world's own story. If Thesis IV is right, this modernist outlook is untenable and all accounts of the world are perspectival.

It is Thesis IV which is central to postmodernist philosophy, for it is this thesis that denies the possibility of a language with a thoroughly context-independent meaning. There is no *lingua universalis*, no pure language of thought. Thesis IV depends on Theses I–III, and so it is these four theses that provide the platform for the postmodernist critique of the unity of truth, rationality and self.

In what follows I shall do two things. First, I shall show in what sense the above four theses are correct. Second, I shall show how these theses are compatible with continuing to believe that there is such a thing as truth and rationality. That is to say, there is a normative concept of truth and knowledge which is compatible with the claim that all accounts of the world are perspectival – Thesis IV. In short, we can learn to live without the world's own story, the absolute conception of the view from nowhere. Truth is humbler than that, but it is still truth. It is still the notion of what we ought to believe. The idea of objective standards of belief survives the loss of the world's own story. To put the point in another, more melodramatic, way: if Nietzsche was right and God is dead, nevertheless truth has survived. Indeed, it is alive and kicking. However, where all this leaves that other member of the Enlightenment trio of big ideas – the self – is another matter.

TRUTH AND PRACTICE

One last idea remains to be introduced before the argument begins. If we thought that truth pertains only to the world's own story we would be bound to accept that truth cannot apply to many of the things of central importance to human life, for example our conception of self, our morals and our politics, unless we account for these in a religious manner. Without the support of a religious foundation, our moral and political points of view, our very notion of our selves, seem to be paradigms of human perspectival thinking. The values which shape our moral and political lives are our values.

This helps explain a common feeling that, in an age which has learnt to live without God, we have forfeited the idea that any one moral or political system has precedence. Without the support of God, how are we to justify one moral perspective over another? In a Godless world, relativism about morals becomes a real and live issue.

But now consider this. If we can preserve a worthwhile notion of objective truth without the idea of the world's own story, then truth can be made to apply to local human stories. Truth can apply to the perspectives that we enjoy and by which we inhabit the world. If that is so, might it not be possible to show that truth can apply to our morals and politics? That is the tantalising option that I shall explore in the closing chapters of this book. If we can legitimise the concepts of truth and rationality without appeal to the idea of the world's own story, then we can have standards of belief other than absolute ones. If this is so, we can have a conception of self other than the absolute and ahistorical concept inherited from the Enlightenment. That is the prize on offer when we learn to live with concepts of truth and rationality more modest than the idea of the world's own story.

The prize is the legitimation of concentrating our attention on our own stories and our own predicaments and averting our gaze from the philosophical misconception that truth must always involve a 'tuning in' to the divine. The prize is the idea that there is truth aplenty to be had right here and now from within the local human perspective. Truth and the power of reason are things we can employ in our human dilemmas about how to live, how to treat one another, how to organise our societies, how to think about ourselves.

This point can be expressed in the following way. To think that truth must be absolute is to think that matters that can only be expressed in local human terms are not candidates for truth. Belief in the idea of the world's own story is the belief that what is real is what is expressible in the world's own story. But from this absolute perspective human life makes no sense. The cosmos as such is indifferent to our follies and foibles. If we want to blow each other to pieces on the battlegrounds of contemporary conflicts, what is this to the cosmos? The world considered in itself offers no guidance on questions of right and wrong. It is not just that the siege of Sarajevo is too parochial for the cosmos, too small an issue. The point is that the world's own story does not and cannot speak to such predicaments, for they are describable only in the perspectival language of our local human histories. It is not that we shrivel in humility before the enormity of the cosmos. Rather, we simply do not figure at all in the world's own story except, maybe, as a momentary cloud of equations governing the behaviour of so many billions of sub-atomic particles.

Of course, if you can sustain a belief in God, you might find some recognition of the human condition from the world's own story. But even in its religious version, it is difficult to square the idea that human concerns matter to the cosmos, given God's apparent indifference to our ever-increasing enthusiasm for blasting one another to pieces.

If we try to tune in to the world's own story we get no guidance on human affairs. The world's own story is silent on the siege of Sarajevo. The world, considered in itself in absolute terms, has nothing to say to us about who we are and how we should live. Recognising the world's indifference to ourselves and our predicaments can bring a sense of despair and a sense of the absurdity of human life. Indeed, it was the great French explorer of the absurd, Albert Camus, who described the world's indifference with the metaphor of the 'unreasonable silence of the world'.[10] But there is another reaction to the moral silence of the world, and it is this reaction I want to explore.

Perhaps the moral silence of the world is not a sign of a lack of objectivity about right and wrong conduct. Perhaps this apparent silence about Sarajevo is simply a function of our looking and listening to the wrong thing. If, in general, truth cannot be identified with the world's own story, then why should we look for the truth about Sarajevo in the world's own story? Rather than trying to tune in to the cosmos for answers about Sarajevo, perhaps we should be listening to ourselves? Perhaps we should be listening to our stories of the world, stories constructed by creatures who are the product of very particular historical and social conditionings? Such perspectival accounts of the world, of ourselves, and of what is happening in places like Sarajevo cannot, by definition, aspire to the world's own story. But if that is a false aspiration anyway, if it is something we can learn to live without and still preserve a normative concept of the standards of belief and of objective truth, then the fact that the cosmos has no answers to the problems of Sarajevo is not a shocking insight that prompts despair. It is the bare and innocent truism that if there is a truth about human concerns, it must be found and expressed in human perspectival accounts.

If we can show that truth can still be made to apply to human judgements and human perspectives, if we can show that nothing profound is lost by turning off the attempt to tune in to either the divine or the secular version of the world's own story, then we can acknowledge the truism that Sarajevo is our problem. It belongs to us, not to God or to the cosmos. Perhaps then we could shake off the despair that so often hinders our attempts to arrive at true solutions to such matters. In a nutshell, if the enquiries and explorations which we are about to undertake succeed, we might make sense of the idea that there is a truth about Sarajevo.

A WORD ABOUT METHODOLOGY

Raymond Williams once observed that 'culture is ordinary'. I think philosophy is ordinary too. That is not to say that I think that its methods and arguments must defer to ordinary language analysis. Rather, I think that the problems of philosophy stem from simple reflection upon the ordinary use of familiar concepts. It takes little reflection to recognise the threat posed by the postmodernist fragmentation of the concepts of truth, rationality and the self. It also takes little reflection to realise the importance of trying to legitimise concepts of truth and rationality that apply to the perspectival claims of human morality.

There are standards of belief, and philosophy can reassure us on this. But the reassurance is required not only by academics. It is required by anyone with half an eye to the state of late twentieth-century society. Accordingly, I have tried to keep the argument that follows as accessible as possible. Accessibility is often gained at the price of simplification. I have simplified many positions, but never, I believe, in a way that ignores the essential point to the argument. However, I need to say something about the methodology of the enquiry before us.

What is distinctive of philosophical postmodernism is the fragmentation of the concepts of truth, rationality and the self. As indicated, this claim is often derived from philosophical theories about language and the way that all our experiences are thick with the interpretative clutter of language and the cultural inheritance our language carries with it. In what follows I shall not provide a step-by-step critique of the philosophical theories of language that have prompted these ideas. I shall proceed in a way that I believe is more accessible and more basic. I shall present the postmodernist critique via a critique of the claims of science to provide a uniform account of truth and rationality. I shall discuss directly the problem of whether or not there can be such a thing as an account of experience which would provide a transparent and uniform concept of truth.

By examining the postmodernist critique in the light of a critique of the role of science in defining the norms of truth and rationality, we can make the issues more accessible than if we detoured via the complexities of twentieth-century theories of language. In addition, this approach takes us directly to what is the key issue anyway: Thesis I above. Most twentieth-century philosophers accept that, in some sense, all experience is a construction, a function of past experiences, theories, histories, presumptions, prejudices and so on. The central philosophical problem that underlies the claimed fragmentation of truth, rationality and the self in postmodernism is the problem of learning to live with the idea that there is no such thing as a transparent experience of reality. All experience is opaque and is affected by all manner of influences many of which appear to have no rational lineage. We need to get clear in what sense, if any, this thesis about experience threatens the claimed fragmentation of our trio of big ideas. If we do that, we can excuse ourselves the necessity of tracing every nuance and twist of the plethora of theories of language now on the market.

There is a more fundamental reason why I have chosen the above method. I have said that the task before us is one of legitimation. We need to legitimise a use of the concepts of truth, rationality and self against the postmodernist critique. To achieve such legitimation it is not sufficient to criticise the theories on the basis of which the postmodernist claims are made. What is required is an alternative picture or model of how these concepts operate. The reason I take this task of legitimation to be so central is because I believe that key parts of the postmodernist critique are correct. What is required, therefore, is a description of how, given the opacity of all experience, the concepts of truth, rationality and self can still have a legitimate role to play in the business of making sense of our lives. This book is, if you like, an essay in descriptive metaphysics. It is an essay which describes the structure of and connections between the key concepts of truth, rationality and self. It is an attempt to provide the metaphysics or model that shows how truth, rationality and the self work; it is a model to replace the defunct model inherited from the Enlightenment.

The most interesting element in this model is the role preserved for the concept of self. However, that part of the argument does not begin until Chapter 8. The reason for this is simple. Until we have a firm grip on the possibility that truth and rationality still have real work to do for us in our conceptual scheme, there is little hope of making credible sense of a cognitivist concept of self. Furthermore, the postmodernist threat is now so pervasive that it is only by a patient explanation of the detailed connections between our concepts of truth, rationality, knowledge and belief, that we can lay it to rest. It also seems to me that this order of presentation aids the accessibility of the philosophical arguments to come.[11]

The argument of this book amounts to a detailed description of what is left of our key conceptual structure if we abandon the pretensions of modernity, if we abandon the idea that the concepts of truth, rationality and self can be investigated in a way that disinherits their historical traditions. The argument I offer is an attempt to describe plainly and simply how our key concepts of truth, rationality and self are, in part, a real historical inheritance and yet still normative concepts. If a plain simple statement of a common conceptual scheme is possible, then it does not matter much if we have ignored some of the latest fashions and theoretical fancies. We will have an account of basic metaphysical presuppositions robust enough to resist whatever theory can throw at it. The task then is to describe a conceptual framework involving truth, rationality and self that despite its historical embedding is normative. Furthermore, it is a description of a conceptual framework that is necessary. It is an account of these concepts that cannot be ignored. If that can be done, and the model produced avoids the real problems that face modernity's version of these things, then the task of legitimation is complete.

I hope that the argument to follow will be accessible to all those who have stopped to ask where we go now in the face of an almost anarchic diversity of beliefs in the modern world. Not least in Europe, political and economic structures are tumbling by the hour as we shed the dead weight of the detritus of social experimentation in the early years of the century. The critics of science are now two a penny, and the general scepticism about the value of the natural sciences has opened the floodgates for all manner of frivolous novelties that offer to explain the meaning of life. The contrasts and impending battles between widely divergent moral outlooks is set to define new vistas in international politics. In every field of human enquiry the options outweigh the sense of probity with which people now face critical choices. Philosophy can act here and offer assistance as we fumble through the changes upon us. But philosophy can only do this if it speaks to all those who understand why it is so problematic to ask, 'What should we believe?'

Philosophy is ordinary and so, very often, are its results. There was a period earlier in this century when analytic philosophy self-consciously adopted a common-sense methodology. An appeal to common sense and ordinary linguistic usage were characteristic marks of how many philosophers conceived their business. I offer no such defence of common sense in what follows.

Common sense is not my method although, very often, it may be my result. This should not be surprising. I have said that I want to legitimise the standards of belief in a way that applies to human perspectives. I accept that the Enlightenment concept of absolute truth is an illusion. That being so, the concept of truth that I set out to defend is the concept that is immanent in our common practices, our common sense of argument, persuasion, interpretation and discursive enquiry.

In other words, although the method does not involve an appeal to common sense, the end result is a defence of what I take to be a shared grasp, a common sense, of the distinction between truth and judgement as we employ that in diverse fields. Our common sense of cognitive purpose is to be protected from the overambition of the Enlightenment that saw knowledge-gathering as the impossible task of reading God's mind. It is to be protected from modernity's secular version of this idea. Above all, it is to be protected from the melodramatic scepticism that says that in the absence of such transcendent standards of belief anything goes. We are caught in a false dichotomy: either there are normative standards of belief that are ahistorical, or we give a descriptive account of ourselves and purposes embedded in history that loses the notion of normative standards of belief. This is nonsense. Between these two extremes there is an enormous level playing field. It is the arena we unreflectively inhabit in our common engagement with the world, the physical, social, moral and political worlds. The point of my argument in this book is to offer reassurance that this engagement is genuine and subject to critical evaluation in the light of something usefully dubbed 'truth'.

If the argument is right we can then resist the siren calls both of the Enlightenment and modernist visionaries and of the postmodern sceptics. The world as seen, the world as engaged, by our common-sense perspective with its attendant particularities and historical, cultural and social conditionings is, nevertheless, the world. It's the only one we have. It may not look much like the semi-divine object of Enlightenment adulation. It is certainly a more confused and chaotic place than that described by the physical mechanics of modern science, although it has considerably more cognitive structure than the sceptical postmodernists make believe. But our view of the world from right here and now is as objective a view of the world as it makes sense to ask for.

Chapter 1

The cosmic register

INTRODUCING THE COSMIC REGISTER

History does not record whether Caesar changed his sandals after crossing the Rubicon, but despite our ignorance we are surely entitled to insist that either he did or he did not. As you read this sentence you do not know if there is someone else who is, at this very same moment, reading the same sentence in another copy of this book. Nevertheless, it seems reasonable to suppose that either there is another reader or there is not. And even if we all agree that Hitler was an evil man, this conformity of judgement is distinct from the fact of whether he was or was not.

In all these cases we see the need to distinguish between what we judge to be the case and the facts of the matter. Our judgements may err or they may track the truth, but either way truth is independent of our judgement. We might be right in our judgements, but equally we might get it all wrong. We might systematically fail to make any true judgements. That can seem a dispiriting thought, but the possibility of such failure is central to our concept of objective truth, for we think that truth is independent of our judgement. Our judging something to be true cannot make it true.

The distinction between truth and judgement is fundamental to the enquiry of this book. Whatever else we say about truth we seem committed to saying that truth is independent of judgement. Our problems begin when we try to produce models or metaphors for this distinction. One way of capturing a powerful philosophical model for the distinction between truth and judgement goes like this.

Let us suppose that there exists a book that contains the answer to everything. All the questions we have asked, will ask and are currently asking are answered in this book. It is the complete book of knowledge. Let us call it the Cosmic Register. It is the record of truth, written perhaps by the hand of God. If there is such a thing as objective truth, truth independent of judgement, then we can think of the truth as what is recorded in the cosmic register. The cosmic register is our model for objective truth. Reading the cosmic register is our model for objective knowledge.

So, do we know anything? Do any of the judgements we make match entries in the cosmic register? That looks to be a difficult question, for if the cosmic register is independent of us – is truly cosmic – how will we ever be able to spot that our judgements are written in the book? Our judgements are only ever earthly judgements written in earthly books, like the one you are now holding. Our judgements are human judgements. Given this model for the distinction between truth and judgement, the distinction between what is in the cosmic register and what is in our minds, our books and our sayings, how can we ever tell that the two correspond? By such reflection we are led from asking 'Do we know anything?' to 'Can we tell whether it is even so much as possible that any of our judgements correspond to the cosmic register?'

The first question sounds like an invitation to say what we know, and most of us think we could respond boringly and long-windedly to that. The second question is more profound. If knowledge requires a correspondence between our human judgements and the cosmic register, the second question makes us realise that whenever we start to say what we think we know, we may be making judgements that fail to correspond at all with the cosmic register. If asked what we know we perhaps start by outlining a scientific theory – Einstein's theory of relativity, say. But the point of the second question is that in doing this we may be doing no more than spinning a web of human invention, turning the wheels within our earthbound web of judgements, a web that fails to engage with the cosmic register. In other words: is knowledge possible?

From about the middle of the seventeenth century it seemed that philosophers had an answer to this question. The answer was affirmative – knowledge was possible. We could read the cosmic register and many of our judgements were entered there. This optimism that not only did the cosmic register exist (there was objective truth) but we could read it (there was objective knowledge) was due to the development of the natural sciences. This development culminated in Newton's crowning achievement of the Enlightenment, a general theory of mechanics for the known physical universe.

Since that time science has taken over the predominant model for knowledge. We have believed in the cosmic register and, furthermore, have begun to understand the language in which it is written. The cosmic register is written in the language of mathematical physics. As the physical sciences have progressed so has our confidence that we can read the cosmic register. Humankind had a destiny, a destiny to read the world aright. The search for God was secularised and turned into the search for knowledge as formulated within the scientific image of the world. From seeking to find communion with God, the modern world shifted towards the idea of seeking to speak the language of the world, the language of the cosmic register. Such is the basis of the modern vision of knowledge and our collective destiny.

This confidence is now being punctured. Many thinkers now question whether knowledge is possible. Even worse, some question the intelligibility of the very idea of objective truth. The optimism of modernity is misplaced. There is no cosmic register. The only registers are human creations for which there is no external standard. If these dents to our cognitive confidence are right we stand to lose the very distinction between truth and judgement as modelled in the image of the cosmic register. In place of the objective truth of the cosmic register, we would then have merely the local standards of truth presupposed by our different theories, religions and worldviews. Truth would not then be objective. It would be relative to our different webs of judgement. And if your web of beliefs brings you into conflict with me, who is to say which of us is right? If we cannot aspire to the revelation of speaking the language of the world, what or who could adjudicate between our different local languages? Without objective truth it seems there could be no room for rational argument with those who confront us from the background of a different web of judgements. Without objective truth we are threatened with anarchy.

To see how these doubts arise and to assess how serious they are we need first to see what was so attractive about the scientific model of knowledge and the idea that the cosmic register is written in the language of mathematical physics. Why is it so common to think that science holds the key to unlocking the cosmic register? The answer to this turns on the way the development of the natural sciences offered a model for the truth/judgement distinction, the model of the cosmic register. The first step to take in this enquiry is to be more precise about this distinction between truth and judgement.

THE BASIC CONSTRAINT

The distinction between truth and judgement is fundamental to the enquiry of this book. The idea that there is such a distinction is, at the least, the idea that when we make a judgement the correctness or incorrectness of it is independent of us. Something does not become true just because you say it or think it. Something does not become false just because I deny it. If you say that there are three apples left in the fruitbowl and I deny it, your saying that there are three does not make it true any more than my denial makes it false. We have a conception of there being a fact of the matter independent of what we both say. It is because of this that there is something to argue about.

The distinction between truth and judgement appears to be entailed by the very idea of making a judgement. The concept of judgement, the idea of saying something or thinking something, commits us to a concept of truth that is independent of us. Without a concept of truth independent of us we could not make sense of the idea of judgement. The concept of truth is a necessary precondition for the very act of judgement. In making a judgement, we lay ourselves hostage to a notion of that which would show us wrong in our judgement. If we judge something to be the case we must have an idea of what would force us to retract our judgement, the state of affairs that would make our judgement false.

To see this point, imagine the following situation. Imagine someone who opens his mouth and makes a noise. Suppose the noise is 'Blurble wangle'. Suppose further that you believe that this person is speaking. He is saying something and you are trying to interpret his language. In the light of what he is doing, the time of day, previous utterances by him and so on, let us suppose that you think that 'Blurble wangle' means 'Dinner is ready'. But now, suppose that having said 'Blurble wangle' this person is then shown that dinner is not ready; the vegetables have not been peeled, and the water has not been boiled. Furthermore, he is wholly unperturbed by the absence of dinner preparations! He shows no inclination to take back the assertion 'Blurble wangle'. He is shown the positive absence of dinner-preparation behaviour. He is shown the lifeless cooking fire, the empty pots, the hunters not returned and the cook asleep in the shade under a tree and still he insists, 'Blurble wangle'! That is to say, you have presumed that his utterance of this noise means that dinner is ready and yet he remains totally unresponsive to all the evidence that dinner is not ready and is not even being thought of!

In such a situation, and in the absence of a long and complicated story about how he might be playing an elaborate trick on you, it simply makes no sense to continue with the hypothesis that 'Blurble wangle' means 'Dinner is ready'. If someone had meant that by 'Blurble wangle', he would have had to retract in the face of the supposed evidence. The force of saying that he would have to retract comes from the point that having an idea of what would make the judgement false is a necessary precondition of making a judgement.

The obvious response in the supposed situation is that we have misinterpreted the speaker and that 'Blurble wangle' means something else, perhaps 'Where's dinner?' Of course, if, as we pursued our investigation of the 'Blurble wangle' speaker, we found that there was no state of affairs to which his utterance appeared sensitive, we would probably come to doubt that this series of sounds meant anything at all. We might even come to doubt whether this speaker had a language![1]

That last claim is stronger than we need for current purposes, but enough has been said to support the following basic constraint:

Basic constraint: Truth is independent of judgement, for it is a precondition of our making judgements that we acknowledge some notion of independent truth.

So far, nothing has been said about this concept of truth other than that it is independent of judgement. But despite the minimalism of the present argument, we can already see the amount of philosophical work that is being done by these concepts. I started this section with the observation that if you say there are three apples and I deny it, the fact of the matter is independent of either of us. Neither of us can make our judgements true at will. And that, I observed, is why we have something to argue about. The work being done by these minimal concepts of truth and judgement can be seen if we vary the example.

Suppose you said that Charlie Chaplin was funny and I denied it. Or suppose you said that eating meat was wrong and I denied it. In these cases, it is harder to see what the independent fact of the matter could be. In these cases we are more prone to suppose that perhaps there is no such thing as these claims being true independent of our judging them to be so. Perhaps, when it comes to judgements about humour and morality there is no truth independent of will? If you find Chaplin funny, that's the end of the matter. If I find meat-eating okay, that's the end of the matter. Once we have said how things strike us there is nothing more to argue about.

In the simple case of the number of apples in the fruit dish, we start by saying how things strike us – you think there are three and I do not – and then we proceed to see who is right. But being right about the matter is making a judgement that, if true, is true independent of our will. We do not make truth. When it comes to judgements about humour and morality it is more difficult to see what this idea of independent truth amounts to. If humour and morality were just a matter of how things strike us, not of how things are, then there would be nothing to argue about in these cases. These would not be areas that were subject to rational methods of persuasion. To convince you about the number of apples in the fruitbowl I provide an argument and some evidence. I appeal to your reason. But if the truth/judgement distinction did not apply in the moral case then where we disagree there would be no point in my trying to appeal to your reason. Perhaps I should appeal to your passions, your feelings, your emotions? I try to 'win you over', but not by methods of rational persuasion that are aimed at truth. Rather I work to get you to see things my way, to feel things the way I do. The whole operation would come to resemble a matter of artistic taste, not of truth.

The apparent contrast between the case of the apples and the cases of humour and morality shows that reflection on the nature of the truth/judgement distinction is a powerful tool for our purposes. Clearly, whether or not one thinks that the truth/judgement distinction applies to moral utterances depends on what else we say about this distinction. It depends on what models we employ in articulating this basic constraint.

The present point that I want to make is simply this. Asking whether or not the basic constraint applies to moral discourse raises precisely the kinds of issues that have dominated moral philosophy and which lie at the heart of the postmodernist claim of the fragmentation of truth and rationality. Ever since Hume claimed that men were creatures of passion not of reason, moral philosophers have wrestled with the problem of where that leaves any notion of moral truth and moral reasoning. Rorty, who has been the clearest advocate of philosophical postmodernism, embraces the label of 'ironist' about values, precisely because he believes that there is no such thing as truth. According to Rorty, our discussions and discourses are to be understood more on the model of imaginative exercises in which we attempt to get people to see things in different ways. They are exercises in which we imaginatively explore novel possibilities and recommend them to one another. However, the 'recommendation' is not the recommendation of reason and truth, but the recommendation of taste and sensibility, of imagination and pathos.[2]

The idea that there is a fundamental division between matters susceptible of truth and reason and matters of passion or sensibility goes back a long way. It is the distinction marked by the ancient Greek concepts of logos and pathos. It is a distinction that has become ingrained in our culture and that manifests itself in the idea that it is science that offers us the way of logos – reason and truth – whereas the arts, music and literature offer us the way of pathos – sensibility.

The remainder of this book is an exploration of the options available to us in the way in which we understand the basic constraint now before us. Despite the minimal point made by acknowledging the basic constraint, in the light of the above considerations it does seem that asking the following questions about it is going to be a good route into the examination of the claims of postmodernist philosophy. We need to ask: what else, in addition to the basic constraint, do we need to say about truth? Does acceptance of the basic constraint commit us to the identification of logos (the way of truth) with the methods of science? Does the basic constraint rule out the possibility that truth might apply to morality? Does the basic constraint force us to accept a sharp distinction between logos and pathos, between truth and sensibility?

It will take the remainder of this book to develop answers to these questions and to acquire an understanding of what the basic constraint commits us to. Our first task is to plot the connection between logos, the way of the cosmic register, and science.

FROM DOGMA TO ENLIGHTENMENT

We need to know the basis for the idea that science can read the cosmic register, the idea that science has the measure of reality. The idea that science has the ability to peer behind the veil of our common-sense view of the world and reveal what is really going on is extraordinarily common. Although many thinkers now question whether science is due such esteem, before we can appreciate the critique of science we must be clear about its apparent virtues. To do this it helps to look back to the origins of modern science as early modern Europe threw off scholastic dogmatism and started on the road to enlightenment.

Like most movements in history, the rise of science does not fall into neat and well regimented epochs. Nevertheless, it is useful to distinguish two important watersheds in the rise of science. The first development was the rejection of scholasticism as early medieval Europe threw off its Aristotelian inheritance. The second development was the arrival of physicalism as the dominant view of the nature of scientific knowledge. This was a view that developed through the sixteenth and seventeenth centuries until, with the full flood of the eighteenth-century Enlightenment, it began to dominate the philosophical community. It still does so today.

The first episode in the rise of science is concerned with the idea that there is such a thing as scientific method. The second episode is concerned with the idea that there is such a thing as the language of science. The rejection of scholasticism was a rejection of bad methods for generating knowledge. Accordingly, the first virtue of science was that it embodied a method suited for generating knowledge; it offered a method for reading the cosmic register.

The development of physicalism was the development of the belief that good methods for generating knowledge required that we operate our science in a restricted language – the language of physical processes. So the second virtue of science was that it offered to generate a uniform description of the world, a description in terms of which all else could be explained and understood. The physicalist descriptions provided by science could be seen as a sort of melting pot in which our different points of view could be melted down to a common currency. The world is a world of matter in motion; the cosmic register is written in the language of the mechanics of this motion. This is the language in which, as it were, the world speaks to itself – the music of the spheres. Instead of the pre-modern idea of seeking communion with the mind of God, the modern world seeks to listen to the clatter of objects bumping into one another.

These two aspects of science are distinct ideas. Taken together they characterise a familiar and common way of thinking about human knowledge. However, there is no requirement that we have to take them together. They did not arise at the same time and there is no necessary connection between them.

BACON: A RECIPE FOR SUCCESS

The idea that there is such a thing as scientific method, a recipe for picking out knowledge from mere opinion, is commonly traced to Francis Bacon (1561–1626). Bacon wanted to spell out the method by which we could arrive at truth. Given that we want our judgements to correspond with what is recorded in the cosmic register, what method should we employ in forming judgements? Bacon thought there was a method which offered a reliable way of picking out truth. He thought it was the task of the philosopher to clarify this method. Once clarified it would enable the generation of knowledge – judgement which corresponded with the cosmic register – to proceed uncluttered by false starts and unhindered by erroneous presumptions. There is much disagreement amongst Bacon scholars over the nature of his recipe for success.[3] Nevertheless, the idea that he thought there could be such a recipe is acknowledged by all, as too is the nature of the problems which beset the 'science' of Bacon's time.

The central problem that Bacon thought threatened the science of his time was dogmatism and, in particular, the authority that Aristotle had come to possess in the scientific community. The wisdom of the Greeks, he claimed, 'has the characteristic property of boys: it can talk, but it cannot generate; for it is fruitful of controversies but barren of works'. Science, he thought, was barren and was making little, if any, progress.

Bacon attributed these problems to two central failures. First, too many thinkers ignored the role of experience and experimentation in their enquiries. Instead they satisfied themselves with the 'giddy whirl of argument', too often starting from first principles accepted dogmatically as part and parcel of the Aristotelian inheritance. Second, where scientists did acknowledge the importance of experiments, their idea of experimentation was shallow. Their appeal to experience was too superficial to provide genuine tests of the acceptability of their theories.

The first failure is the most important one. Bacon lived in a time when arguments in support of a theory were conducted with almost total disregard for experimental facts. Too often it was considered sufficient to support theories by appeal to the authority of learned authors from the past. Aristotle was the favourite authority. This meant that if it could be shown that a theory was derivable from the views of Aristotle, that was counted sufficient to show the theory to be true.

In terms of our image of the cosmic register the problem with this is obvious. We want to know if we are able to read the cosmic register, but the key test available in Bacon's time is whether our views correspond with the works of Aristotle. The adequacy of that test turns on whether Aristotle had read the cosmic register right. But in accepting the works of Aristotle as articles of dogmatic faith there is no hope of measuring the adequacy of the appeal to Aristotle's authority. Clearly, if our task is one of trying to read the cosmic register and of looking for a recipe for successful reading, it does no good if our only recipe is to read the works of other enquirers. The general problem concerns whether any of the works of man have succeeded in reading the cosmic register and, if so, how they have succeeded. Bacon's critique of the dogmatic acceptance of the Aristotelian science of his day is well founded. The only recipe for success that his contemporaries employed was to test the coherence of their views with the views of Aristotle. That cannot begin to measure the success of a theory in terms of its correspondence with the cosmic register.

Bacon's concern with the inadequacy of experimentation in those rare instances where it was undertaken flows from his identification of the problems associated with dogmatism. Where experiments occurred they were not used as independent tests of theories. Instead, experiments were conducted as confirming showpieces. They were used to confirm a theory already passed fit due to its coherence with the dogmatically accepted Aristotelian view. Experiments were conceived with no serious intent to test the experimenter's theory. Theories were measured for their adequacy in conforming to the accepted view. Experiments were mere frosting on the cake of this incestuous relationship between the Aristotelian inheritance and the theories of Bacon's contemporaries.

If Bacon's chief diagnosis of the ills of the science of his day lay in the charge of dogmatism, what was his recipe for avoiding this dogmatism and achieving success in reading the cosmic register? It is here that we find disagreement amongst modern Bacon scholars, disagreements that would take us too far off course if we were to try to pursue them here. One point, however, is clear. Whatever else is true of Bacon's recipe for knowledge, it is clear that the role of experience and experimentation is central. That is the key to his critique of scholastic dogmatism. It is not enough to test our theories in terms of their coherence with respected authorities like Aristotle. They must be tested against the benchmark of our common experience through repeatable and rigorous experimentation.

It is on the question of the exact role experience plays in Bacon's thought that modern scholars disagree. The traditional interpretation of Bacon took Bacon to endorse a simplistic model of the generation of knowledge in which all that had to be done to generate knowledge was for us passively to sit back and let the world flood into our experience. On this interpretation, the Baconian accumulation of knowledge would be acquired in a highly mechanistic way. On this account, experiments are seen as conduits through which knowledge is accumulated rather than as critical tests of theories. Bacon is then seen as replacing a simple-minded reliance on the dogmatic acceptance of authorised texts as the conduit of knowledge, with a simple-minded reliance on experience instead. The reliance on ancient authority is replaced with a reliance on an untutored induction on experience.

I doubt that this account of Bacon is right. Indeed, I suspect that recent work that claims Bacon as a precursor of many modern ideas in the philosophy of science is probably much nearer the mark. The modern view of Bacon sees him advocating

a much more sophisticated and complex role for experience and
experimentation in the accumulation of knowledge. It is an
account that has Bacon anticipating ideas about the growth of
scientific knowledge that have become associated with Popper's
philosophy of science.[4]

On this modern view, Bacon's chief insight lay in his advocacy
of a critical use of experience and experimentation to test theories. He did not believe that a simple induction on experience
would automatically generate true theoretical knowledge. He
believed that although the generation of theories was not a
straightforward mechanistic process, it could and should be sub-
jected to certain heuristic rules. This means that Bacon accepted
that theoretical claims 'go beyond' observational claims; a theoretical claim refers to features of the world that are not experi-
enceable by untutored sense experience. The idea that the claims
of theoretical science 'go beyond' the claims of untutored
common sense is an important point. We shall have need to refer
back to this on a number of occasions, so it is as well that we be
clear about what the point is here.

To say that theoretical claims go beyond the claims of sense
experience, or observational claims, is to make two related points.
The first point is an epistemological one, concerned with the
nature of knowledge. If a theoretical claim goes beyond observational claims then this means, epistemologically, that there is
no valid derivation of the theoretical claim from observational
claims. This can be expressed by saying that the theoretical claim
is a stronger claim than the observational one, for, if it is true, it
commits us to more than the observational claim.

The second point is a semantic one, concerned with the meaning of theoretical science. In this sense, to say that theoretical
claims go beyond observational claims is to say that the meaning
of the former cannot be captured in the meaning of an observational claim or any set of observational claims. This means that
there is no way of reducing talk about unobservable theoretical
entities to talk about observable entities. Philosophers and scientists have, on many occasions in history, attempted just such
reductions, but if we accept that theoretical claims go beyond
observational ones such reductions must fail.

These two points, the epistemological and the semantic, are
related. It is because the theoretical claim is semantically stronger
than the observational claim that it makes a claim that is not

derivable from observational reports and so, from the point of view of our observations, it is a harder claim to justify. These points can be illustrated with an example.

Suppose we visit a physics laboratory in a modern university and are confronted with a cloud chamber. This is a device employed for detecting and monitoring the paths and collisions of invisible particles. When a high energy particle, say an alpha particle, crosses the cloud chamber it leaves a vapour trail that marks its path. The particle itself is invisible. It is too small to be detected by ordinary light, but the disturbance its path makes in the cloud chamber is visible. On seeing this result we can make two distinct claims.

First, we might report:

(1) A vapour trail has passed across the cloud chamber.

This is to make a very weak claim about the world. (1) says no more than that the world looks a certain way. However, to report:

(2) An alpha particle has passed across the cloud chamber

is to make a much stronger theoretical claim about the world, a claim that is not deducible from the observational claim. If you believe the theoretical claim is true you are committed to much more than if you merely assented to the observational claim. If you believe the theoretical claim you are committed to the existence of certain kinds of invisible particles. The semantic point of saying that (2) goes beyond (1) is that the meaning of (2) is not reducible to (1) or sets of statements like (1). The epistemological point of saying that (2) goes beyond (1) is that (1) is a much more secure claim about the world, a claim that gives only tenuous support for the stronger claim in (2). It is relatively easy to agree that (1) is true, but it requires considerable sophistication of both intellect and equipment to have warrant for believing that (2) is true.

I think it is clear that Bacon believed that theoretical science goes beyond mere observation and so cannot be based upon observational claims in any simple or mechanical manner. Nevertheless, he put forward rules for the formulation of theories on the basis of experience. These rules were designed to show how we could rule out some theories and advocate others through a series of critical experiments. The rules were designed to weed out the weak from the strong theoretical hunches. His account of how to reach a theoretical understanding of the phenomenon of heat is a good example of this method.

However, despite the availability of this heuristic, Bacon's chief insight concerns the critical role experiments play in his scientific method. Hypotheses are made, for example, about the nature of heat, and are then tested with crucial experiments designed to sort out which hypotheses will stand critical examination and which will not. That is the key to Bacon's method, the critical employment of experiments in the testability of theories.

This highly undogmatic methodology does not have an accepted label. I propose that we call it 'critical empiricism'. The 'empiricism' in the title signals the break with the dogmatic rationalism of Bacon's contemporaries who, in measuring the adequacy of their theories, relied solely on a test of compatibility with the Aristotelian inheritance. The 'critical' signals that the appeal to experience and experimentation is not an appeal to experience as an unchallenged conduit for knowledge. Experience cannot be like that. No experience on its own could deliver the idea that heat is due to the excitation of invisible particles of matter; it takes experience informed by theoretical hunches to get to that.

We can summarise the basic tenets of critical empiricism in two claims:

Critical empiricism:
1 The advancement of scientific knowledge requires our making theoretical 'guesses' which go beyond the evidence supplied by our senses.
2 All theoretical claims must be subject to experimental testing.

The first claim is a metaphysical point. It presupposes the idea that reality is independent of our experience and judgement. It assumes that our claims about reality cannot be reduced to reports about our experiences. The second claim makes the epistemological point that our claims about reality need to be supported by evidence. Critical empiricism may seem an intellectually undemanding doctrine. Does it not merely summarise a very common-sensical view of the world and of the way we gather our knowledge of it? If critical empiricism seems very common-sensical that is in part a reflection of the enormous influence philosophers such as Bacon have had upon common sense. Despite this, critical empiricism has grave problems. But, for the moment, let us accept that it appears to capture something very fundamental to our idea of the proper way of going about the business of finding out how the world works. It offers a credible first approximation of a recipe for success in reading the cosmic register.

SCIENCE, KNOWLEDGE AND *SCIENTIA*

Does critical empiricism capture the method of science? The simple and important answer to this question is that it all depends on what we mean by 'science'. Nowadays we are inclined to use the term 'science' to refer to a particular institutionalised search for knowledge concentrated on our investigations of the natural, physical world. We sometimes clarify this by speaking instead of the 'natural sciences' or the 'physical sciences', but, by and large, 'science' is used to refer to those activities that engage in physical investigations of the physical world. This usage has the important and often unnoticed consequence that for any branch of enquiry to be accorded the status of 'science', it must deal with the phenomena it investigates in a way that fits within an overall physicalist view of the world. A good example of the operation of this constraint is psychology. There is a common presumption that, as a science, this discipline only came of age when it found the vocabulary to discuss the investigation of human cognition in a manner continuous with the physical and chemical discussion of the rest of the physical universe. Hence, the common tendency to view the hard end of psychology, in neurophysiology, computer simulations of intelligence, etc., as those parts of the discipline most scientific. On this view, social psychology has yet to earn its reputation as a science.

This view is unwarranted. In terms of the tenets of critical empiricism, it is little more than confused prejudice. Critical empiricism as so far outlined offers a recipe for uncovering knowledge with no restrictions on the domains in which that recipe may be applied. It is a modern confusion to think that science must be restricted to a description and understanding of things physical. The root of the term 'science' lies in the Latin *scientia* and this carried no such connotation in favour of knowledge of the physical universe. *Scientia* would be better translated simply as 'knowledge'. It is *scientia* which is picked out by critical empiricism. Critical empiricism offers a method for arriving at judgements which correspond to entries in the cosmic register. It does this irrespective of how those judgements might be framed in the language of physics, chemistry, human cognition, morality, religious faith, or whatever.

So, if we restrict 'science' to the physical sciences, critical empiricism does not capture the method of science. What it captures is the idea of a general method for arriving at judgements that are true – entries in the cosmic register – with no presumption that in order for a judgement to be one that mirrors the cosmic register it must be stated in a particular language. It may be the case that, in order to subject our theoretical claims to experimental testing, we will have to frame those claims in the language of physical processes. But if that is so, that is not something which mere reflection upon the idea of a recipe for success – a general methodology for knowledge – shows to be so. As such, the idea of critical empiricism is neutral on the question of whether all knowledge must be expressible in the language of the physical sciences. Critical empiricism is neutral on the question of whether the cosmic register is written in the language of mathematical physics.

On its own, critical empiricism offers a recipe for arriving at truth however we may subsequently think that truth is written or expressed. The idea that the truth about the world can be captured wholly within the restricted language of physical events and processes is an idea that signals a later development in the history of the rise of science.

LOCKE AND THE LANGUAGE OF SCIENCE

By the time John Locke published his *Essay Concerning Human Understanding* at the end of the seventeenth century, the idea that the activity of science was primarily an investigation of the physical universe had acquired wide support. In his 'Epistle to the Reader' Locke famously remarked that his role was that of an under-labourer to the sciences. Locke was widely read and well-connected with the scientists of his day and grasped the importance of the advances that were being made in scientific knowledge. Locke accepted that scientists were beginning to unravel how the world worked and took his philosophical task to be the description of the conceptual apparatus that made this achievement possible.

By the time Locke came to write his essay the probings and explanations of the physical world provided by scientists were gaining an impressive cumulative effect. In 1609 Kepler had published his first two laws of planetary motion explaining the apparently irregular movements of the planets. In 1610 Galileo revealed the observations made with a telescope that convinced him of the truth of the idea that the earth moves around the sun. In 1616 the English physician William Harvey discovered the circulation of the blood. By the second half of the seventeenth century Newton had begun his discoveries. In 1665 he discovered the laws of gravitation; in the following two years he discovered the composition of white light and a new branch of mathematics – calculus.

Locke saw his job as one of analysing the range and scope of human cognition to explain how these achievements had been possible. It is clear at several stages of his analysis that he assumes that the real world is to be identified with the world as described in the physicalist language of his scientific friends, the burgeoning club of associates who founded the Royal Society in 1660. It is from these thinkers onwards that the idea begins to take hold of the cosmic register as a work written in the language of physics. The cosmic register becomes an exhaustive account of the total matter of the universe in motion. The beginnings of this move towards the metaphysics of physicalism is seen in the corpuscular theory of matter and Locke's celebrated distinction between primary and secondary qualities.

Locke's distinction between primary and secondary qualities is best thought of as a distinction between the qualities that figure in a scientific description of the world and those that only figure in our ordinary common-sense descriptions of the world. It is a distinction between two different languages. Common sense tells us that ripe tomatoes are red and grass is green. However, the description of these items provided by science has no room for the qualities of redness and greenness. Colours do not figure in the scientific description of the world; they are not part of that language. From the scientific description what we learn is that tomatoes have a particular kind of fine-grained surface structure. This causes them to reflect electromagnetic radiation of a specific wavelength; a ripe tomato reflects light of a wavelength of around 7,000 ångström. Whereas common sense says that tomatoes are red, science tells us that they have a particular molecular structure that affects the kind of light they reflect.

As such, this distinction makes manifest the point that there are some properties which common sense tends to find important, like colour, and yet which science ignores. Why should this be so? The difference between these two kinds of descriptions appears to be this. The scientific description, which concentrates on the purely material properties of things (like size, shape, motion), provides a description of the world which is not restricted to the way the world affects us. In contrast, to describe an object as coloured is to describe it relative to the way that objects affect us. This is an important difference.

The language of science is a language that sticks purely to the material, or mechanical, properties of things. As such, it claims to be a language with universal application. In contrast, the language of colours is a language with a very limited application, for it describes objects only in terms of the effects objects have upon us. This seems to be the way Locke saw the importance of this distinction. On the view born in the Lockean corpuscular theory of matter, the world is a world of matter in motion, a flurry of particles moving around and colliding with one another in all sorts of ways, but fundamentally governed by the laws of mechanics. This is the corpuscular theory of matter. The whole of the material universe is one large mêlée of particles jostling one another. What then happens when we look at a ripe tomato? Locke's answer goes like this.

When confronted with a ripe tomato, light particles bounce off the surface of the tomato in ways governed by the fundamental mechanics of matter in motion. These particles (light corpuscles) travel away from the tomato in all directions. Some of them reach our human eyeballs. When they do so, they have an effect upon the human eye that is, once more, governed solely by the mechanics of matter in motion. This effect causes further transmissions of particles along the optic nerve to the visual centre in the brain. All this activity is the activity of matter in motion. The activity is concluded when, within the brain, this activity gives rise to an experience of redness, an experience which looks to us as if we see an object splashed in red. Locke has nothing much to say on how this final stage of the physical process produces the experience of redness and, as we shall see, this is not without problems. But taking the overall picture of this process at face value the conclusion we seem drawn towards is simple. Colour is not a property of the real tomato. Colour is a feature only of our subjective experience of real objects, like tomatoes, that have the ability to produce this long sequence of effects upon us. In short, colour is an effect the world produces in us; it is not an objective feature of the world. A similar analysis can be given for Locke's other secondary qualities, for example taste and sound. The bitterness of an almond, to take one of Locke's own examples, is, like its colour, an effect produced within our minds; it is not an objective property of the object.

There are two important points to be noted about the possibility of this kind of physical explanation of colour experience. First, by concentrating on the material properties of things and the mechanics of their interaction science is able to give an explanation of colour vision. The sort of story sketched above explains the experience of colour and does so in an economical way. The economy of the explanation means that the phenomenon of colour experience can be brought within the same explanatory framework as all the other phenomena investigated by physical science. The unification of explanation achieved supports the thesis of the unity of science.

The unity-of-science thesis is the claim that science can be thought of as one uniform attempt to capture the whole of reality within a single framework of explanation. For this to be possible, we must expect that psychology will be reducible to physiology, physiology reducible to chemistry, and chemistry reducible to physics. The laws of physics, the laws governing matter in motion, are to be seen as the fundamental laws that define the boundaries of scientific explanation. The outline sketch of an explanation of colour vision above is an example of just such an attempt to bring all phenomena within the range of physicalist explanations. Adherence to the unity-of-science thesis entails adherence to the idea that if something is not capturable within the scientific image of the world, it ain't really there. Science then becomes the grand narrative which defines the world's own story.

That brings us to the second point to be noted about the outline explanation of colour vision. Properties, like colours, that common sense ascribes to the world but that turn out not to figure in the scientific explanation of worldly goings-on, are not then real properties. Colours, and a whole host of properties that commonsensically we ascribe to things, are merely subjective effects that the world produces in our minds. The scientific explanation of how these effects are brought about only confirms the suspicion that such properties are not part of the real world. They are part of the world of subjective experience. In so far as common sense leads us to think that colours are objective features of objects, common sense is subject to illusion. All that is really out there are objects with propensities to produce certain sorts of effects in us. The propensities by which objects achieve this are fully describable in the physicalist language of physical science.

On the picture we are putting together, colours are not the only example of properties about which common sense is subject to illusion, confusing objective properties of things with the subjective effects of reality upon the human mind. Aesthetic and moral values are other good examples. From the scientific point of view, the moral property of kindness is not an objective property of an action, but rather signals an effect certain sorts of actions are prone to have on us, namely that we have a certain sort of emotional response. So moral values are not objective properties of the world. Morality is not objective. Moral claims are concerned with the emotional responses we have to a world that is morally inert, just as colour descriptions are concerned with particular psychological responses we have to a world that is colourless.

The idea that there is such a thing as the language of science, and that it is the language of matter in motion as captured by physics, presents us with a powerful metaphysical image. It is the image of the objective world conceived as matter in motion laid out before us with a whole range of properties relegated to the status of psychological effects located within the human mind. Science offers the prospect of uncovering the way this objective world works and revealing the illusions of common sense, such as our untutored tendency to believe that colours and values are part of the fabric of the world. They are not. They are part of our subjective view of the world. Although science offers us great power and explanation, in revealing the illusions of common sense it offers also what Max Weber called 'the scientific disenchantment of the world'. In this modern materialist image of the objective world, science replaces the gods and demons of earlier magical and mystical images of the universe with a materialist debunking of all that is mysterious. The modern physicalist expects quite soon to bring the whole of creation within the range of the scientific field of explanation. In doing science we may be talking the language of the world, but we rapidly discover that it is a peculiarly restrictive language. If that is the language of the world, there is not a lot out there.[5]

SCIENCE THE GREAT PRETENDER

Once we ally the idea of the recipe for success to the idea of the language of science we have a powerful model of the supremacy of science. It is science which will define what is real and what is not. Through its recipe for success science has the ability to read the cosmic register. Through the idea of the language of science, science effectively ensures that any claim not expressible in the language of physicalism cannot figure in the cosmic register. Claims of morality do not correspond with entries in the cosmic register, for they are written in the wrong language. Therefore, there are no objective truths in morals, just as there are no objective truths about the colours of objects. In both cases claims about these things are mere opinion, subjective preferences perhaps, but not judgements with a corresponding entry in the cosmic register. In the modern world our destiny is to see the world stripped bare, with no objective colours, values, needs or emotions. In learning the language of the world we find the world lacks all these things that seem important to us. In learning the language of the world we learn a vision of how things really are, a world consisting of frenzied clouds of particles in motion.

Despite the enormous power of the image of science as the arbiter of what goes in the cosmic register and what does not, nothing has been said so far about why we should accept this role for science. If we accept the idea that there is such a thing as the recipe for success – a methodology for uncovering knowledge – why should we restrict the application of the recipe to judgements made within one particular and highly specialised language, namely the physicalist language of physics? This is the central question. For the moment there are a number of points that can be made in defence of the pretence of science as final arbiter of truth and falsehood.

Perhaps the most obvious point to be made in defence of the scientific view of the world is the observation that science has enjoyed an enormous success so far. The success is a success in explanation, prediction and control. Science has taught us how diseases are spread, why water droplets have a maximum size, why a feather and a stone fall with equal acceleration in a vacuum and yet, when dropped from a tower, one falls quicker than the other. Indeed, the range of our explanations is as broad as the range of our inquisitiveness. Wherever we have asked 'how?' or 'why?', sooner or later, with perseverance, some good luck and occasional flashes of genius, we have come up with the answer.

The range of answers that we have acquired to our puzzlements about the world is matched by our increasing success in predicting the future course of events. Even weather forecasters now get a lot right. We can predict with hair-splitting accuracy the position of planetary orbits and projectiles we have sent into space. We can predict the precise point of impact of terrestrial projectiles (invariably military ones) with an accuracy often beyond the power of resolution of the human eye. We can predict the course of disease, the growth of crops. We can even predict such recherché events as the bending of light by objects with large gravitational fields and still get it all right.

It is this predictive success that has given us the power to control our environment, a power that would not have been ours without the achievements of science. Like all power, this is a power that we have abused and not always wielded with wisdom. But despite our frequent foolishness and despoiling of the environment, there has been enormous benefit from our collective power. We can control most diseases even if, for political and economic reasons, we do not always decide to do so. Similarly, we have the power to defeat starvation given the control that our scientific knowledge has given us over crop development, both in terms of the production of disease-resistant strains of basic food crops and the control of their natural pests. Indeed, we have clearly conquered our environment even if we have not always recognised this or been wise conquerors. Even large-scale natural disasters like hurricanes can be predicted with enough accuracy about their timing and location to give some protection.

The practical consequences of our scientific achievements in terms of the growth of explanation, prediction and control add up to an impressive argument in favour of accepting the scientific view of the world. For many people this is reason enough to accept the idea that the cosmic register is written in the language of mathematical physics. However, there is a more important point to be made in defence of the supremacy of science as a means of reading the cosmic register.

THE WORLD'S OWN LANGUAGE

The central idea behind the cosmic register is the idea that truth is independent of judgement, and that is what makes it objective. Truth concerns what is objectively the case however we may think about it. The idea behind the notion of a recipe for success is the idea that it is a recipe for detecting truth amongst the distortions of human dogma. We need a way of sifting out the dogma in order to arrive at judgements that match the objective truth. The concern for knowledge is a concern to sweep away the veil of our ignorant and sometimes dogmatic illusions to arrive at an account of what is really going on. We can express this by saying that our concern is to arrive at an account of the world that transcends our limited and perhaps erroneous point of view. The cosmic register expresses truth that transcends the limitations of human judgements. Now, is it not by working with the physicalist language of the physical sciences that this transcendence is made possible? In other words, is it not the case that it is the very minimalism of the physicalist descriptions, stripped of the thicker complex vocabulary of morality, aesthetics and so on, that makes the search for objectivity possible? The very sparseness of the scientific physical outlook, in ignoring the complications and clutter of our commonsensical point of view, has enabled us to apply our recipe for success and achieve knowledge. The language of science is a language that describes the world independently of the effects (colours, values, etc.) that the world has upon one particular species, namely ourselves. As such, the language of science is the language of objective truth, for it provides a way of describing what is going on independently of our particular point of view, the view of untutored common sense.

The idea that there is something special about the language of science that makes it ideal for a description of the world that transcends our limited points of view is important. It is the idea that there is such a thing as a unique language for describing the world as it is in itself. For such a language to be possible it must have a very special property. I shall say that such a language is transparent.

To say that the language of the cosmic register is transparent is to say that judgements found in the cosmic register must be judgements which 'stand alone'. That is to say, they must be truths which can be expressed in a way that is independent of anyone's particular point of view. What makes the cosmic register a register of truth that is cosmic is the idea that the judgements recorded in it could be read by anyone. The entries in the cosmic register must be entries that can be made fully explicit and recorded in full in a language that would be transparent to anyone who tried to read it. So, judgements that are entered in the cosmic register must be judgements that can be fully expressed in a language in such a way that nothing is left to be misinterpreted or misunderstood by the reader. The cosmic register must say the same thing to any reader who confronted it. Only then will it be cosmic. So, a transparent language is one the meaning of which is fully expressible in the language's symbolic system so that there is no further interpretation required in order to understand a sentence of the language. Therefore, there is no scope for different creatures, or different kinds of creatures, to understand such a language differently. A transparent language offers, if you like, a self-interpreting description of the world. It is the world's own language.

The very idea of the cosmic register of absolute truth presupposes a language, a system of concepts, that could be understood by any kind of creature no matter how that creature was constructed, what kind of mind and perceptual systems it had, and what its history and culture was. The language of the natural sciences, in particular mathematical physics, is the prime candidate for such a language. It is a transparent language.

This explains why Locke should have thought that colours were not real. The language of colours is not a transparent language, for to describe a ripe tomato as red is to describe it in a way that could only be understood by certain types of mind – those with the appropriate perceptual system. However, to describe a tomato as spherical is, perhaps, to describe it with a concept that is transparent. For any creature that acknowledged the existence of the external world, no matter what perceptual systems it had, it would have to grasp differences in shape between objects. Spheres present a different kind of obstacle to a creature's movement through space from the kind of obstacle presented by a cube. Therefore, just so long as a creature is able to detect the differing space occupancy of objects in the environment, it will possess concepts of shape. Of course, it may not possess exactly the same shape concepts as ours. For example, for some creatures the difference between perfect cubes and other rhomboids may not be particularly salient. Nevertheless, any creature which understood the general principles of space occupancy would surely have the capability to discriminate between such differences in shape. However, unless a creature is equipped with a similar visual system to the human one, it will not grasp the concepts of colour.

In summary then, the language of the cosmic register must be transparent. This means that it is a language the content of which is fully captured in the symbols used. It might seem that that is a feature of all languages, but that would be a mistake. The point is simply this: the sentence

(1) Tomatoes are red

only carries a meaning for creatures, like ourselves, who are appropriately equipped with the right kind of visual system. Only such creatures are able to interpret this sentence. In contrast,

(2) Tomatoes are spherical

carries a meaning that can be grasped by any kind of creature. Of course, the sentence at (2) is a human sentence, a sentence of a particular human language, English. Nevertheless, its meaning is transparent, for its meaning could be captured in any language whatsoever. This is not the case with (1). The meaning of (1) would not be expressible in the language of creatures with only a monochromatic visual system, for it seems plausible to think that such creatures would lack colour concepts.

To put this point in another way: The meaning of (2) can be fully captured in the language of mathematical physics and that, so the hypothesis goes, is a language in principle we would expect any kind of rational creature to understand. It is the language of mathematical physics that provides the transparent language of the cosmic register. In that language we would not have the expressive power to express the meaning that creatures like ourselves express with (1).

The language of science offers clear and unambiguous questions to put to the world, questions that can receive a simple yes/

no answer recorded in the cosmic register. For example, to ask whether a tomato is at a particular place is surely to ask just such a question, a question with a simple yes/no answer. However, to ask if the tomato is red is not such a question, for the answer you get to that question is relative to the kind of creature who asks the question and the kinds of effects tomatoes have upon them. Indeed, it is a question that can only be asked in certain specific and local languages. Colour vocabulary should not then figure in a language suited for asking questions of the cosmic register and, of course, colour vocabulary does not figure in the materialist language of science.

Let us summarise this discussion as follows:

> The language of the cosmic register is a language that is fully transparent. It offers descriptions of reality that are independent of any interpretation placed upon the language by different kinds of creatures. The transparent language of the cosmic register is, if you like, a self-interpreting language, for there is no possible ambiguity or scope for interpretation and misinterpretation about what such a language says. It is the language of the world; it is the world's own language.

One kind of ambiguity that rules out a proposition's potential entry in the cosmic register is the ambiguity that arises when a proposition makes a claim which is incomplete, for it is a claim that only describes the world relative to the effects it has upon certain sorts of creatures. To ask if the tomato is red is to ask an ambiguous, because incomplete, question, for the tomato is not objectively red. Redness is a subjective effect tomatoes have upon certain creatures. As we shall see in the next chapter, there are more ways in which a proposition can fail to be transparent than the case of propositions about colour.

There is then something very appealing about both the claims of scientific success and the idea that science has made these achievements within a language that is transparent. Such a language is suited for acquiring objective knowledge as modelled in the idea of the cosmic register. Science offers to describe the world not from my point of view or from your point of view; it offers to describe the world not from our point of view or from the point of view of any other kinds of creatures; science offers a transparent description of the world. It offers the absolute conception of the world. This is a description of the world in its own terms. Our destiny, according to the modern image, is to speak the language of the world – to learn the world's own story – and it is by doing science that we can achieve this destiny. Science possesses not only the recipe for objective knowledge, but the language in which such knowledge (truth independent of our point of view) must be written.

In its pursuit of explanations science has continued to rid the world of mystery and put everything in its place. Later in this book we shall look at the issue of whether the success of science has rendered religious faith an unnecessary piece of excess baggage in our understanding of the world. The common view that the success of science threatens the demise of faith is supported if we accept the identification of objective knowledge with truth written in the transparent language of physicalism. This is a view that has come to dominate much of our western culture. It is the view that there is such a thing as the cosmic register – the world's own story – and that this is a book written in the language of mathematical physics. It is a view the challenges to which will occupy the rest of this book.

Two issues will now dominate our enquiry. First, is such an ideal of objective knowledge possible? Is it really possible that there could be such a thing as a transparent language, let alone that we might achieve the revelatory state of learning this language and the knowledge it expresses? Second, if we think this goal is out of our reach, what goes in its place? Postmodernists say that there is no universal transparent language. But does that mean that the ideal of the cosmic register is to be replaced by a babble of chattering? Is the semi-divine role of the scientists who thought they could speak the language of the world to be replaced by the anarchic chaos of the chattering classes? These questions need answering. The rest of this book examines these questions and shows where some of the answers lie. The first job is to start the process of undermining the idea that there is a universal transparent language of the world and that it is the language that scientists speak.

Chapter 2

Mind – the final mystery?

INTRODUCTION

I have outlined reasons for thinking that there is such a thing as objective knowledge and that this comes from speaking the world's own language. This is an idea of knowledge as fully expressible within the language of the physical sciences. The eighteenth-century confidence in the Enlightenment project that human reason could learn the absolute truth about the world grew into the modern vision that this truth would be expressible in the transparent discourse of science. We have a model for this: the model of the cosmic register. That model is now challenged. It is time to introduce the problems and arguments that now threaten to chip away the very foundations of knowledge, and science in particular.

The postmodernist threat, especially in the hands of Rorty, arises out of a direct challenge about the nature of language. Language has been one of the central preoccupations of twentieth-century thinkers. Language has taken over the role 'Ideas' played for earlier thinkers as the vehicle of thought. The idea that there could be a transparent language, one that required no interpretation, goes against the grain of most contemporary theories of language. All meaning is interpretative, so the contemporary slogan goes, and perhaps there is no end to the interpretations possible of any given piece of language. No wonder then that contemporary literary critics have given up trying to fathom authors' intentions, for between reader and author lies an infinitely deep layer of interpretations and counter-interpretations.

However, rather than review contemporary theories of language directly and try to unpeel the complex philosophies which prompt such views about language and interpretation, I shall take a more direct and simple route. I believe that the key postmodernist insights are more accessible if put first as a critique of science. In this chapter I shall review the threat to the scientific enterprise that comes from insisting that science cannot explain everything.

The first threat challenges the ability of the physical sciences to unravel all the workings of the universe. It is a challenge to the universalism of the scientific enterprise. This threat starts when we ask whether knowledge has to be restricted to what can be expressed in the language of science. It also introduces us to some preliminary ideas about that most difficult of the Big Ideas of the modern meta-narratives: the self.

THE STUFF OF MIND

A central stumbling block to the continued progress of science's ability to explain the totality of the universe is the mind, and the nature of consciousness. The fact that there is a difficulty with fitting mental phenomena within a materialist view of the universe is a familiar idea. It is part of our common cultural inheritance. The thought that minds are made of a kind of stuff radically different from material objects goes back to Plato and clearly infuses the dominant western religions. However, although the idea that the mind might prove to be one mystery too far for the physical sciences is a readily recognisable thought, we need to examine the reasons why the mind seems to pose an ineradicable problem for the scientific explanation of everything. There are two basic reasons why mental phenomena seem to present a barrier to further scientific progress. I shall call these the naïve reason and the sophisticated reason for the mysteriousness of the mind.

The naïve reason is endemic in the account of colour experience outlined in the previous chapter. In sketching the physical explanation of colour experience I employed the idea of a sequence of physical events starting with the reflection of light waves by a ripe tomato. Following the mechanical effects of the motion of these waves we then considered their effect on the human eye and the consequent physical excitation of nerve firings along the optic nerve from eye to brain. Within the brain further nerve excitations take place and various nets of neurons charge up and pass on their minute electric charges to other neurons. Now, it is tempting to think that however far we trace this sequence of physical events we will not have fully explained colour experience until, at the end of this chain of events, we say something like: the physical event of neurons firing causes the mental event of the tomato appearing red. That is to say, it is tempting to think that however far we analyse colour experience physically, no account of neuronic excitation can actually be what it is to see redness. The experience of redness is a mental phenomenon; it is a matter of something looking a certain way, not simply a set of neurons firing.

This naïve reason for the mysteriousness of the mind amounts to a refusal to countenance the possibility that mental events – like experiencing colour, or thinking a thought – could possibly be material events. How could a set of neurons experience colour? How could the electrical excitation of a neural net be a complete account of an orgasm? These questions look to be deep and problematical. It is one thing to analyse an experience in terms of a sequence of physical events like nerve activity. However, the objection is that, sooner or later, if the analysis is to capture what having a mind is really like, it will have to make a leap and postulate a mental event at the end of the physical chain of causation. The postulation of the mental event as something after the completion of the sequence of physical causation is the postulation of a range of objects and events outside the scope of the physical world. In short, it amounts to the postulation of a whole new world.

If this two-worlds view is right, the material world investigated by the physical sciences is only half the story; in addition there is the world of mind. So, on this account, the cosmic register is a two-volume work. One volume covers the goings-on of the physical world as described in the language of science. The other volume covers the world of thoughts, experiences, wishes, hopes, the emotions and all the complexities of conscious existence. This two-worlds view is Cartesian dualism, for it received its definitive statement in the works of Descartes.

Cartesian dualism is the thesis that there are two radically different kinds of stuff in the universe, two very different kinds of things. This is expressed by saying that it is a substance dualism. On this view, there is material stuff from which material objects are made; and there is mental stuff from which minds are made.

Many philosophers since Descartes (including Locke) have been Cartesian dualists. They have denied the possibility of science extending its domain to include explanations of mental life. There are more kinds of stuff in heaven and earth than are dreamt of in the scientific view of the universe. However, this two-worlds view of Cartesian dualism is problematic.

The most serious problem with Cartesian dualism is that it leaves minds detached from the rest of reality. It seems to require the image of the physical universe proceeding according to physical laws with minds existing on a detached plateau above and beyond contact with material things. Minds are conceived as some kind of ethereal audience upon the material world. Despite the popularity of this imagery, this detached account of the mind renders any connection between mind and matter utterly mysterious.

Whatever else minds do, they have effects upon the material world. We make plans and decisions and move our bodies accordingly. Similarly, events in the world have an effect upon our minds. If I step on a pin I feel pain. But on the two-worlds picture of Cartesian dualism there is no possible mechanism by which the two worlds can be connected, for the whole point of postulating two worlds is to tear minds apart from the material world. The whole point of insisting that the cosmic register comes in two volumes, not one, is to insist that there is no translation manual between the two, for if there was there would be no need for two volumes in the first place.

This problem is called the problem of interaction. If there are these two radically different worlds containing items formed out of radically different kinds of substance, then how could it ever be possible for the two to interact? I think that the problem of interaction on its own is sufficient to discount Cartesian dualism as a serious option, although there are other equally telling objections to the position. I do not then believe that Cartesian dualism provides us with a sound reason why we should think that the mind poses an insoluble barrier to scientific progress. However, that does not mean that it is going to be easy to accommodate mental phenomena within the scientific view of the world. Indeed, I believe we have little or no idea of how such an accommodation might be achieved and this is because of the issues that are raised by the sophisticated reason for the mysteriousness of the mind.[1]

THE LANGUAGE OF MIND

The sophisticated reason for the apparent mysteriousness of the mind and why it seems to present an obstacle to the achievement of a scientific explanation of everything concerns the concept of a perspective, or point of view. Minds are things with a perspective upon the environment. Spelling out what this amounts to touches upon issues already addressed about the peculiarity of the mental. However, the point I now want to consider has a subtle but very important difference.

Cartesian dualism is a two-worlds view. It is a view which says that there are two different kinds of substance. The sophisticated reason for thinking that mental phenomena fall outside the reach of scientific investigation is rather a two-language view. It is a view that claims that certain features of mental life cannot be captured within the materialist language of science, but does so without postulating an extra substance. Instead, it involves a dualism of properties, but properties that are properties of material things. The key to this challenge is the idea that in order to express what mental life is like, we need to talk about properties of things over and above the properties referred to within the language of science. The language of science only allows for physical properties of things: shape, size, mass, motion, etc. So, rather than say that there is an extra kind of substance which defines an extra world, this option says that there are properties of the world other than the purely physical properties referred to in the language of science.

Now, this might suggest that rather than say that the cosmic register is a two-volume work with each volume about a separate world, the present option says that there is only one cosmic register (one world) but that it is not written in a uniform language. There is one register, but there are different ways of speaking or writing within it. However, this is not quite right, for to say that the description of mental phenomena requires a separate language to the language of science, means that this separate language cannot be a transparent language in the sense defined in Chapter 1. Therefore, the language of mind is not a cosmic language. If this is right, this critique of the limitations of scientific explanations takes us right to the heart of the critique of the idea of the world's own language.

Let us express this position in terms of what it means to say that minds have a perspective. The key point is that in under-standing this idea we have to express it in ways that cannot be captured in a language referring only to physical properties – the transparent language of science. There are other non-physical properties that objects have and these properties define the idea of a perspective.

The key idea here is the idea that the meaning of talk about mental life cannot be reduced to the meaning of talk about physical events and processes. The language of mental descriptions is irreducible. There are two ways in which this irreducibility is manifest, both of which help to capture the idea that having a mind is having a perspective or point of view on the world. The two manifestations of this irreducibility concern the irreducibility of sensory qualities and the irreducibility of perspectival thinking. I shall look at each claim in turn. Both these aspects of what it is to have a perspective turn on the idea that in describing mental phenomena we are forced to employ a language that fails the test for entry to the cosmic register introduced in the last chapter. Talk about the mental is not transparent.

SENSORY QUALITIES

The irreducibility of sensory qualities amounts to this thought: having a mind involves having a point of view upon the world in the sense that it involves experiencing the world in a certain way. For example, we are members of a species that has evolved colour vision. Providing the apparatus is working correctly, we experience the world visually as a world of colour. To describe our experience of the world in terms of the way it appears visually to us is to describe it as coloured. Colour qualities are qualities that characterise, in part, the kind of experience or point of view that a typical human being has of the world. I shall say that colour qualities are sensory qualities, for they are qualities that characterise the particular perspective or point of view possessed by creatures like us.

We might contrast our perspective with that of other creatures. Take the case of bats.[2] Bats are creatures with very poor visual systems. However, bats have a keenly developed sense of hearing that provides them with a sonar system for finding their way around the world. We locate ourselves in the environment largely in terms of the way things look, including the colour of things.

Bats locate themselves in the environment in terms of the way things sound. If we are confronted with two obstacles one of which is nearer than the other, we would say that one looked nearer than the other. The bat, in the same situation, would experience one as sounding nearer than the other. Visual qualities like colour, light and shade dominate the way we experience the world. For bats, it is the sonar qualities of objects that predominantly characterise the way they experience the world. Sonar qualities are, for bats, the sensory qualities that define their perspective on the world. For them, the world sounds a certain way where we would say it looks a certain way.

Now, why should we think that such sensory qualities are irreducible properties defining a perspective on the world that cannot be expressed in terms of the language of science? The answer to this comes from trying to consider the following question: 'What is it like to be a bat?' Suppose we wanted to answer this question. Suppose we conducted a detailed scientific investigation into the physiology of a bat's sonar system. Suppose we discovered how the system operates. We calculated how the detection of sonar echoes is managed by the bat's auditory systems and how this produces sequences of neural activity in the bat's brain. Suppose we could give a complete scientific account of everything that goes on when a bat detects that one object is nearer than another. Now, with all this information to hand, are we anywhere near being able to say what it is like for one object to sound nearer than another? It is difficult to see how all this scientifically expressed knowledge could answer that question. The neurophysiology tells us only what happens physically when a bat detects that one object is nearer than another. It seems to tell us nothing about what it is like for one object to sound nearer. We are inclined to say that it does not tell us what it is like 'from the inside', so to speak, to be a bat. Similarly, it seems plausible to insist that a complete neurophysiology of our colour visual system would not be enough to tell an intelligent bat what it is like for one object to look nearer than another.

Let us change the example to one nearer home. The idea that sensory qualities are irreducible qualities which define the perspective of our experience means that, even if we possessed a complete neurophysiology of colour vision, we would not be able to explain fully to a congenitally blind person what it is like for a ripe tomato to look different from a lettuce leaf. To do that we would have to talk the language of colours, the language of sensory qualities, and that is a language that the congenitally blind person does not understand. Why? Because they do not have the same experience – perspective or point of view – as the person with a normally functioning visual system. In other words, colour talk is not transparent. Merely giving the congenitally blind person sentences about colours does not give them understanding of colours. For an understanding of colour, they need also the ability to have certain kinds of experiences and that is precisely what they lack. Just so, we do not understand the language of the bat, the idea that one object might sound nearer, or sound more spherical than another. And the bat, no matter how intelligent it might be, would not understand the idea that an object could look nearer, or look spherical, for their experience is predominantly an auditory one, the sensory qualities of which are sonar qualities. At the heart of this critique of the limitations of scientific accounts of the world is the following assumption:

> Part of the meaning of concepts required in order to characterise conscious experience is not transparent. These concepts cannot be encoded without loss into language. Understanding these concepts presupposes the ability to have certain sorts of experience. The sorts of experience concerned are defined by the sensory qualities that characterise them.[3]

Note that this argument for denying that science can capture the perspectivity of the mind does not commit us to Cartesian dualism. It does not commit us to a two-worlds view with an extra substance. It commits us only to the idea that not all the things that are true of this world are expressible in the transparent language of science. Some of the things that are true are expressible only in a language that includes sensory qualities and these are qualities, like colour, that do not figure in the language of science.

The irreducibility of perspectival thinking is a separate point. In addition to thinking of the idea of a perspective in terms of those sensory qualities that define the kind of experience we have of the world, there is another sense to the idea of a perspective which is more fundamental. It is also more difficult to express. The idea of perspectival thinking is concerned with the way that we literally experience the world from a particular position.

PERSPECTIVAL THINKING

Consider the fact that I am currently sitting at a particular place in the world – my desk. We might express this fact by saying that Michael Luntley is at a certain point picked out by an agreed coordinate system. Of course, it is normally sufficient to pick out someone's position by referring to the room he or she is in, or whereabouts within the room, for example by the fireplace, at the piano, etc. Such descriptions of location are rather like crude coordinates. We could, if we had the time, replace such descriptions with a precise coordinate system.

Now, it is an integral part of the kinds of descriptions that science offers us of the world that it offers locations of objects that are replaceable with precise coordinates. The provision of precise coordinates is characteristic of an objective location of an object, a location that says where the object is in a way that is not subject to further interpretation or misinterpretation. In principle, that is the aim in giving locations of objects within the scientific point of view. When science locates an object it does so with a description of the general form: (1) 'Object O is at position x, y, z, t', where the term O unambiguously picks out the object, and the variables x, y, z, t give the spatio-temporal coordinates of its location. The availability of such locations is what guarantees that the questions science puts to the world are questions with simple yes/no answers. Such locations are transparent.

Now, contrast the above sort of location with the kind of location that is typical of a thinking, conscious agent. Consider first the sentence, (2) 'Michael Luntley is in his office.' This is a sentence that is, in principle, of the same form as (1). However, from my point of view, I can express the fact expressed at (2) by saying, (3) 'I am here', and (3) is a very peculiar way of locating an object. It is a way of locating an object that is peculiar to objects with consciousness, with a perspective or point of view upon the world. I am the only person for whom (3) adequately expresses my position. From the point of view of everyone else, where I am is better expressed in (2). However, in order to capture the idea that I am a mind with a literal perspective upon the world, we need the availability of expressing location given in (3). It is a way of locating objects which is essentially first-personal. It is not a way of locating objects which unambiguously locates them in the manner of scientific location. Indeed (3) is the most extreme example of a sentence which is not transparent.

This point is easily seen. Suppose a friend phones you from a call box somewhere and you ask where she is. If all your friend says in reply is 'I am here', you have no hope of finding her although, from your friend's point of view, it might be a perfectly adequate location. Possession of your friend's 'I am here' sentence does not, on its own, tell you where she is. The meaning of your friend's self-location is not fully expressible in the symbols used. To understand the meaning of her thought you need much more than the sentence. In addition, you need the ability to locate her by vision or some other means.

Locating oneself by saying 'I am here' differs from locations of the form of (1) both by employing a reference to the object that is not transparent – the pronoun 'I' – and by giving the object's position in a non-transparent way, the word 'here'. 'I' is ambiguous because it does not uniquely pick out one object. The object picked out by 'I' depends on the circumstances in which it is used. We can all use 'I' to refer to ourselves and if we ask, in the dark, who has just entered the room, to be told 'It is I' generally leaves us firmly unenlightened. Similarly, when lost in the desert, to be told that here is where we are is scant comfort, for 'here' can be used to pick out any place in the whole universe. Which place it picks out is, once again, dependent on the circumstances in which it is used.

The expression of object location in (3) is then an expression the success of which is dependent on circumstances of use. The expressions involved – 'I', 'here', as well as 'you', 'there', 'now', 'then' – are what philosophers call indexical expressions. They are not part of the language of science for they do not provide us with transparent unambiguous questions to put to the world. Simply to ask 'Am I here?' does not suffice to frame a question to which the cosmic register could be expected to have a simple yes/no answer. The question only makes sense given the circumstances of its use. As such, questions expressed with indexicals are not suitable for use as objective scientific questions. If science speaks the language of the world, then indexical questions are not questions that can be expressed in the language of the world! However, it is only by using such indexicals that we can adequately capture the literal perspectivity of conscious experience. It is by saying 'I am here' that I best capture what it is like, from the inside, to be this particular person with this particular perspective or point of view on the world. To say 'Michael Luntley is in his office' only describes the facts from the external point of view. Therefore, a language suitable to describe the nature of consciousness and having a perspective must contain indexicals. But, therefore, it must be a language which is not capable of framing transparent unambiguous questions of our cosmic register. The language necessary to capture the character of consciousness is necessarily an opaque language, a language incapable of framing transparent questions with simple yes/no answers.[4]

IS THE MIND A MYSTERY?

I have outlined two senses of the idea that having a mind is having a perspective on the world, both of which threaten the universalism of the scientific enterprise. The irreducibility of sensory qualities to physical qualities and the inexpressibility of perspectival thinking in terms of transparent locations of persons give two senses in which a language suitable for expressing claims about our mental lives cannot be part of the transparent language of science. Now, what follows from this? Does this show that the mind presents an insoluble mystery for science?

If the arguments of the last two sections are correct then the following claim is true:

> Either we must deny the reality of consciousness as we experience it, or we must amend the model of objective truth and knowledge as outlined in the model of the cosmic register in the last chapter.

The first option here is the one we must take if we stick with the physicalist outlook of science as sketched in the last chapter as the way of reading the world. But this option seems fantastic. It is the option of saying that our concept of reality is exhausted by those claims that can be accommodated within the cosmic register. This option rests on the assumption that in order to figure in that book a proposition must be expressible in the transparent language of physics because that is the world's own language. But if we stick with that we would have to conclude that conscious experience itself was an illusion, consciousness was not real! That does not appear to me to be a credible option.[5]

Of course, there is plenty of scope for the idea that many of the things that appear to us to be true are not. There is plenty of scope for the thought that how things appear to us need not be the same as how they really are. We are frequently deluded by the appearances of things. But the idea that we might be deluded about the very facts of consciousness seems altogether too absurd.

If that is so, we must take the second option above. We must amend the model of the cosmic register as presented so far. In particular, we must concede that there are things we want to say about the world that are not expressible within the language of mathematical physics. Perhaps we should say that the cosmic register is not written in a single uniform language, for those truths that express our nature as conscious agents seem not to be expressible in the language our natural sciences have developed. However, it is not clear that it makes sense to think of the cosmic register as a multi-lingual work. The whole point of calling it the 'cosmic' register was to signal the idea that it encoded the world's own language. The cosmic register is a device for marking the idea that there is such a thing as the way the world is in itself, a way describable in one unique transparent language. But a language fit to describe consciousness has to be our language, not the world's language. A language fit to describe consciousness must be a language that can describe the life of creatures with a perspective or point of view. The language of the cosmic register is the language of no particular point of view, an absolute language. When we look at ourselves we do not seem to fit into the world as defined by the cosmic register. There is no place for creatures with a perspective in a world described in a non-perspectival way. Acknowledging the reality of our own mental lives is to recognise a reality that is not describable in the terms of the cosmic register. If our mental lives are part of a reality that is recordable at all, they are describable in human registers, registers that describe the world from our point of view, not the transparent world's own point of view. An account of our mental lives will have to be recorded in human language, not the language of the world.

If the above argument is right then we have endorsed Thesis III mentioned in the Introduction. Thesis III is:

III There is no single language suitable for reporting all the things we want to say about the world.

The shift that comes from accepting Thesis III has two consequences. First, in challenging the idea of the cosmic register – the revelatory knowledge which many thought it was our destiny to unravel – we are forced to recognise that there are many more things that can be said than could be fitted within the scientific picture. Second, the more different languages we allow, the more we are threatened with a chaotic cacophony of chattering. If we replace the cosmic register with a plurality of human registers, will we lose our grip on the concept of truth altogether?

So far we have looked at arguments which suggest that this constraint only operates with regard to mental phenomena. The idea that science may not have exclusive rights to the whole truth has been premissed on the claim that we cannot understand mental phenomena within the scientific image. However, the idea that science might not be the whole story is generalisable. I want briefly to examine this idea, but there is a sting in its tail. Recognising the possibility of kinds of description other than the transparent scientific description of the world opens up the general sceptical argument which threatens to undermine the very idea of truth. Having chiselled away at one fragment of the pretence of science, we find that there are no foundations at all for our confidence that there is such a thing as truth, no matter how it is written. That is the threat to which we are being drawn.

EXPLANATORY FRAMEWORKS

The point about the mysteriousness of mental phenomena and the difficulties in expressing truths about mental life in the language of science reveals the potential for explanatory frameworks other than the scientific one. What is suggested is the idea of alternative frameworks of explanation that offer equally valid explanations in their own right. Science might adequately offer explanations of physical phenomena within its own materialist explanatory framework, but perhaps there are other frameworks. This idea challenges the concept of the cosmic register as I introduced it in the last chapter, for it claims that what counts as a simple question with a yes/no answer depends on the framework or language in which the question is posed.

To ask 'Am I here?' or 'Is the tomato red?' is not to ask questions with simple yes/no answers from the point of view of the scientific framework of explanation, but it may be to ask questions that from the point of view of consciousness are in order and possess simple yes/no answers. So, in addition to the transparent scientific explanatory framework that has so captured our imaginations, perhaps there are other explanatory frameworks which we should now consider?

This is an idea that has been taken up by thinkers from a variety of disciplines.[6] For example, some distinguish three main explanatory frameworks: those of science, of psychology and of religion. The point of distinguishing the explanatory framework of psychology from that of science in general is to make room for the phenomenon of consciousness and to allow that there are facts about our mental lives which cannot be captured within the materialist language of science. By distinguishing a separate explanatory framework for psychology our mental lives are protected from reduction to physical processes. Similarly, by insisting that there is a further separate explanatory framework that covers our spiritual life, we protect religious views from the challenge of science. If there are such separable explanatory frameworks then science and religion are not in competition. They describe the world from radically different points of view. Therefore, the claims of science cannot show the claims of religion to be false; nor, for that matter, can science show them to be true.

However, before we think that this generous proliferation of explanatory frameworks is an inexpensive and useful way of remodelling the image of the cosmic register we must be aware of the problems it generates. By allowing a proliferation of different languages and different explanatory frameworks we are inviting into our midst a scepticism that threatens to undermine not only science, but the simple idea of truth; that threatens not merely to replace the cosmic register with a set of human registers, but to cast doubt on the idea of there being any truths even if they are expressed in human terms.

Consider this: suppose we accept the possibility that there are explanatory frameworks other than that of the natural sciences and that these frameworks have an equal claim to validity. Suppose we accept the frameworks or registers defined by the opaque languages of human interests and points of view. What can we say if someone offers an explanation that looks as if it competes with the scientific one, but which they say belongs to another explanatory framework? Suppose a witch doctor says that an epidemic is caused by bad spirits and can only be defeated if the spirits are appeased with sacrifice. Suppose the medical doctor says that the epidemic is caused by a water-borne infection and that the communal feast following the sacrifice will only exacerbate the spread of the disease. Who is right? Suppose that you are told by your doctor that your backache is caused by degeneration of the nerves in the spinal column and bed-rest plus drug therapy is the only hope for cure. But suppose also that you are told that the problem arises from an imbalance in Chi forces within your body and that pursuit of deep breathing exercises will cure this imbalance and relieve the pain. Who is right? Suppose a modern physicist tells us that the universe began with a big bang, at which point space and time were brought into being and have been expanding ever since. But suppose also that a creationist insists that the world was created by God in 4004 BC. Who is right?

If we allow explanatory frameworks to proliferate, then, in each of these cases and in hundreds of others, we give scope for the protagonists to protect their competing claims by saying that they are viewing the world from different explanatory frameworks. What is right, what is true or false, can then only be made sense of from within a particular explanatory framework. But if that is the case, there is no such thing as the truth, that which is objective and independent of our particular points of view. The relativisation of truth that comes from accepting the proliferation of explanatory frameworks obliterates the idea of objective truth. Not only does it obliterate the cosmic register, it obliterates any notion of truth that is independent of judgement. Truth will depend on your point of view, the explanatory framework from which you view the world. Truth would then become fragmented. In essence, that is the worry that shakes the modern confidence that we might discover the truth. It is a worry that threatens the very idea of truth.

It is the above worry that we now need to examine. The idea of allowing explanatory frameworks other than that of science looks tempting, for it allows us to preserve the reality of our mental lives without assuming that this must be expressible in the language of science. The possibility that there are valid explanatory frameworks other than that of science is one we should not give up. It is an idea that takes the 'cosmic' out of the 'cosmic register'. It is the core challenge to the idea of a transparent language of the world. But before we can make use of the idea we must examine the radical sceptical threat that has now been sketched. For the idea that there are more things to be said than can be written in the language of mathematical physics raises the issue of what standards there are, if any, to what we say and think. Without the cosmic register as a standard, who or what is to monitor our claims? If there is no transparent language of the world, there can be no transparent experiences of the world either. What we find in experience will not, and cannot, be transparent.

The idea that there are more things in heaven and earth than are dreamt of in the scientific image is comforting. The absolute conception of the cosmic register does not tell the whole truth. But with what right can we say that these other things we wish to talk about, our mental lives for example, are things in the world, when we have lost the cosmic register as our model for the world? In the next four chapters I shall locate and examine the epistemological problems that arise when we give up the idea of there being a transparent language of the world.

Chapter 3

No Archimedean point

INTRODUCTION

In the last chapter we saw how science's claim to be able to deliver the whole truth can be loosened. When we think about the nature of our mental lives and what it is like to be creatures who are conscious of their surroundings, it can seem impossible to fit an account of consciousness within the scientific worldview. We saw how we could accommodate consciousness by admitting more worldviews than the merely physical. By proliferating the number of explanatory frameworks we can, perhaps, hope to provide a better and richer account of what is going on in the world. The cosmic register of transparent facts represented in a transparent language becomes a collection of human registers written in opaque perspectival languages.

This idea of accepting explanatory frameworks or languages in addition to that of physics raises a serious threat. If facts about our mental life cannot be described in the transparent language of physics but require their own opaque language, the assessment of the truth of a claim about our mental lives cannot be made by physics. If a claim can only be properly expressed within one explanatory framework, then so too can it only be assessed as true or false from within that framework. If these extra explanatory frameworks are not transparent, there will be no universal transparent account of human experience that could serve as a general criterion of truth or falsity. What that amounts to is the following thought:

No Archimedean point: There is no criterion of truth external to our different explanatory frameworks; truth can only be measured internal to our frameworks.

Archimedes said that with a fixed point and a sufficiently long lever he could move the entire world. The above thought says that there is no fixed point from which we can adjudicate between the different explanatory frameworks at play in the world. There is no criterion of truth that, like an Archimedean point, stands outside our different explanatory frameworks.

The 'No Archimedean point' thought is no longer the seemingly harmless idea that there are more things in heaven and earth than are dreamt of in the scientific worldview. It is a thought that threatens to obliterate the idea that there is any such thing as truth independent of the languages and judgements we make. If all measures of truth are internal to an explanatory framework or language, then if proponents of different worldviews are in competition there is no matter of fact concerning who is right. Truth is internal to their different frameworks, truth is relative. Not only is the cosmic register lost, so too is the idea of a normative standard of truth and falsity.

If this is so, disagreement is not a case of people differing in what they believe about a common world, for that idea is premissed on the notion of truth independent of judgement. For that to be a tenable idea it must make sense to think of truth as something independent of our explanatory frameworks, our systems of judgement. But if truth is only measurable internal to a given framework, then the cosmic register is lost. Without the cosmic standard we are left with the competing cacophony of different human registers. That seems to be the threat once we accept the rejection of the transparent language of science. That rejection is the core of philosophical postmodernism.

The concept of postmodernism, however, is vague. One of the central claims made by writers such as Rorty and Lyotard is the rejection of the cosmic register. Postmodernism starts with the rejection of the idea of a universal language fit to describe the whole of reality. Instead there is a plurality of languages. This is seen most immediately when thinking about consciousness. In addition, there are the languages of morals, of aesthetics, of economics, of social life, etc. None of these ways of describing our selves, our lives and our worlds seems plausibly reducible to the scientific image. These languages that we have developed are central to our conception of ourselves as creatures with minds, values, feelings and relationships. The existence of the plurality of languages is the key postmodernist insight. However, although this plurality means that we have lost the standard of truth supplied by the cosmic register, does it mean that there are no standards at all to what we say?

Most postmodernists are unclear on this point.[1] On the face of it, even if we acknowledge that there is no universal transparent language, it does not mean that there are no standards by which we should measure what we say when we speak in the many tongues required to capture the complexity of human existence. For example, if I say that an apple is red, although I describe it from a very human point of view, there is still some sense of what I say being true or false independent of what I think. The simple idea of truth, as captured in the basic constraint of Chapter 1, p. 28, requires that what is said, no matter which language it is expressed in, if true, is true independent of my thinking it. Or perhaps even stronger, no matter how expressed, what is said, if true, is true independent of any of us thinking it. That seems to be a very basic notion of truth. Is it something that survives the loss of the cosmic register? Whether or not it does survive that loss is the issue of whether or not there are any standards left us once we give up on the impossibly high standard of the cosmic register. The issue is whether or not postmodernism entails relativism.

The idea that truth might be deflated to a relativised concept, our cosmic register deflated to an array of different human registers between which there is no rational choice, has been and continues to be extraordinarily influential. Although this is a deeply problematic idea, it can seem attractive because of the intellectual protectionism that relativism offers. For example, many early anthropologists assumed that so-called 'primitive' peoples must have had 'primitive mentalities'. This was thought to explain why they persisted with their magical worldviews, explanatory frameworks that envisage a world populated with spirits, witches and demons. From the standpoint of the relativist this is just cognitive imperialism. Who are we to judge the efficacy of the magic beliefs of primitive tribes? According to our scientific worldview their beliefs may be false and even rather silly. But perhaps that is to make an unfair judgement, a judgement that attempts to assess their beliefs in a way that is external to their explanatory framework. If we make the effort and work our way inside their explanatory framework, then we will find nothing wrong in the belief in magic, witchcraft, etc. Isolated within their own explanatory framework such peoples are then protected from the advancing imperialism of western science.[2]

Such a line of thought is now very popular and familiar. Its anti-imperialism makes it thoroughly fashionable, for who would dare admit to imperialism? The problems with this liberality about truth are also obvious and familiar. Relativism entails that we can never criticise someone from a different culture, world-view or explanatory framework. Criticism, like the assessment of truth, must be internal to a framework, not external to it. And although as good liberals we may hesitate to criticise the views of another, to rule out the possibility of any critical engagement with the beliefs of others seems a recipe for the end of all knowledge and learning. It would amount not only to the end of the Enlightenment project that assumed that by rational criticism and the critical appeal to experience we could learn to speak the language of the world; if all criticism and debate turns out to be internal to our different explanatory frameworks, the most we can ever do is work out the intricacies of the different ways we think the world works. If criticism cannot take us outside our frameworks, we lose even the simple idea of truth.

The Enlightenment thought that the only credible standards of judgement were cosmic, that we would be like Gods in our ration-ality. Modernity thought we would be like scientists, that our rationality would match the world's own story. The postmodern-ists say that rationality is human, the standards of judgement are human standards. We view the world from human perspectives. If that is so we cannot aspire to read the works of God and sing the music of the spheres. We must simply and with humility learn to read ourselves and our world. The full-blown postmodernism that embraces relativism then says that once we accept that the world is ours, the standards are human, then there are really no standards at all. There are habits of the mind, there is an inheri-tance we acquire. On such an account we would lose the norma-tive notion of what we ought to believe. The normative notion would be replaced with a mere description of the beliefs we have inherited. We inherit many worlds and if some of them conflict there is no escaping our inheritance to see if one is better than the other. That looks like relativism. But it is more than that.

Extreme postmodernists are not really relativists about truth, for they think that there is really no such thing as truth at all. This is anti-rationalism. It is a position which denies that there is any normative notion of what we ought to believe, but just the assembly of historical facts about what we do believe. There are no norms of rationality, only habits of the mind.[3]

In this chapter I shall show how this radical anti-rationalism arises and outline the deep philosophical reasons why it is so commonly embraced. I shall start with the core reason why it is an option. I shall then examine a couple of cases in which people have been tempted to take the anti-rationalist position.

EXPERIENCE – WHAT'S IN IT FOR US?

In the light of the above thumbnail sketch of the anti-rationalist position and the problems with it, one might think that the simplest response would be to deny the proliferation of explanatory frameworks with which I introduced the problem. However, that will not do. I introduced the idea of an explanatory framework to capture the idea of ways of describing the world other than the scientific way. But the anti-rationalist problem arises even if we consider a narrower notion of explanatory framework, a notion that is used to distinguish between different theories within science. The possibility of setting up the anti-rationalist position within the worldview of the natural sciences shows that anti-rationalism is threatened by something very fundamental, more fundamental than the idea of different explanatory frameworks as I have used that idea so far. I think this is right. Anti-rationalism looks more dramatic when considering examples where we challenge the scientific view of the world with, say, the magical view of a primitive tribe. Nevertheless, the core anti-rationalist threat arises earlier than that. The threat of anti-rationalism comes from a simple point about the nature of experience, a point that gives a critique that goes right to the heart of the apparently banal and commonsensical position I called critical empiricism in Chapter 1.

In Chapter 1 I characterised critical empiricism in the following way:

Critical empiricism:
1 The advancement of scientific knowledge requires our

    making theoretical 'guesses' which go beyond the evidence
    supplied by our senses.
  2 All theoretical claims must be subject to experimental testing.

I noted that critical empiricism had the appearance of a rather
obvious and minimal concept of correct methodology, a methodology suitable for reading the cosmic register. Nevertheless, the
idea appears fundamentally flawed. The first component of critical
empiricism is unproblematic. Let's accept that theoretical claims
go beyond the evidence supplied by our senses. If we do not
accept that, it is difficult to make much sense of our scientific
endeavours. Accepting the first component of critical empiricism
is to note that, in doing science and in engaging in any attempt
at knowledge, when we make a judgement we take ourselves to
be saying something that is aimed at a truth independent of
judgement. The evidence may prompt us to make a claim, but
what is claimed is a judgement that is aimed at a truth beyond
the mere evidence.

    It is the second component of critical empiricism that generates
difficulties. The second component says that we must look to
experience to test our theoretical claims. However, there is no
such thing as a theory-neutral account of experience. All experience is theory-laden. Our reports of experience are always reports
that presuppose the truth of some theory or another. This
means that there are no observational reports of the world that
can play the role of independent tests for our theories. The
common-sense view is that we make theoretical hypotheses and
then test them against the objective benchmark of experience.
However, that benchmark, our observational reports of experience, is not neutral. Our account of experience is rich with theoretical assumptions and interpretations. So, in measuring the
adequacy of a theory against experience what we are really doing
is measuring the adequacy of that theory given the assumption
that some other theory or group of theories is true. There is no
Archimedean point from which we can achieve a genuinely neutral and objective assessment of theories. It is this point about
experience which underpins the denial of a transparent language
of the world's own story. In the previous chapter we saw how, if
there was such a thing as the world's own story, it would not
capture central features of human life, for example our consciousness. The present claim about the nature of experience shows

that there can be no such thing as a transparent language. If all experience is interpretative, based on prior assumptions, then so too is all experience of language and meaning. There can be no such thing as a pure self-interpreting language. There can be no such thing as a pure uninterpreted raw experience.

Experience can provide no Archimedean criterion of truth. Experience cannot provide an objective test between two competing theories, worldviews or explanatory frameworks. That is what the claim about experience amounts to. In what sense is it true? To see this let us examine two cases where this claim about experience has been thought to threaten anti-rationalism. The first case is one where anti-rationalism arises within the scientific explanatory framework and the problem is the lack of a criterion to judge between two competing scientific theories. The case here is the debate between a Ptolemaic and a Copernican account of the solar system. The second case is one where anti-rationalism arises because there is no criterion to judge between two competing explanatory frameworks. The second case is then a case where the competing claims do not offer different theories within, say, the language of the natural sciences, but one where they offer competing claims that operate within radically different languages for describing the world. The second case concerns whether the magical-cum-spiritual worldview of the Azande tribe of the southern Sudan can be shown to be false from the viewpoint of western science.

PTOLEMY VERSUS COPERNICUS

One of the key moments in the history of human knowledge was the Copernican revolution, the point at which it was realised that the earth was not the centre of the solar system. Copernicus pointed out that the earth, rather than being at the heart of the cosmos, was simply a ball of matter in orbit around the sun. It is difficult now to appreciate the enormity of this change of view.[4]

The Ptolemaic view of the solar system had man at the centre of things. Man was on earth and the sun and the stars and all the other heavenly bodies were in orbit around us. In contrast, in the Copernican picture of the solar system, man is relegated to life on a rock in orbit around the sun. The enormity of this shift in view is not just a matter of its significance for our understanding of the cosmos. The cultural, religious, social and political consequences of accepting a worldview with humankind relegated to the periphery were enormous. It is no wonder that Galileo found himself confronted by the Inquisition and was forced to recant his Copernican views. The Copernican revolution not only introduced a sea-change in our view of the universe, but also in our view of ourselves.

Prior to Copernicus, humankind was at the centre of the cosmos – a state of affairs created by an omniscient and benevolent God. It was appropriate then that God's voice on earth, the Catholic Church, should appropriate the authority to tell us what was credible and what was not. To the minds of those who exercised such authority, it was literally incredible that we should be relegated to the sidelines. If we were so relegated was it not likely that the Church would be next?

Of course, as history turned out, that is exactly what happened. What was really swept away with the Copernican revolution, however, was the reliance on dogma and authority. Coming to recognise that we inhabited a small ball of rock in orbit around a much larger sun turned out to be a liberating thought. It freed the human mind from the dogmatic authorities that insisted that humankind had a pre-eminent position in the universe. In so doing it implicitly recognised the idea of the universe as something going on independently of us and our thoughts and dogmas. Perhaps the universe was going on independently of us to the extent that we were merely crawling around the surface of a lump of matter orbiting a modest star in a lazy backwater of an average-sized galaxy within a galactic cluster no different from a billion others, in no particularly important position within the total infinite space of the universe. Such self-effacement before the majesty of the universe has paid handsome dividends in terms of knowledge. It has encouraged us to recognise the independence of the universe from our concerns and enabled us to investigate its nature without always assuming that it was a place specially created for us to play around in.

The Copernican revolution was important. It is difficult to imagine the path of the Enlightenment and the development of science having been the same, or even having occurred at all, without Copernicus' challenge to the Ptolemaic view of the cosmos. However, if it is true that experience can give no theory-neutral adjudication between competing theories then we have to ask, 'In what sense does experience show that Copernicus is right and Ptolemy wrong?'

Consider, for the moment, our ordinary earthbound observations. Which observation is it that shows that Copernicus is correct in claiming that the earth is orbiting a stationary sun? It is, of course, no surprise that early cosmologists thought that the sun orbited the earth, for that is just the way it looks! There is no simple observation that adjudicates between the two cosmologies. A Copernican and a Ptolemaic cosmologist standing together on a hillside at dawn will not agree on what they are seeing. The former sees the earth turning, the latter the sun moving up over the earth. Do not think that you can get them, given their different theoretical presuppositions, to agree on a common observational claim that might adjudicate between their theories. Of course, that is not to say that they cannot find something to agree on, merely that it will never be sufficient to count as a criterion of who is right and who is wrong. For example, they will surely agree that the earth's horizon and the bright ball of orange are gradually separating and moving further apart. But whether or not that amounts to an earth turning relative to a stationary sun, or a sun moving relative to a stationary earth, is not settled by finding that thin level of observational agreement.

So, with regard to the observations available there is no observation that shows that Copernicus is right and Ptolemy is wrong. Observationally, all that is available is a series of statements about the relative position and motion of the sun, the earth, the planets, the stars and other heavenly bodies. The Copernican revolution was not based on an observational advantage that pointed out something that the Ptolemaic system had missed. Rather, it was based on the fact that, given the Copernican hypothesis that the heavens were not rotating around the earth, a simpler and more elegant mechanics would accommodate the agreed observations of the relative position and motion of all the bodies concerned. The situation then was this: observationally, the Copernican and Ptolemaic cosmologies were equivalent. Both accommodated the agreed thin level of observations about the relative position and motion of the sun, the earth, the stars and the planets. There was no neutral observation available that would vindicate Copernicus and falsify Ptolemy. What was available was the fact that the Copernican hypothesis gave a simpler and more elegant model of the mechanics of the solar system.

In particular the following point was significant. If one stuck to the Ptolemaic viewpoint, in order to accommodate the agreed thin level of observations about the relative position and motion of the planets, one had to postulate increasingly complex patterns of movements of the stars and planets as they orbited the earth. The Ptolemaic system was not contradicted by the observed relative movement of these bodies, but it was required to postulate ever more complicated accounts of their orbits in order to preserve the sightings of relative position. In particular, the simple idea that the earth lay at the centre of things with the planets, stars and sun orbiting in perfect circles had to be amended. That simple earth-centred model did not fit the observations of relative motion. But the observations of relative motion did not show that the earth-centred view was false; they merely showed that it must be more complicated than previously supposed. In particular, the observations showed that the stars could not be moving around the earth in perfect circular orbits, but rather must be moving in epicycles on their orbits. If the Ptolemaic view was right, the stars must be pirouetting in little epicycles as they orbited the earth.

The key point to all this is the simple claim that, regardless of the agreed low-level observations concerning the relative motion of the relevant bodies, the Ptolemaic view could always be made consistent with those observations. The general claim concerning the limited role of experience in adjudicating theoretical disputes is then this:

The limit of experience: No set of agreed observations can, of its own, falsify a theory. Whatever observations are agreed, any theory can be made compatible with them.

Therefore, there was no observation to which the Copernican could point and say, 'There, see that, your theory is wrong.' The best the Copernican could say was something like: 'My theory gives a more elegant and simpler model of the mechanics and movements of the stars underlying the agreed observations of relative motion.' And to that, the Ptolemaic can always respond, 'What makes you think that the universe is a simple and elegant place?'

The Copernican versus Ptolemaic debate can now seem academic and fanciful. We followed the Copernican view and has not history shown us right in this? That thought is tempting and looks true, but what we have to consider is this: is our belief in the correctness of the Copernican view something that is rationally justifiable, or is it something that has an irredeemably irrational base? If we were confronted now with a modern Ptolemaic, is there an argument or set of observations that we could put to them to convince them of their error? Given the limit of experience, it is not clear that there is any ground for a rational critique of the Ptolemaic.

Perhaps it might be thought that, if we came across a modern-day Ptolemy, we could put him in a space-ship and take him into orbit around the earth, or even to the moon. Then he would simply see that he was wrong. It may well be that no earthbound observation could show our Ptolemaic to be wrong, but once we take him into space, matters are a lot easier. This seems a very obvious thought, but it still does not work. A modern-day Ptolemy with sufficient ingenuity might protest that the observation from the spacecraft does not falsify his view. All he needs to do is to add to his theory an assumption about the way in which our observations of the planets and stars are distorted by high-speed travel of the kind enjoyed by spacecraft. Of course, this is getting to look a little silly now. We point to something as straightforward as the view of the earth and sun as seen from the moon, and our Ptolemy replies with a claim that our observations are being distorted by our high-speed travel. Our Ptolemy is simply making ad hoc assumptions in order to save his theory.

All that is true, we hope. But what justifies us in saying that this latter-day Ptolemy is irrational? That is the question to which there seems no clear answer. For sure, his position is now buttressed with ad hoc assumptions, just as it was in early modern Europe with the assumption that the stars moved in epicycles. But is it always irrational to make ad hoc assumptions in order to save a theory?

What is frustrating about the latter-day Ptolemy is the way in which he seems to be treating his theory more as an article of faith than an empirical hypothesis. Whenever we point to an observation we think is significant and shows his position to be false, he responds with an ad hoc assumption to protect the position. Continuing these responses requires greater and greater ingenuity on his part, to the point where we tire of his inventiveness and ignore his theory. But does that mean that the rise of the Enlightenment and the development of modern science crucially started from a point not at which Ptolemaic ideas were shown to be false, but a point at which people simply got tired of arguing with Ptolemaics and turned their back on them? We like to tell ourselves that the Enlightenment occurred when we shook off our inherited dogmas and, forgoing our inheritance, started to work things out from scratch, from the foundations. But perhaps all we did was swap one set of inherited beliefs for another? Is Copernicanism merely an inheritance? That is the worry – that our present cosmology lacks a rational foundation. That is the key anti-rationalist challenge.

More generally, even if you think that it is too incredible to believe that the Ptolemaic view could still be defended (although recall that that is what the Catholic Church once thought about Copernicus' idea), the structure of the debate between Ptolemy and Copernicus is mirrored throughout modern scientific enquiry. As medical scientists compete to find a cure for AIDS, the observations they call upon to defend their favoured analyses presuppose a host of complex theoretical assumptions. If another researcher's analysis threatens your own, the available options for attacking the competitor's analysis are virtually unlimited. The complexity of the theoretical assumptions now brought to bear in most modern science means that the path from agreed observations to verification or falsification of a theory is long and tortuous. Therefore, the limit of experience is a real and serious challenge to the integrity of science as a rational activity.

We are inclined to think ill of the Catholic Church for its persecution of Galileo and its obstinacy in refusing for so long to accept the falsity of Ptolemy's view of the cosmos. We say that it was too dogmatic. Its concerns were not to do with truth and knowledge, but more to do with politics and the preservation of its power. We may think all that. We may think that we are better than that and above such crude power politics in our search for knowledge. But the problem is this. We have no way of showing that we really are any better than the medieval Catholic Church in this respect. What we cannot show is that what is credible and incredible for us is simply a matter of pure reason and testing by experience. Given that what is available in experience is never enough to settle matters rationally, perhaps we are still pursuing the old-fashioned power politics for which we are inclined to despise the early Catholic Church. That is the worry.

In summary, the conclusion this example shows about how

much, or how little, is available in experience is this: there is no purely rational decision procedure which takes us from an account of experience to an account of which of two competing theories is true. Where two or more theories are in competition, then, in so far as we can agree on which observations are true, such agreement does not force us to accept one theory rather than the other. The decision is not forced by experience.[5]

This example shows that the idea that experience can force us to revise our science is false. Experience alone does no such thing. That is a salutary thought to bear in mind in thinking of the history of science. We are tempted to think of that history as a history of rational turns and advances in which experience taught us to drop one theory in favour of another. The limit of experience reveals that experience is not such a demanding teacher. Experience alone cannot force us to change our minds. The history of science is perhaps still as much a history of changes prompted by all sorts of considerations we take to be extraneous to rational thought – cultural, religious, social, political and economic factors have been and still are at work in the decisions we take in shaping our science.

Nevertheless, although this example shows that there is no simple rational criterion of truth, it does so with regard to debates within science. The Copernicans and Ptolemaics could still be thrashing it out, but at least they would be agreed that they differ over theories about a uniform class of events. That is to say, although the example may prompt the thought that the truths of cosmology are relativised to your basic assumptions, the protagonists are at least agreed on the language of observation. The relevant observations are observations about the motion of material objects. It is simply that when all the observations are in, that settles nothing. The next example is more radical, for it is an example in which there is no agreement on the language of observation.

SCIENCE VERSUS WITCHCRAFT

The Azande tribe live in the southern Sudan. They have a rich system of beliefs in magic and witchcraft. The Azande recognise the sorts of observations we would typically make of the world. They recognise that in a drought the crops are likely to fail. They recognise that there are discoverable regularities about the way the material world works. They experience the material world in ways recognisable to our ordinary experience. However, in addition to thinking that the world is made of objects describable within the explanatory framework of physical science, they believe that there are other frameworks of explanation and description that apply. In particular, they have a rich explanatory framework concerning the operation of magic in the world.[6]

The Azande system of beliefs about magic is not just an option among competing theories. The Azande magic beliefs are not simple candidates for scientific theories, for these beliefs introduce novel concepts and methodologies for investigating the world. They do not introduce novel options within the scientific framework of understanding, but rather they introduce a novel framework of understanding. This is best seen if we consider an example.

The influence of witchcraft and magic permeates the way the Azande believe the world works. They see magic and witchcraft everywhere. The appeal to magic and witchcraft is not a last-resort appeal when all else has failed. Their concepts of magic and witchcraft concern matters which, for them, permeate the whole of reality. They are matters which influence normal daily life. A now infamous example of this is the Azande chicken oracle.[7]

When the Azande want to settle some matter of fact they will often resort to the chicken oracle. The oracle, which is a ceremony that has to be performed by the witchdoctor, is a magical means of discovering factual truth. An example would be this: Banda charges his wife with adultery; the matter is brought to the tribal elders who consider the evidence available; on hearing the accusation and defence, the elders then demand the oracle be consulted to settle the matter; the witchdoctor performs the oracle.

The performance of the oracle proceeds in the following way. The witchdoctor prepares a poison called *benge*. The idea is then to see whether or not a young chick dies on being given a dose of the *benge* that borders on a lethal dose. Before administering the poison it is decided how the question is to be put to the oracle; for example, if the chick dies, then Banda's wife did commit adultery. Suppose that that is the way the question is posed to the oracle. Matters do not rest there. For the oracle having been performed in that manner, the ceremony is then repeated with the question reversed. So the Azande have a control upon the operation of the oracle. If the first chick has to die to show that adultery took place, a second chick, on being administered the same dose, must live to confirm the result.

The two-stage operation of the chicken oracle might seem to place an intolerable strain upon the credibility of the idea as a means for discovering whether or not someone committed adultery. If the first chick dies, so too surely will the second? But note, first, that the dose administered to both chicks is a borderline lethal dose, so there should be a 50–50 chance of getting an agreement between the two runs of the test. More importantly, if we are quizzical about the efficacy of such a procedure because we think that if one chick dies of such-and-such a dose then so too must the other, that shows that we are thinking about the situation in the wrong categories. The whole point of the oracle, for the Azande, is that it is a way of revealing forces in operation in the world in addition to the normal causal connections we recognise. We might not be able to see how two causally identical situations could give different results – one chick lives and the other dies – but for the Azande the situations are not identical, for the whole scenario is wired into more than merely the causal regularities of the world. It is wired into the magic of the world.

Well, the Azande might say that, but it still seems odd that a procedure such as this could have survived so long. There must have been plenty of occasions on which either both chicks died or they both lived; that is, occasions on which the oracle failed to give a clear result. Of course, we would think that, if we refused to acknowledge the possibility that the whole affair is governed by more than the laws of normal causality. The Azande, nevertheless, acknowledge that there are plenty of cases in which the oracle fails to give a clear result. However, their belief in the oracle and in magic and witchcraft in general is not shaken by this. How can this be so? Does not this show that they are fundamentally irrational?

The Azande have a series of explanations to which they can appeal if the oracle misfires. Perhaps bad *benge* was used? Perhaps the *benge* had been influenced by a witch? Perhaps the whole ceremony had been subject to the malign influence of a witch? And so on. Once again, to the scientific mind this can sound silly. We are tempted to make the charge that such responses are ad hoc and illegitimate. You would not catch a scientist behaving in that manner, would you?

At the level of the school science laboratory, budding scientists never get exactly the right results. We do not say that this shows that the science they are learning is wrong. We say that they made a mistake. Perhaps their test tubes were not clean enough? Perhaps their chemicals were impure? Perhaps their thermometers were not calibrated accurately? And so on. Even within our most expensive research laboratories we work with quite elastic margins of error. Every scientist has a rag-bag collection of anomalous results, findings that simply do not fit in with what is believed and which are ignored and assumed to be due to faulty equipment, dirty test tubes, and so on.

Given these parallels between the scientist and the Azande, it seems that what we are faced with here are two radically different and fundamentally opposed ways of viewing the world. If you work exclusively within the scientific worldview you will refuse to find credible the idea that if one chick dies and the other lives the explanation for this involves magic. The explanation must lie, you will say, in there having been a small difference in the strength of the two doses of poison. As for the idea that this whole operation might be a relevant way of finding out whether or not someone has committed adultery – that is a non-starter. On the other hand, if you work with a worldview which sees magic and witchcraft in every corner of the world there is nothing incredible in the oracle failing on any given occasion. That just shows how pervasive the influence of sorcery is. The failure of the oracle, and it does fail at times, does not refute the Azande beliefs; if anything, it confirms them.

This example shows two different and incompatible worldviews between which there appears to be no bridge. In particular, there is no experience to appeal to in order to see whether or not the Azande account of the operation of the oracle or the scientific account is correct. Everywhere the Azande look they find experience full of the influence of magic and witchcraft. Nowhere the scientist looks is there any experience like that. The Azande and the scientist literally live in different worlds, and have very different experiences. There is no route, certainly no rational route, from one world to the other. You must first embrace the worldview of the Azande in something not unlike an act of faith before you can begin to see the world the way they see it. And should you do that, you will need to lose that insight, that whole frame of explanation, in order to regain the scientific worldview. Switching between the two will be like a gestalt switch; not a rational manoeuvre, but a pre-rational commitment. Rationality begins only once that commitment is undertaken – it does not govern the making of that commitment.

... AND THE WALLS COME A-TUMBLING DOWN

The simple common-sense view enshrined in the modest position I called 'critical empiricism' says that our theories must be tested against experience. We like to think of experience, observation and experiment as the foundations for our knowledge about the world. The above two examples show that there are no such foundations. It is, in principle, possible to amend any anomalous observation in order to preserve a theory. Experience does not provide the secure foundations with which to reject or support theories that 'critical empiricism' supposes. That is the core challenge to the modern idea of trying to understand the way our world works. The Enlightenment project of building human knowledge upon the secure foundations of reason and common experience is in ruins. The foundations are gone. The structures that we in the west have developed are perhaps no more than castles of our collective imagination.

This challenge consists of two claims. First, even if we agreed on a single uniform explanatory framework for all knowledge, there would be no foundational set of observations that would determine which theories were true and which were false. So, in so far as they are constrained by experience and observational reports, Ptolemy and Copernicus could be arguing still. Experience is not a matter of the passive reception of raw given data about the world. Experience is always a matter of interpretation, interpretation based upon prior theoretical assumptions. Common sense tells us that experience is clean and neutral and provides an objective foundation for distinguishing between one theory and another. Unfortunately, common sense is wrong. We have now reviewed the argument for the claim advertised in the Introduction as Thesis I, namely:

I All experience is based on interpretation.

Second, not only does experience not provide a neutral foundation within, say, the scientific worldview, but it provides no foundation for choosing between the scientific worldview and that of other competing explanatory frameworks. If experience is always a matter of interpretation based upon prior theoretical assumptions, some of those prior assumptions may introduce radically different explanatory frameworks with radically different methodologies. An example of this is the assumptions that provide the interpretations that shape the Azande experience of the world, a world that includes not only physical objects in motion but witches, magic and sorcery. If experience alone does not provide a foundation that shows that Ptolemy was wrong, neither does it provide a foundation for showing that the Azande chicken oracle is mistaken. If we insist that a scientific account could explain everything that takes place in the chicken oracle, are we not merely airing our prejudices, the basic assumptions that colour the interpretations that we have learnt to place upon experience? Similar thoughts then apply in other areas. When scientists and para-scientists disagree about the cause of crop circles are they both merely airing their prejudices? When conventional medical practitioners and homeopaths disagree about the cure for some ailment are they merely airing their prejudices? When a Christian liberal and an Islamic fundamentalist disagree about the *fatwa* on Salman Rushdie are they merely airing their prejudices? The possibility that no truth-telling is going on at all in these cases is raised once we accept the loss of foundations. The loss of foundations here is the point advertised in the Introduction as Thesis II:

II There are no secure foundations for knowledge.

Can the enterprise of trying to read the cosmic register survive this loss of foundations? The answer has to be that it cannot, for if Theses I and II are correct then we have lost the basis for believing in the possibility of the transparent language of the world. If all experience is interpretative, there can be no transparent experience, or self-interpreting experience. But then there can be no transparent self-interpreting language either, for it would be impossible to experience a language with such meaning. There is no single language suitable for reporting all the things we want to say about the world. And that last remark is Thesis III, which we arrived at in the previous chapter.

Can our simple concept of truth survive if the lack of

foundations allows scope for so many different and incompatible explanatory frameworks? This is a difficult question. There are issues here which modern philosophers are still very unsure how to answer. Quite what the options are here is unclear. But this much at least is clear: if some notion of knowledge built upon human rather than cosmic standards is still possible, the route to discovering it will have to be much more cautious than the optimistic faith in reason and common experience that we inherited from the Enlightenment. That faith is unwarranted. It is an inheritance. As such, it is potentially an arational inheritance. In the first instance, we must see whether this loss of foundations threatens anarchy. If this is the basis for postmodernism, how much are we committed to? That is the job we start in the next chapter.

Chapter 4

Nothing is certain, nothing is known?

INTRODUCTION

Knowledge looks to be out of our reach. There is no experience
that does not rely on prior interpretations. Experience, our observations and experiments, cannot provide a transparent window
upon the world, even less the basis for a transparent description
of the world. The most rigorously controlled scientific experiment
is still a confrontation with the world via the mask of a complex
web of prior assumptions, many of which are highly theoretical
and concern the operation of sophisticated technology. There is
available no transparent reading of the cosmic register, for there
is no such thing as a transparent language. All experience and all
meaning is larded with several thick layers of interpretation.
There is scope for an interminable argument about the appropriate language in which our accounts of ourselves, our lives and
our world are to be written. Not only is there no transparent
reading to show whether Ptolemy or Copernicus was right, but
there is no transparent reading to show that the explanatory
framework of witchcraft does not have entries in some legitimate
register. There is then the possibility of radically incommensurable readings being offered, with no way that experience or
reason could adjudicate between them. Knowledge looks to be
out of our reach.

In this chapter I want to clarify further the nature of this
problem. First, I shall show that the lack of secure foundations
for our knowledge does not show that knowledge is impossible.
However, it does show that it is going to be difficult to tell
whether we ever have any. That is to say, the lack of foundations
does not show it is impossible to have standards of belief, but

it does suggest that the enterprise of trying to gain something usefully called 'knowledge' is fragile.

Second, I want to show that when we realise the degree to which all experience is based upon prior interpretation, to the extent that language itself is but a mask through which we experience the world, then the fragility of our knowledge can seem to reach breaking point. If language itself is a mask through which we interpret the world, and if it is not possible to step outside our language, there seems little hope of there being any such thing as truth or objective knowledge independent of our languages and explanatory frameworks.

KNOWLEDGE: A BUILDING WITHOUT FOUNDATIONS

Buildings without foundations do not always fall down. However, they are prone to collapse if disturbed. If there is no raw experience prior to interpretation and theory, there is no objective foundation for our knowledge. Does this mean that our attempts at knowledge must collapse, or does it merely mean that they are much more precarious than we had supposed? That is the first question we need to settle. More exactly, we need to be clear in what sense knowledge lacks foundations. Having done that we will need to see whether the point about the limits of experience constitutes a disturbance that would bring about the collapse of our attempts at knowledge.

One sense in which we have to accept that knowledge lacks foundations concerns the slack between the observations that we can agree on and the theoretical claims we want to make. Although it is true that all experience is based upon prior interpretation, there are many reports of experience on which we can and do agree. For example, although Ptolemy and Copernicus would disagree on whether they saw the sun moving or the earth turning, they would agree that the horizon and the sun were moving progressively further apart. There are also many other things on which they agree. However, this agreement, no matter how large, does not settle their theoretical differences. Between their agreed observational reports – the experience they have in common – and their competing theoretical claims there is an insurmountable gap.

What this amounts to is the following:

Given an agreement on a set of observational claims, there is no mechanical procedure for determining an agreement on theoretical claims.

This means that whatever agreement we may enjoy at the level of observational reports, to proceed from that agreement to a settlement of a theoretical dispute requires a leap. There is no algorithm for determining the truth or falsity of theoretical claims on the basis of an agreed set of observational truths. We could not expect to build a machine into which we could feed the agreed observations and that would then churn out the theoretical results.

One sense in which it is true that knowledge lacks secure foundations is then just this: no knowledge claim can be demonstrated to be true on the basis of experience and reason. No matter how much evidence we amass in support of a claim, no matter how convincing the reasons to which we appeal, there is still a gap between all that and a demonstration of the truth of the knowledge claimed. Even if we were given all the evidence and the supporting reasons, it is still conceivable that the claimed knowledge would turn out to be false. The lack of foundations then amounts to the following: from an account of all the true agreed observational claims that there are, there is no hard and fast recipe, no mechanical procedure, for arriving at an account of which theoretical claims are true and which are false. More exactly, there is no effective decision procedure for determining the truth or falsity of a knowledge claim on the basis of experience. Let's capture this sense of the lack of foundations for knowledge by saying: there is no mechanical recipe for knowledge.

It is important that the point is put by saying that there is no 'mechanical recipe' for knowledge. As we saw in Chapter 1, Bacon thought there was a recipe for knowledge, but he did not think it was a mechanical procedure. He thought that there was a set of rules, application of which would remove dogma and generate knowledge. Bacon did not think that the application of these rules was mechanical – their status was more as a set of heuristic guidelines to assist in the removal of the foggy veil of dogma.

So, given a complete list of agreed observational claims there is no mechanical recipe for churning out knowledge claims. Gaining knowledge is not a mechanical process. So, despite all the evidence so far in, it is still conceivable that Copernicus was wrong. Of course, to say this is to stretch the notion of what is conceivable beyond the limits of normal credulity, but that just shows that what we normally find credible is a function not just of what experience and reason have told us. What we ordinarily find credible is a function in part of our faith in the continuing success of science. The basis of our beliefs about the solar system is an inheritance; it is not experience and reason.

How worrying is it that knowledge lacks foundations in this sense? The answer we give to this question depends, in part, on how high we set the standards for knowledge. Clearly, if we assume that for something to count as knowledge it must be demonstrably true, provable beyond doubt, then the lack of foundations would show that knowledge was impossible. Also, if we assume that for something to count as knowledge it must be something that can be known with certainty, then the lack of foundations would show that knowledge was impossible. However, it is not clear why we should make such strong assumptions about knowledge.

If the lack of foundations for knowledge amounts to the thesis that there is no mechanical recipe for knowledge, does this really amount to any more than the observation that all our knowledge is fallible? If so, surely that is correct? Our knowledge is fallible. Recognising our fallibility, the fact that for any claim we make it is possible that we could be shown to be wrong, is surely not a problem but a recognition of our humility? Indeed, if we think about it further it would seem odd, if not presumptuous, to think that we could be infallible in our knowledge claims. We are not that good. So, if the loss of foundations amounts to no more than a recognition of our fallibility, what's the problem? It is possible that Copernicus got it all wrong, but I bet he did not![1]

However, we cannot leave matters there. The discussion so far merely shows that for so many philosophers to have got worried by the lack of foundations for knowledge they must have been worried about something worse than merely the lack of a mechanical recipe for knowledge. I think that that is right. The lack of a mechanical recipe for generating knowledge on the basis of some set of agreed observations amounts only to the claim that there is no valid deductive inference from the truth of the set of agreed observations to the truth of the theoretical claim.

Before focusing on the sense in which the lack of foundations for knowledge is a more serious threat than that, we need to clarify further what we mean by knowledge.

KNOWLEDGE: A SOCIALLY TRANSMITTED CONDITION?

What then do we mean by 'knowledge'? If we mean possessing true beliefs about the world that can be known with certainty because they can be supported by deductive arguments from premises that are themselves necessary, then we would have to accept that there is no such thing as knowledge. But why on earth should we mean something as contentious as that? The whole threat of postmodernism would look rather silly if it was dependent on such a contentious concept of knowledge. So let's start with something weaker and more commonsensical and then locate the threat to our ordinary common-sense notion of knowledge.

Knowledge is a matter of having a true belief that has been obtained in a non-accidental way. To say that the belief is true is to say that the belief corresponds to, or mirrors, how things are in the world. So far, our image for this idea has been the idea of the cosmic register. My belief is true if it is a belief that in addition to being recorded in my head is also recorded in the cosmic register. But if the cosmic register is a book written in the language of the world, there is no such book. We need then a weaker concept of knowledge. Of course, we may have to conclude that no weaker concept is available, and that is what we shall try to settle in this chapter. But if knowledge is possible without the cosmic register, our model will have to be a weaker one.

Therefore, let us say that, regardless of what we think about what causes our belief, to have knowledge is to have a true belief brought about in a non-accidental way. To say that the belief has been obtained in a non-accidental way is to ensure that knowledge is not just a matter of possessing true beliefs. For a true belief to count as knowledge it cannot be an accident or a matter of luck that I happen to believe it. My having the belief and the fact in the world must be connected in some way.

For example, suppose I count the number of people in a large room and arrive at the belief that there are thirty-two people there. However, suppose I missed someone out but counted wrongly, so that I do have a true belief for there *are* thirty-two people in the room. In such an example I have surely been too lucky to count as having knowledge. Although my belief is true, in that it mirrors the facts, that it does so is a lucky accident. Because of that it is implausible to say I know that there are thirty-two people in the room.

Now the above looks close enough to our ordinary concept of knowledge, although it says nothing about the nature of truth. Truth cannot be what is in the cosmic register, for we have lost that. But we can still acknowledge some notion of truth as: that which is the case independently of whether I, or anyone else, thinks it. What we want when we want knowledge is to have a belief that mirrors the facts and that this belief be one that we hold because it corresponds with the facts.[2] All we have done now is to spell out a little more carefully the idea of knowledge. We have remained neutral on the issue of what constitutes the facts. We have left open the possibility of facts being a varied realm including things that can only be reported in a plurality of different non-transparent languages. But having spelt this out we can note a number of important facts about knowledge and the lack of foundations for knowledge.

Given what we mean by knowledge, the lack of foundations for knowledge does not show that knowledge is impossible. The fact that there is no mechanical recipe for knowledge does not show knowledge is impossible. However, it does suggest that we cannot know that we have knowledge. This means that, despite the lack of foundations for knowledge, we may know many things because we have beliefs that are true and that we have because they are true. However, we would not know that we had knowledge. The point can seem sophistical, but it is important and reveals the true nature and seriousness of the postmodernist predicament.

Given what we mean by knowledge we need to distinguish between knowing something and knowing that we know that something. For example, there is a distinction between knowing that there are thirty-two people in the room and knowing that you know there are thirty-two people in the room. You will know the first thing just in case you have the true belief that there are thirty-two people in the room and you have that belief because of the fact that there are thirty-two people in the room. But, for all that, because of the lack of foundations for knowledge you will not know that you have this knowledge. This just shows that if knowledge is having a true belief which you have because it is true, then this is something you can have without knowing it! That can sound odd, but the following image may help.

Knowledge, thought of as true belief that you have because of the fact which makes it true, is like a disease. It is something with which you can be infected without knowing that you have it. Knowledge is an infection you acquire from your contact with the world and, in more cases than not, with other people. Knowledge is a socially infectious condition. You bump into the world and other people and you come away infected with knowledge. That is a useful image for thinking about knowledge. It captures the idea of knowledge as true belief caused by the fact that makes the belief true. Most important of all, it captures the idea that knowledge is having beliefs about something independent of oneself, something objective.

Perhaps it will seem that if that is what our image of knowledge amounts to, then this is too weak a concept of knowledge. Certainly, unless we add the idea that the facts can be represented in one uniform transparent language of the world, this concept of knowledge is much weaker than that which defined modernity. It is a concept of knowledge that allows that the world is a complex place. The world is, in many ways, our world, a world that has room for us with our perspectives and points of view, rather than the transparent world of matter in motion. Perhaps it will be thought that if that is all that knowledge amounts to we are dodging the real problems about knowledge that postmodernism threatens? This is not true. Indeed, accepting that the above clarifications of our concept of knowledge are right only goes to show how powerful the postmodernist threat is.

Far from weakening the threat, the above clarifications enable us to mark more precisely what the threat is and how it appears unanswerable. I said in the last chapter that the examples that revealed the limits of experience were different. The Ptolemy versus Copernicus example was an example of a potentially interminable debate within the explanatory framework of science. The Azande witchcraft versus western science example was an example of a potentially interminable debate between two competing explanatory frameworks. This difference means that there are two problems about the lack of foundations for knowledge, only one of which we have so far located.

TWO PROBLEMS ABOUT KNOWLEDGE

So far, the lack of foundations for knowledge means that there is no mechanical recipe for producing knowledge. This does not mean that there is no knowledge, but it does mean that there is no criterion for knowledge. It means that we cannot show that we have knowledge although, for all that, we might know a lot. Lacking an effective criterion for knowledge shows that we cannot know that we know. If knowledge is like an infectious condition arising from contact with the world and with others, then it is something for which there is no guaranteeing symptom. Knowledge is an infection that produces no effective symptom that shows that we are infected. This does not mean that we are not infected, but it does mean that we cannot show that we are. If things stood just at that, it is not clear there would be any general problem about knowledge even given the lack of foundations. However, there is a problem about knowledge.

Let us distinguish between what we might call the first-level and second-level problems about knowledge. The first-level problem about knowledge is this: can we tell from amongst the beliefs we hold which of them are cases of knowledge and which are not? Given the lack of foundations for knowledge it seems that we cannot tell which of our beliefs are cases of knowledge and which are not. Remember, if a belief is knowledge, then it must be true and we must hold it because of the fact that it is true. However, given the lack of foundations for any given belief that we hold it is always possible that it is not true. But that means that for any given belief of ours it is possible that it is not knowledge. Whatever we do in sifting out the mistakes in our beliefs it is always possible that we have done the sorting wrong. We have no way of sifting amongst our beliefs that is guaranteed to sort out the ones that constitute knowledge.

The idea of trying to sift amongst our beliefs to find the ones that constitute knowledge is what I mean by a first-level enquiry. Essentially, it is an enquiry to find out which, if any, amongst our beliefs are the ones that we ought to hold on to. However, we can have no general criterion to pick out the beliefs we ought to hold on to; that is what the lack of foundations amounts to. Of course, this does not mean that we are completely bereft of ideas of what to do in seeking knowledge. If you want to know how many people there are in a room, it's a good idea to start by opening your eyes! The present point is that there is no general criterion that will apply in all cases and effectively sift out knowledge from ignorance. That is the first-level problem about knowledge.

This first-level problem does not show knowledge to be impossible. On the other hand, it does not show that knowledge is possible either. What it shows is that if knowledge is possible we cannot expect philosophers or anyone else to come up with an effective decision procedure for filtering out the knowledge from amongst the different beliefs we all hold. Given the lack of foundations, philosophy can have no pretence to supply such a criterion. Not only is there a limit to experience that shows the lack of foundations for knowledge, there is also a limit to what we can expect of philosophy and philosophers. No philosopher can come up with a criterion for knowledge, a general method or effective recipe for spotting which of our beliefs are knowledge.

In the light of much of the history of philosophy this first-level problem is serious. Indeed, seen from the perspective of the pretensions of much of philosophy's history, it is calamitous. Philosophers have long thought that they could describe a criterion for sifting out knowledge from amongst our beliefs. If you expect that much from philosophy then you must learn to live with disappointment. In particular, a criterion for knowledge that historically has been important in western culture, namely that we should believe in the results of science, is unwarranted as a criterion. From the perspective of a philosophical tradition that has taken upon itself the task of providing a criterion of truth this problem can appear dramatic. However, it is not the end of the world. It is not a problem that signals the thought that there is no such thing as knowledge at all. It is a problem that says that we can never devise an effective recipe for telling which of our beliefs count as knowledge and which do not. Without such a criterion it is possible that we know nothing, but it is also possible that we know a lot. However, the full postmodernist challenge takes us further than this and raises the more serious second-level threat that not only is it possible that we know nothing, but it is impossible that we know anything, for there is no such thing as the belief we ought to hold.

Suppose for the moment that you could live with the idea that philosophy cannot provide an effective criterion for solving the first-level problem about knowledge. That problem was: can we tell which of our beliefs are ones that we ought to hold on to? The second-level problem is the much more profound: can we tell whether there is such a thing as that which we ought to believe? Where the first-level problem asks if we can tell which of our beliefs are true, the second-level problem asks if there is such a thing as truth at all. If there is no such thing as that which we ought to believe – the truth – then there is no such thing as knowledge. So why should anyone think that this second-level problem is forced upon us? The answer lies with the second case of a lack of foundations illustrated in the last chapter, the case where we have an interminable disagreement between two competing explanatory frameworks.

If we are agreed on the basic explanatory framework, the basic language for describing experience, then the lack of foundations for knowledge only shows that we cannot know that we know. For all that, it is still possible we know a lot. If we are agreed on the way in which we should describe experience, but we disagree only on what we should say next about what is beyond experience, then it is still possible that we know a lot. Although we cannot provide an effective criterion to prove Copernicus right and Ptolemy wrong, at least we are assured that, whichever of them is right, the issue is about the movement of large lumps of matter in space. We still retain the idea that, regardless of whether we have got any knowledge about the world, the world at issue is the world of matter in motion. So, as long as we consider the problem of the lack of foundations for knowledge from within one explanatory framework, we have no reason to suppose that knowledge is not possible. Although we might not be sure quite where or how, we are nevertheless still in touch with the world.

Put this matter another way. If there is no competition about what the appropriate explanatory framework is, we are not threatened with the idea that we might have totally lost touch with the world. If there is only one explanatory framework, then although we may have no criterion for singling out which of the claims within that framework are true, we have no reason to doubt that the framework itself offers a way of describing the world that captures something real. Think of an explanatory framework as a language. The point is that if there is only one candidate language, then although we may not know which sentences are true and which false, we have no reason to doubt that the language in general offers a way of talking that mirrors the way the world is. If there is no competition for the language in which the world is to be described, then even if we cannot tell whether we are describing it correctly, at least we are talking the right sort of way. We are speaking the language of the world. That is why the lack of foundations within an explanatory framework does not close off the possibility of knowledge.

However, as we have seen, the lack of foundations for knowledge has a dimension beyond that of not being able to prove whether it is Ptolemy or Copernicus who is right. The lack of foundations in the second-level sense is not just that there is no effective criterion for truth, but that there is no agreement about the language or explanatory framework in which we should describe our experience and begin the search for truth. As long as we assume that there is only one explanatory framework or language, we do no harm to think of that language as the language of the cosmic register. That amounts to saying that that language offers a transparent medium for recording the truth, or, the explanatory framework offers a transparent medium for discovering what is going on in the world. However, once we allow that there are competing explanatory frameworks we have to accept that these languages are not transparent. They cannot be transparent, for in being alternative competing ways of conceptualising experience they can no longer be seen as media for reading something beyond experience. If there is nothing in common between the spirit- and witch-populated experience of the Azande and the physicalist description of experience of the western scientist, then there is no scope for seeing them as different experiences of something common. Now, does the loss of the idea that these explanatory frameworks provide experiences of something in common entail the loss of the idea of truth as independent of experience? That is a difficult question and one that requires care in how we answer it.

The acceptance of a plurality of non-transparent languages does not, of itself, entail the loss of a notion of objective independent truth. The idea that there exists a plurality of non-transparent languages is compatible with there being independent truth as long as the different explanatory frameworks are not in competition. In contrast, a plurality of explanatory frameworks that were incompatible with one another would entail loss of the idea of independent truth. However, if the different explanatory frameworks complement rather than compete with one another, there is still room for the idea of truth to gain purchase – although the notion of truth could no longer be the transparent truth of the cosmic register.

Therefore, it is only if the proliferation of explanatory frameworks provides frameworks that are incompatible with one another that we lose the idea of that which is independent of experience. Only then do we lose the idea of truth. We would then lose the idea of that which we ought to believe, that which makes up knowledge. Knowledge would be impossible.

BEYOND THE LIMITS OF PHILOSOPHY – THE NIHILISTIC TENDENCY?

As long as there is only one explanatory framework, one language in which to seek knowledge, then although language is a medium, a mask that disables us from reading the world directly and unproblematically, it is still hopefully a mask through which we read the world. As long as there is only one medium, even if there is no criterion for when the messages in that medium should be retained as knowledge, we can still hold on to the idea that the language is a medium through which we can contact reality.

Even if we accept extra explanatory frameworks, these may amount to ways of reading the many facets of the world. As long as the proliferation of frameworks is a proliferation of modes of understanding and explanation that complement one another, we can still hold on to the idea that in all this it is truth and knowledge that we are after. That is why, at the end of Chapter 2, I remarked that it was a liberating thought to countenance the proliferation of explanatory frameworks beyond the explanations offered by the physical sciences.

However, if we acknowledge the possibility of incommensurable languages, then the pursuit of truth and knowledge is lost. If we acknowledge the idea that there can be interminable disagreements about the very language in which we are to describe experience, language is no longer a medium for investigating something beyond. In that scenario there is nothing in common between the competing languages that could possibly exist beyond language. That is why, in the last chapter, I said that in a very real sense the Azande and the western scientist seem to inhabit different worlds. There is no conception of a common reality for which their competing languages might be no more than alternative media.

That is the second-level problem that characterises the anti-rationalism of the postmodernist predicament. It is the problem that the languages we employ in describing our experience can no longer be seen as media for talking about something beyond language. This is a problem we are faced with as soon as we accept the proliferation of languages or explanatory frameworks that are incommensurable. Language ceases to be a fallible medium through which we experience the world. Different languages turn out to be the media through which we construct and inhabit a plurality of worlds. If those worlds are incommensurable, there is no common language in terms of which a resolution of their differences can be achieved. Knowledge, that which is true independent of judgement, is then impossible.

Note that we have now come to the full-blown postmodernist predicament without having to accept anything contentious about the nature of knowledge. Indeed, we refused to assume that real knowledge required certainty or demonstrable proof. We assumed only that knowledge was the humble matter of having a belief that is true and that one had the belief because of the fact that it was true. This is, I think, our ordinary common-or-garden concept of knowledge and it is this, not some fancy construct of speculative philosophy, that has got us into trouble. The postmodern predicament, although a philosophical problem, is not merely a problem for philosophers and those who attend philosophy seminars. It does not require the suspension of ordinary ideas about truth and knowledge to get the postmodernist predicament going. The problem is not an academic problem. It is a problem that arises from reflection upon our ordinary concept of knowledge.

We have now located two separate problems. First, there is the problem of the lack of foundations for knowledge. That is the problem that within any given explanatory framework there is no effective recipe for sifting out knowledge from false belief. In addition, there is the 'knowledge is impossible' problem. This second problem is the problem that if there are competing alternative explanatory frameworks for experience, the idea of objective truth and knowledge drops out of our picture altogether. This is the anti-rationalist thought that we cannot criticise and rationally adjust our worldviews; we can only inherit them.

I have suggested that it is perhaps beyond the limits of philosophy to do much to address the lack-of-foundations problem. That is a serious matter. It means we have no secure handrails left to guide us in our search for knowledge. The confidence with which we have ripped the physical world apart and then, in trying to glue it back together again, have tried to understand how it all works, has been misplaced. Given the lack of foundations we have been far too sure of ourselves. The very ordinary-looking and humble notion I labelled critical empiricism is too presumptuous for an account of how to search for and collect knowledge. Where we have assumed that we were boldly going forth and grasping what made the world tick, it now looks likely that we were stumbling like so many drunks in a dark alley late at night.

However, plenty of drunks still make it home. The full postmodernist predicament suggests that there is no home to head for; there is no such thing as what we ought to believe. Matters are serious enough with the lack of foundations for knowledge. But, the proliferation of competing explanatory frameworks does not dent our confidence – it shatters it. There seems to be little room to escape the problems we have now distinguished. In particular, how can we avoid the total loss of truth and rationality without returning to the discredited idea that the language of physics constitutes the transparent language of the cosmic register? That is to say, how can we avoid the full-blown postmodernist predicament except by denying that there are alternatives to the physicalist description of our experience of the world?

It may be the case that it is beyond the limits of philosophy to provide a criterion for knowledge that would solve the lack-of-foundations problem, but matters are truly desperate if it is beyond the limits of philosophy to address satisfactorily the full-blown postmodernist predicament. If we cannot answer that, a kind of nihilism is all we are left with. We will have no grounds for criticising those who speak in other tongues, those who adopt competing explanatory frameworks. We will have no scope to criticise so-called para-scientists and they will have no basis on which to criticise the status quo. We will have no resources to criticise fundamentalists wherever they occur, nor they to criticise the liberals who tolerate blasphemy of one kind or another. We will have no grounds to criticise those who grow rich offering deep-breathing cures for life-threatening and wasting diseases like AIDS. And such people will have no scope to criticise received medical science and show what it misses out and why. We will be beset by anarchy and chaos. We will have no notion at all of what we ought to believe. We will have only the traditions of belief into which we are born, those traditions that feel comfortable and familiar. If we ask whether they are right or not, we will get no answer. That silence is the silence of anti-rationalism. It is a profound nihilism. It is a silence that is now insinuating itself into the general consciousness in these postmodernist times.

The idea that we are all postmodernists now is a vague idea. The label 'postmodernism' can stand for many things. Some postmodernists stress the lack of foundations for knowledge; some are prepared to countenance the anti-rationalist nihilism of the loss of all knowledge. It is important that we keep these two issues separate. As it is commonly used, 'postmodernism' seems to be a label for a position that assumes one or both of the problems we have focused upon. I shall use 'anti-rationalism' as the label for the position that holds that there is no such thing as truth and knowledge. This is the position that holds that all belief is relativised to our different inherited languages or explanatory frameworks. What we have to do now is see whether it is within the limits of philosophy to address the problem of anti-rationalism. Does the postmodernist rejection of the idea of a single uniform mode of explanation and description of the world – and in particular the scientific model as a way of reading the cosmic register – have to proceed to this nihilistic anti-rationalism?

In Chapter 2 I introduced the idea that perhaps the truth was to be expressed in many tongues; that is to say, perhaps not all truths are written in the language of the physical sciences? However, it now seems that it is the very idea of proliferating explanatory frameworks or languages that introduces the nihilistic tendency. The nihilism arises when the proliferation is understood to introduce a plurality of explanatory frameworks as competitors, rather than complements. That is why we seem pressed to return to the single language of physicalism in order to escape anti-rationalism. In the next two chapters I want to open up the possibility that we can find a way between these two extremes. We need to see if there are standards by which we can measure our progress other than the daunting standards of the cosmic register.

In other words, we need to see if the second-level problem of anti-rationalism is something that can be tackled within the limits of philosophy. Even if philosophy is impotent in addressing the lack of foundations for knowledge, perhaps it can ward off anti-rationalism. But we must not forget this: even if we ward off anti-rationalism, we are still left with the first-level predicament that there are no foundations for knowledge. This means that from now on, we are going to have to proceed with much greater caution and humility in investigating the world, ourselves and our place in it.

Chapter 5

A web of our own conceit?

THE LANGUAGE OF THE WORLD

Modernity rose upon the idea that we could learn the language of the world. If we could strip away the distorting influences of our various human perspectives and look at the world transparently, we would learn to speak in the language in which the world speaks to itself. We would achieve a picture of the world that would be a picture from no particular point of view. We would escape our inherited beliefs and work out how things were from scratch. Such a conception of the world and such a conception of knowledge is impossible. That is the key postmodernist challenge.

There is no such thing as a language that strips bare our human predicament and gives us a glance of the world transparently conceived. All the meanings that we acknowledge are human meanings. The world we inhabit is a world as we understand it. It is a world experienced through human concepts, for there is no such thing as a transparent experience or a transparent language. There is no such thing as an experience that directly dials into the world as it is in itself. There is only interpretation, interpretation based upon earlier interpretation based upon earlier interpretation. Our interpretations, the forms through which our experiences are shaped, are inherited. If there is no transparent experience, there can be no point of view from which we can, at a stroke, disinherit our human perspectives and achieve direct contact with reality. We can never learn the language of the world; we will never learn the music of the spheres. Modernity has been a conceit. We mistook our human earthly languages for something divine, something cosmic. We thought that a way of describing the world that we had constructed matched the language of the world. It does not. There is no such thing as the language of the world.

If the human languages we employ include languages that offer radically incompatible accounts of our experience, and if there is no universal common tongue in which to settle our differences, there is no fact about who has the best story to tell. Perhaps all that we ever do when we talk about the world is spin comforting stories to help us sleep at night? Perhaps there is no rational choice to be made between competing languages? All the different languages we inhabit are mere webs of our own conceit, inheritances from our various histories. So much by way of recap.

THE END OF PROGRESS?

Since the Enlightenment, the ideal of knowledge has been built around the idea of progress. We believed progress would occur as we learnt to speak ever better approximations to the language of the world. The development of knowledge was meant to be a development as we learnt the grand story of the world. There was a single story to be told, told in a uniform language. If we persevered, then with time, considerable effort and good luck we would unravel that story. The modern version of this idea centred on the claims of science to give us the world's own story. The end of modernity signals the end of this belief in a single uniform story of the world. The great story has been replaced with a plurality of local human stories. There is no story of the universe. There is only a plurality of local tales. What then becomes of progress? Where do we go from here?

Some postmodernists would say that there is nowhere to go. The very idea of progress is unwarranted once we are rid of the ideal of the cosmic register and the language of the world. We should not ask what we should believe next if we are expecting to make a rational choice. What we believe next will depend on all sorts of factors including aesthetic factors, social factors, individual psychologies and so on. What we believe next will not be a matter of who is telling the truest story. It can only be a matter of who is telling a story we like the sound of!

It is not clear that such versions of postmodernism are stable. Even Rorty wants to speak of 'better' descriptions of the world and that sounds as if he means a 'description that is more accurate'. He would, however, deny that. He says that, for example, although there are cases where the scientific account of the world is better than others, this notion of 'better' really means no more than that, for the case in hand, science meets our human needs better than some other account. For example, if we want to know where a projectile will land if thrown into the air, then science is the best way of arriving at an accurate prediction. You will do better listening to the scientist than reading tea-leaves.

However, if Rorty really means that the sense in which science is better at prediction and control of projectiles is only an instrumental sense, namely that it is better given various needs we have, it is difficult not to see this as a form of anti-rationalism. If the only measure of the value of a story or belief is a measure relative to some need or desire that we have, then that is to say that there is no notion of a belief being better than another because one is true and the other false. Certainly Rorty will insist that if we mean by truth, 'correspondence with the cosmic register' or 'part of the story of the world written in the world's own language', then we cannot say one belief is better than another because it is true in that sense. But the present issue is distinct from all that.

Let us agree that we give up on the world's own story, the thing written in the language of the world. Throw away the cosmic register. Having thrown away the conceit that we might see the world from nowhere, what notion of truth and progress, if any, is left? It does not take much effort to realise that postmodernism still operates with ideas of truth and progress. Nevertheless, many postmodernists, such as Rorty and Lyotard, in their desire to distance themselves from the Enlightenment ideal of knowledge, are hesitant to advertise the fact.

If Rorty says that science gives a better account of why a projectile will fall to earth at one point rather than another, he takes this to mean 'better, given our interests and desires in prediction'. But, of course, matters do not end there. For if that is what Rorty means, then it is easy to ask why the scientific account is better in this instance. It is difficult to see how there could be any answer to this other than that the scientific account, in this instance, is true. It is because the scientific account is true that it is better at predicting the trajectory of projectiles than an account that involved reading tea-leaves. Remember, saying this does not commit us to reinstating the cosmic register, but only to recognising the following point.

Suppose that we calculate the trajectory an apple will take in falling to the ground if the wind blows. That calculation is useful to us; it meets certain needs. To say that it meets those needs because it is true is to say no more than this: the apple would have taken that trajectory anyhow, whether or not we had made the calculation. That is to say, the claim about the apple's trajectory is not made true by us. If it is true, it is so independently of our thinking about it. When the wind blows the apple will fall, whether or not we are thinking about it, calculating it, or had even developed the resources to calculate it. Apples were falling from trees long before Sir Isaac Newton was impressed by the event.

To recognise this is to recognise a very simple and humble notion of truth. It is the idea that what makes a claim true, in this case a claim about the trajectory of an apple, is not what we think. It is what happens. Such an obvious and simple concept of truth is not obliterated by our argument against the cosmic register. It is a concept of truth that is presupposed when Rorty says that, for certain things, science has a better account than other systems of thought. Of course it does, but that is only because, in certain fields like apple orchards, science has discovered something that is true.

There is then a simple but important notion of truth still at work within postmodernism. Why are postmodernists reluctant to acknowledge this? Furthermore, is it a concept that could fuel a new notion of progress? Clearly, modernity's ideal of progress, in which we learn more and more of the world's own story, is no longer an option. But is a humbler notion of progress concerned with getting more things right in our limited human stories available here?

Postmodernism is a name for a large number of beliefs, but the thing we have so far fixed on, the rejection of the cosmic register model of knowledge, is central. Many postmodernists resist the idea of truth altogether; they think it smacks too much of the semi-divine mysticism of the cosmic register. In doing this, they run the risk of embracing anti-rationalism. At the same time, most postmodernists, and Rorty is certainly one of them, reject the charge of anti-rationalism. However, without a concept of truth, that is the charge that sticks.[1]

We need to see a way out of this impasse, for there is something right in the critique of modernity. There is also something profoundly right in the idea that some concept of truth must be sustained. That is to say, the key insight of postmodernism must be separated from the heady intoxicating brew of anti-rationalism; the 'anything goes' position that can provide no account of why you would be daft to look to your tea-leaves to work out where the apple is going to fall.

A major step in seeing how we can accept the critique of the transparent cosmic register, and save our sanity by admitting that apples fall from trees whether we think about them or not, is to look at the following question. In what sense are the different languages and explanatory frameworks at play in the world today our languages? That is to say, in what sense are they all webs of our own conceit? If we can show that there is a clear sense in which they are not conceits, perhaps we can then apply simple truth to such languages? To do that we must be clear about this notion of simple truth. So, first: the simple truth.

THE SIMPLE TRUTH

Postmodernists often sound as if they do not believe in the concept of truth at all. But why then do they wear seat-belts in their cars, go to the dentist when they have a toothache, or go to the bank manager for a loan? There are many things that we believe about the world and, in so doing, we show our commitment to a simple concept of truth – the idea that things go on independently of our thinking about them. Whether I think about it or not, the money in my bank account continues to decrease as I write my cheques. Like it or not, I cannot stop this happening simply by ignoring it. I know this is true.

This simple and commonsensical concept of truth is central to all our actions. Of course, this is not to say that we have the truth in all our actions. Rather it is to say that it is impossible to make sense of our lives without the idea that things happen independently of our thinking about them. We do not need to concentrate on science and the physical world to see that this is so.

The facts about my bank account are not physical facts. They could never have been written up in the cosmic register. A cosmic accountant with the transparent view of the cosmos would never have seen my bank account. The very idea of a bank account only makes sense within a human story, a human perspective in which the movement of little pieces of paper has come to have such importance. It is of no comfort to me to be told that from the point of view of the cosmos – in the language of the world – there is no fact concerning the state of my bank account. The facts about the state of my bank account are human facts. They are facts shaped by all sorts of complex human conventions, but for all that they are still facts. They are things that will not go away no matter how hard I try to ignore them. These are facts that I cannot ignore. They impinge upon me. They are things that I ought to believe, for they are true.

There is a variety of things that will not go away. Even in our moral lives we find it hard to resist the idea that when it comes to the things that really matter, there is some fact of the case. Why else do people get so passionate about animal rights, apartheid, prisoners of conscience? Is it not because they feel that, on these issues, their beliefs are true? Whether you like it or not, whether you think about it or not, is not apartheid wrong? People who think it is wrong do not just take that as a belief that is useful. They are passionate about it because they think they are right. Of course, it is notoriously difficult to see how we can have clear rational arguments in such matters. The present point is simply to note the readiness with which we all assume that there are standards of correct belief, even in matters of morals.

Morals, as also our beliefs about bank accounts, did not figure within the cosmic register. The modern scientific image of the world that evolved from the Enlightenment banished all that from the world. Matter in motion was the sum total of the truth – there could be no truth about morals and bank accounts. The concept of simple truth is a much humbler idea. It comes from acknowledging that when we make a judgement, there is a notion of whether or not what we have said is correct independently of what we happen to think. So, if I judge that there is a balance of £2,000 in my bank account there is an issue about whether that is correct which is independent of what I think. Unfortunately, that point is simply right. I cannot control my bank balance by thought alone. And although the similar idea is much harder to sustain in the case of our moral judgements, the ease with which we make the same assumption is striking. When engaged in a moral argument we assume that one party is right and the other is wrong even if we cannot see a way to convince the other party that they are mistaken. Just as with the beliefs about the bank account, we cannot control the truths of morality.

The concept of simple truth is the idea that things are thus and so whether or not we choose to think that they are. It is the notion of truth implied by the discussion of the basic constraint in Chapter 1, p. 28. The present point is that this notion of truth is something that can survive the loss of the cosmic register and the idea of a transparent language of the world. The range of things to which simple truth applies includes the state of bank accounts, apples falling from trees, possible moral questions, the rate of inflation, the colour of my true love's hair and so on and so forth. Apart from the apple, none of this could have been captured within the cosmic register. These are all facts which can only be spotted from a human perspective. But they are still facts.

To the above argument, the following complaint might be made. It will be said that all I have done is observe that we appear to endorse a distinction between truth and judgement, but that I have not legitimised that distinction. That is to say, it might be objected that complacent reminders about our common-sense notion of truth cannot justify our appeal to simple truth. Common sense might be wrong. This is a fair criticism. I think it amounts to the following correct observation: in the absence of the model of the cosmic register we need some account of what the truth/judgement distinction consists in. The fact that we normally act as if such a distinction was well grounded does not show that it is. There must be an account of the truth/judgement distinction; we must have an account of the distinction between right and seems right. After all, it might seem to me that I have £2,000 in my bank account, but it seeming so to me does not make it so. What model then is left for conceptualising this distinction? That is the question we are now left with. And note, this question is a metaphysical question. It asks for an account of the distinction between truth and judgement. It is not an epistemological question that asks how we are to pick out true judgements from among the erroneous ones.

It is at this point that we have to provide the alternative metaphysics to replace the cosmic register. Note that by 'metaphysics' I mean no more than a model of what makes our thoughts and utterances true or false. I have appealed to a simple concept of truth, the notion of things being thus and so independently of our thinking that they are. This is a concept that we readily employ throughout our normal discourse. The question is: is the concept of simple truth legitimate? That is the question that requires a metaphysical model of truth to answer it.

IN DEFENCE OF TRUTH – THE REAL THING

We need an argument to show that the concept of simple truth is legitimate. What I am calling our concept of simple truth is the concept of things continuing to exist independently of our thought about them. It is our simple everyday concept of the truth/judgement distinction. I judge that there is £2,000 in my bank account, but I acknowledge that there is a fact of the matter independent of my judgement. That is a simple example of the common grasp of a distinction between truth and judgement. Is it legitimate?

In order to provide legitimacy to simple truth, I shall consider truth in one very basic domain: our thought and talk about material objects. The argument I am going to give is a transcendental argument. Transcendental arguments are arguments that unveil the conditions necessary for something; for example, the conditions necessary for experience, or the conditions necessary for thought. Kant introduced the idea of a transcendental argument with an argument about the conditions for the possibility of experience.[2]

A transcendental argument is always of the form: for X to be possible, Y must be the case. Y is the condition necessary for X. If we know that X exists, then the argument shows that Y must be the case too. One traditional problem with such arguments is that in trying to construct them, how can we be sure that the condition Y is the only condition that makes X possible? It may be that some other kind of condition is available. If so, the argument from the existence of X to the existence of Y is invalid.

Another way of representing what a transcendental argument is helps avoid this problem. Transcendental arguments are arguments that show, given that X obtains, certain other things, Y, must also be accepted, for these are commitments that cannot be denied, given X. So, rather than argue that, say, the existence of the external world is a necessary condition for the possibility of experience, we can represent the transcendental argument as saying: an understanding of the concept of experience commits us to a belief in the existence of the external world. On this account we can think of a transcendental argument as unpacking the conceptual commitments of accepting X. The end result is still the same. The conceptual commitments of accepting X are beliefs about Y, something which is necessary if X is to be possible.

I shall legitimise simple truth by offering a transcendental argument about the conditions necessary for thoughts about material objects to be possible. This means that it is an argument about the sort of model, or metaphysics, to which we are committed if we accept that we are able to have thoughts about material objects. It is an argument that unpacks the metaphysical model which is presupposed by our ability to have such thoughts.

Note that the starting point for this argument is the claim that we have thoughts about material objects. That is all that I require to legitimise simple truth. So let us start with the observation that we can entertain a thought such as:

(1) The chair is black.

What follows from our ability to think a thought like (1)? The answer, I think, is that our ability to think a thought like (1) only makes sense within the context of our commitment to a certain conceptual scheme. The conceptual scheme is one that conceives of objects existing independently of us in an objective framework of space and time. That is to say, our ability to think about material objects presupposes our acceptance of the notion of the material world as an arrangement of entities in objective space and time. Our concept of a material object is of something that can only be made sense of within the objective spatio-temporal framework.

That then is the claim. The argument goes as follows. First, if we can think a thought like (1), we must be able to distinguish (1) from the weaker thought:

(2) It looks as if there is a chair which is black.

The difference between these two thoughts lies in the different strength of the commitments they introduce. If you think (2) you are not committed to any hypothesis about what your experience would be like in a moment's time, or if you were to move. After all, you might think (2) on the basis of seeing a hologram image and the projector might be turned off. Also, the image might not be visible if you were to move to one side. Therefore, it is possible to think (2) with no particular commitment to what you ought to think next as time elapses or as you move. However, this is not possible with (1).

The thought at (1) is the thought that a chair is black. It is not just a thought that something looks like a chair and it looks black. What differentiates (1) from (2) is the fact that (1) is a thought about a material object. But how can we mark this difference? The answer lies in plotting the richer commitments that are made in thinking (1) compared with thinking (2). For example, if you think that there is a chair before you, as opposed to just thinking that it looks as if there is a chair before you, are you not thereby committed to the following idea: in the absence of any special intervention, the chair will still be there in two seconds' time. Note that the thought at (2) does not entail this, for (2) is compatible with the world not looking as if there is a chair there in two seconds' time. This is because the thought at (2) allows the possibility that, for example, someone turns off the hologram projector in two seconds' time. In other words, if after two seconds it no longer looked as if there was a black chair before you, this would not cause you to retract your thought at (2). It would, however, cause you to retract your thought at (1). If, after two seconds, the world no longer looked as if there was a chair there, that would be reason to think you had been mistaken in thinking (1). It would not be reason to think you had been mistaken in thinking (2). Therefore, thinking (1) commits you to more than thinking (2). In particular, in the absence of any further explanation of where the chair has gone, it commits you to the continuing existence of the chair.

The commitments of (1) are richer than this, though. Thinking (1), as opposed to thinking (2), also commits you to ideas about what would happen if you were to move. If you are only thinking (2) that commits you to no particular thoughts about how the world would be were you to move to one side. If it is a hologram image you are looking at, there is no commitment as to how it would look if you were to move one step to the right. Not so in the case of (1).

If you think that there is a chair in front of you then, in the absence of any explanation to the contrary, you must expect that, were you to move one step to the right, you would still see a chair, albeit from a slightly different angle. Thoughts (1) and (2) differ in their commitments with regard to a notion of objects existing in an objective spatial framework. Moving one step to the right and losing sight of a chair is, other things being equal, good reason for retracting the thought that there was a chair in front of you. It is not a good reason for retracting the thought at (2).

In summary, having any sort of thought involves having some notion of what would make your thought false. That idea was argued for in Chapter 1, p. 28. The above considerations show that in order to differentiate the thought about the object – (1) – and the thought about how things look – (2) – we need to differentiate the different notion of what would make such thoughts false. The notion of what would make (1) false requires a conception of objects as persisting in space and time. That is the metaphysical model that is necessary in order to distinguish between the thoughts at (1) and (2). We must be able to distinguish between the thoughts at (1) and (2) in order to be able to have thoughts about material objects. Therefore, the metaphysical model of objects as persisting in space and time is necessary in order that we be able to have thoughts about material objects. The model of the world continuing independently of experience is something we are committed to on acceptance of our ability to have thoughts about material objects. Everyone accepts we have thoughts about material objects; that is not in question. Therefore, the idea of simple truth as outlined is legitimate. It cannot be questioned without denying that we can have thoughts about material objects.[3]

Note that this argument only legitimises simple truth for thought and talk about material objects. The argument does not provide a general legitimation of simple truth for all kinds of discourse. The legitimation of simple truth can only proceed case by case as we look at different discourses and explanatory frameworks. Later in this chapter I shall indicate how simple truth about colour talk can be legitimised. In Chapters 8 to 10, I shall sketch a legitimation of simple truth for discourse about moral and political values.

Can postmodernism admit the facts of simple truth? Can we give an account of the truth/judgement distinction while accepting the demise of the cosmic register? If so, can there be any progress in our talking about these facts? If postmodernism can admit these facts then it offers a radically new world for us to live in.

The world of the cosmic register was devoid of most of the things humans find interesting, the state of our bank accounts, moral issues, the rate of inflation, the colour and smell of one's lover's hair, and so on. If postmodernism can give us the resources to talk purposefully once again about these things, it has much to offer. So, to rephrase the questions: can postmodernism admit the simple truth? Does the simple truth offer any hope of progress?

To the first of these questions it is now possible to answer 'Yes'. To the second question, however, it is far less likely that anything like the notion of cumulative progress that figured in the Enlightenment story is available. Sketching an answer to the first question will occupy the rest of this chapter, for it requires that we show that the legitimation of simple truth given above can, in principle, be extended to languages that are perspectival.

ALL LANGUAGES ARE NOT OURS

Postmodernism teaches us that there is no such thing as the language of the world, the language that describes the world as it is independently of the way we experience it and conceptualise it. Descartes's great mistake was to think that it was possible to develop such a language. He thought it was possible to shake off our inherited beliefs all in one go and achieve a pure and transparent reading of the world. He failed. He failed to escape our human stories. Indeed, he only gave the appearance of success in so far as he drew heavily on the resources of one of the most familiar human stories of all time, the story of God. Without God, Descartes had no credible concept of reality or knowledge. And most people now agree he had no credible argument for the existence of God either. So, if we accept that we cannot escape our human perspectives, do we have to accept that all our perspectives or languages are ours in a way that makes knowledge impossible?[4]

In the last chapter we discovered that if there was agreement on a single language or explanatory framework, the lack of foundations for knowledge would not show it impossible. Rather, if there was such agreement on a common language we would have to acknowledge with due humility that we had no mechanical recipe for churning out knowledge. However, we have also agreed that there is no universal transparent language. There is no uniform transparent account of experience. The ideal of absolute knowledge is lost. However, although there is no universal transparent language, there may yet be human languages or perspectives that enjoy a universal employment. There may be languages and ways of looking at the world that we all employ. If so, then although they will be useless for describing the ideal of absolute knowledge and writing the world's own story, they would do fine for expressing simple truths, the simple truth about our stories. We could have simple knowledge, knowledge of simple truth. It would not be a case of mainlining the world's own story. It would simply be a matter of telling our own stories correctly.

So, are there any languages, explanatory frameworks, that enjoy a universal assent? On the face of it there appear to be a number of such explanatory frameworks. All cultures and societies talk about the motion of physical bodies. All cultures and societies talk about the inner life that comes from having a mind. Most societies have some talk about and some sense of a religious life. All human societies talk about the colour of objects found in the world. Apart from the first, these are all explanatory frameworks distinct from the one that modernity thought hooked up with the world's own story. If there is simple truth to be had within these frameworks, it is nothing like the truth recorded in the defunct cosmic register. It is simple truth from a human perspective.

So, the thought is this: if there are languages that are not really just options, but they are ways of speaking and thinking that we all employ and have to employ, then there is scope for some notion of knowledge and truth within those languages. The key idea is of explanatory frameworks which are necessary in order to make sense of experience. In the terminology introduced in the previous section, these will be explanatory frameworks that are transcendental requirements. As such, they will be frameworks that gain common assent. This idea is compatible with the key postmodernist challenge to the cosmic register. Of course, the fun really starts when we try to settle whether or not some language is an optional extra. How are we to decide whether or not the language of witchcraft and sorcery is an optional extra, something that does not have to be used in making sense of experience? The Azande will say that without that language they cannot make sense of their experience, for their experience is constituted by their language. To try to demarcate between languages that are necessary in order to make sense of experience and languages that are mere optional extras is no easy matter. Perhaps it is impossible? Before we try to settle that, let us look instead at what is available if there are some languages the application of which we do agree on. We might have scope for radical disagreement over which languages are optional extras, but there might nevertheless be agreement on some languages that none of us think of as mere options, languages that we all use in describing our experience.

PUTTING THE COLOUR BACK IN THE WORLD

In the scientific image of the world, the world has no colour. In the scientific language there is no colour vocabulary. As we saw in Chapter 1, this means that colour is thought of as an effect, something that belongs within the human mind. It is not part of the fabric of the world. Do we have to think of colour this way, as a subjective effect?

Colour is clearly a human way of describing things. As we saw in Chapter 2, colour is a sensory quality, one that characterises the peculiarly human visual perspective of the world. That is why the cosmic register stripped colour out of the world's own story and dumped it into the mind. To describe an object as coloured is to describe it from a very particular point of view, the point of view of a certain kind of creature with a certain kind of conscious experience. However, it does not follow from this that colour is subjective and resides only in the mind. The phrase 'in the mind' is ambiguous. Rather than try to disambiguate all the different things people might mean by that, consider the naïve view about colour.

The naïve view about colour says this: colour concepts only occur within human languages, within the languages of creatures with the appropriate sort of conscious experiences. That is to say, colours are sensory qualities; they are characteristic of the way we experience the world. Nevertheless, for all that, they are real properties. They are properties of the world not of the mind, for colour is a property of objects that only certain kinds of minds can detect. If you have not got the right sort of mind you will not be able to detect, or understand talk about, colours. But, on this naïve view, what you will not be able to detect is something about the world, namely that it is coloured. So, on the naïve view, objects are really coloured. Not everyone knows that, for there are creatures who lack the right sort of consciousness to hook onto the fact that colour exists. Bats, for example, do not know about colours.

Note that the naïve view agrees with the postmodernist debunking of the supremacy of the scientific worldview. The naïve view about colours says that there are more things in the world than are dreamt of in the scientific image. Also, because of this, the naïve view agrees that whatever the world is, it is not something that is describable in the world's own language. It is describable in the human language of colour talk. The world then, on the naïve view, is not the world as it is in itself. It is not the world as seen and described in the semi-divine vision of the cosmic register. It is the world as seen from a distinctively human perspective. For all that, it may be that it is a truth about the world that, so described, objects are coloured. The colour is out there in the world and not in our minds.

Now, the coherence of the naïve view about colour does not, of itself, legitimise simple truth for colour talk. What the possibility of the above naïve view does is remove the reason for thinking that there is good reason for us not to abide by the common-sense view that the world is coloured. Essentially, the point about the naïve view is that it shows that acknowledging the sense in which colours figure only in human perspectives on the world is compatible with thinking that colours are objective properties of the world. To say that an object is, for example, red, is to make a very specific and non-transparent claim about the object. To say an object is red is to say something like:

(1) x is red = x is such that under conditions c it will produce in creatures of kind k a certain sort of experience e.

To say that an object is red is to describe it from the point of view of a particular kind of creature as viewed under appropriate conditions. However, none of this entails that colours cannot be objective properties of objects. What appears to threaten that idea is a very specific way of understanding the last part of (1), the idea that x produces a certain sort of experience.

Many philosophers hold a representative theory of experience. A representative theory of experience is a theory that holds that the immediate objects of experience are not external objects, but internal ideas or sense-data. In general, a representative theory of experience holds that the contents of an experience, or of a mental state, can be characterised independently of the environment. Now, if one holds a representative theory of experience one will then hold that (1) entails the unreality of colour. For on a representative theory of experience, the experience produced by the red object will be thought of as something like an arrangement of sense-data. If that is the kind of experience that, say, ripe tomatoes produce, it is then tempting to think that the redness is literally a property of the sense-data and not of the tomato. The tomato has the power, under appropriate conditions and relative to the appropriate kind of creatures, to produce a certain sort of experience. What it produces is a red sense-datum. If that is your theory of experience and perception, then acceptance of (1) will be incompatible with the naïve view about colour.[5]

The representative theory of experience is a philosophical theory. There are alternatives. For example, on a direct realist theory of experience, it is held that it is possible to have experiences in which the object of experience is the external object. From such a point of view, the experience the ripe tomato produces in the appropriate kind of creature will be an experience as of redness. That account leaves the redness firmly out in the world, all over the tomato.[6]

In summary, acknowledging the non-transparent human relative character of colour descriptions of objects is compatible with thinking of colour as on the naïve view – as a real property of objects. It is only if a specific theory of experience and perception is added that we have reason to doubt that colours are real. The representative theory of experience is contentious. Many philosophers favour a direct realist theory of experience. Therefore, the legitimacy of continuing to talk of the world as a coloured place is not seriously challenged by the postmodernist critiques that we have examined.

There is something very liberating about the postmodernist critique of the idea of reading the cosmic register. If we stay wedded to the cosmic register we are stuck with a conception of the world that has no colour, no value, no meaning and no people! We are stuck with a conception of the world in which we can find no place for ourselves, our interests and our perspectives. But once we drop the cosmic register, can we not rebuild the world in the simple sense of allowing that things that are perspectival are nevertheless features of the world? Of course, if we do that our concept of 'the world' loses the stability it had under the Enlightenment project, but we are going to lose that anyway. However, the loss of that is not the loss of all stability.

In so far as we all agree that objects are coloured, in so far as we share that language or perspective, then the world is a stable coloured place. And our agreement here is not accidental, it is transcendental. Acknowledging that objects look coloured is necessary in order to give an accurate account of human experience. That's the way the world looks to humans. Fail to note that fact and you have failed to capture something intrinsic to the normal human perspective. On the naïve view of colours, the necessity that we acknowledge the role colours play in our experience is shown to be compatible with the thought that our experiences are experiences of the way the world is. The colour is in the world. On the naïve view we begin to find some place for ourselves and our projects within the world. If we can learn to take our eyes off the distant horizon, the idea of the world's own story just out of view and beyond our reach, perhaps we can regain some stability in the foreground and middle distance. The world is coloured.

The naïve view amounts to no more than applying simple truth to our talk about colour. Grass is green whether or not we see it or think about it. It always has been green. It was green long before humans evolved, for even then it was true that it was such as to produce, under appropriate conditions, for creatures of the appropriate kind, the experience as of greenness. That's the simple truth about grass. If we can lose the impulse to try to think of the world in terms of the cosmic register, if we can lose that pretension, we can regain the common-sense notion of a world of colour.

THE WORLD ACCORDING TO US

In a sense, modernity taught us to feel embarrassed about the way we talked. We are inclined to say that apples are red, that stepping on a pin is painful, that murder is wrong, and so on. This talk was an embarrassment for, if modernity was right, it failed to make any genuine claims about the world. Such talk was merely the ramblings of our obsessive concern with the effects the world had upon our inner subjective lives. Our minds, and the colours, the pains, the values that they contained, had no place within the world's own story. Well, modernity and, before that, the Enlightenment, got it wrong. It is the notion of the world's own story that turns out to be an embarrassment. It is the cosmic register that we need to relinquish, not our humble human registers and human stories. The only notion of the world we have is the concept of the world as seen from human perspectives. From such perspectives, the world is coloured. Perhaps it is also full of minds and pain? Perhaps it is also full of value?

The key postmodernist critique turns the tables on the world as conceived in the cosmic register. The simple truth may be no more complicated than that apples are coloured in addition to being things that fall from trees in trajectories describable by science. Science is just one of the human perspectives on the world.

The idea that the world may be correctly described not only in the language of science but also in the language of colours, perhaps also the language of conscious awareness, is an idea we have met before. It is the idea, first encountered in Chapter 2, of there being different explanatory frameworks. By accepting the scope for these different languages or perspectives we can no longer be talking about a cosmic register. We have lost the idea of the world's own story. We have lost the idea of knowledge expressed in the absolute perspective of a transparent language. If we still have knowledge when we employ the different explanatory frameworks of colours, conscious experience and others in addition to the framework of the sciences, then the knowledge we have is always from a perspective. It is knowledge and truth about the world as seen by us. It is not the world according to God or whoever is supposed to sit at the Archimedean point enjoying the point of view of the cosmos. It is the world according to us.

The fact that such a simple concept of truth, knowledge and the world is still available to postmodernists shows that the target of their critique is not so much science as the presumptuous way that some philosophers have tried to tell the history of science. The key flaw in the modernist worldview was not science. It was the erroneous belief that in doing science we were dialling into the very fabric of the world and that anything not expressible in the language of science simply did not belong in the world. However, if we lose the philosophical image of the world's own story, we can regain the common-sense world of colours, minds, feelings and perhaps values. Recognising that this is possible shows why postmodernists such as Rorty do not want to give up doing science altogether. What we need to give up is the erroneous image that suggested that doing science was the only worthwhile pastime.[7]

Of course, what is conspicuously absent is any general model for simple truth, simple knowledge and the world as understood from the point of view of our common-sense preoccupations and interests. No general metaphor will do here. There is no image to replace the faulty metaphor of the cosmic register. Indeed, it is a preoccupation with metaphorical imagery that has led us astray ever since the Enlightenment. It was the preoccupation with thinking that our human points of view were in some sense inadequate and needed to be transcended that caused the problems. In trying to escape our human points of view we needed a metaphor to describe what we wanted. So we had the cosmic register to capture the elusive notion of the world's own story.

It is these speculative philosophical images that we need to shed. If we do so we can regain the field for common sense. We can regain the idea that knowledge is something lived rather than a speculative revelation. Knowledge comes from an immanent contact with the world as experienced by us, not from a mystical union with something divine. Averting our gaze from that siren imagery offers a liberation of human enquiry possibly greater than the break with dogmatism that signalled the Enlightenment. But it also offers a liberation that does not require us to give up talking about the truth. It is simply that the truth is no longer gilded with connotations and imagery of the divine. It is simple truth.

We need to be clear about what the argument so far has achieved. The argument has been an argument about legitimising the possibility of combining the idea of truth and perspectivism. That possibility is not foreclosed by the criticism of the idea of the transparent language of the cosmic register. I have argued that simple truth legitimately operates upon our common language for talk about material objects. The cognitive status of such discourse is legitimised. However, the legitimacy of employing simple truth to such discourse means that the way is open to enquire whether it can also operate with respect to other richer discourses, for example moral discourse. That is the direction in which we are heading.

Not all postmodernists will accept the possibility of simple truth. The possibility of continuing to talk of simple truth is dependent on our being able to find some common languages with which to construct our common sense. There are two problems here. First, might not a postmodernist claim that, for example, the language of science is just one language among many? Second, if science is just one option among a variety of options available it will be difficult to find any languages, or explanatory frameworks, that we all agree on. That is to say, it will be difficult to find a language that, although not a universal transparent language in terms of which all truths can be expressed, might nevertheless be a language common to all. And if there are no candidates for languages common to all, anti-rationalism is still a threat. We will have to accept that truth is not the simple truth that comes from describing the world correctly, even if from a human perspective. We will have to accept that it is our human perspectives that make things true. It is that thought which conflicts with the simple truth and which lies at the heart of anti-rationalism.

Postmodernists tend to be unclear on these points. What we need to investigate is whether it is right to think that science is just another language among a variety of alternatives. I think that there is a sense in which science is a common language, one that enjoys universal assent, but also that this does not conflict with the central postmodernist challenge. In the next chapter I shall offer some suggestions about how we might clarify the two problems just noted. Not all postmodernists would agree with the clarification I offer, but I think that is only because they have, to date, been unclear themselves on what they wish to say. However, it is important to note two points. First, I am going to offer a finer-grained clarification of arguments than postmodernists typically provide. Second, I will do so in a way that is compatible with most of the critiques postmodernists typically offer against science and the possibility of a transparent language of the world.

We have seen that, in principle, it is possible that we can still talk of truth, knowledge and the world from within postmodernism if we can find some language or languages that gain universal assent. We now need to know if there are any explanatory frameworks that are universally accepted as necessary in order to make sense of experience. This is the issue of whether all languages are equally valid games we might play with no commitment to play any particular one or set of them, or whether some can be shown to be essential components of the true stories we tell about ourselves and our world.

Chapter 6

Whose game is it anyway?

INTRODUCTION

The story of the cosmic register was a story about how, if we did our science well enough, we could learn to play the world's own game. We would learn the world's own language and discover the rules by which the world worked. However, it transpires that the languages we speak are our own languages. We have been playing our own games all along. Does this matter? Indeed, as we look around the different languages and explanatory frameworks on offer in the world today, do we see clearly identifiable languages? Do we see clearly separate games that people play with no crossover or overlap? If the games people play are really different games with little or nothing in common, then even the humble notion of simple truth loses its grip upon us. If there are no language games in common then there is no truth about the world at all. We would lose the simple truth and be faced instead with the anarchic chaos of a plurality of chattering.

The question then is this: amongst all the languages and explanatory frameworks we find in the world can we find any scope for the idea that some of them might be true, or be capable of talking the truth, because they are universally accepted as necessary in order to make sense of experience? If not, we shall have to retreat to the anti-rationalist position of simply observing that all this diverse chattering is going on and acknowledging that nothing more than that can be said.

IS SCIENCE JUST ANOTHER GAME?

It is the elevation of science to a modern secularized language of God that is the prime target for the postmodernist critique of the idea of a transparent language and transparent experiences. However, if we accept this critique we do not need to deny the power and scope of science. However we may describe it and whatever metaphors may spring to mind, the history of science is still a history of a staggeringly successful series of achievements. No one will deny that. However, the anti-rationalist does say that science is just another game, just another way of looking at the world. There is room to be a good deal clearer and more explicit about the sense in which this is right.

In one sense that we have already acknowledged science clearly is just another game. If science is demoted from being the language in which the cosmic register is written, then it becomes just one of the languages or explanatory frameworks through which we make sense of our experience. However, that poses no threat of anti-rationalism. The idea that science is 'just another game' that needs examining is something more dramatic. It is the idea that, when considered in the light of competing explanatory frameworks and worldviews, science is just one among several different options between which there is no rational choice.

That last characterisation introduces anti-rationalism. It is the idea that there is no rational choice between, for example, the worldview of science and the worldview of the Azande. One might see the world the way the scientist does in terms of the mechanical causation of matter in motion. On the other hand, one might see the world as the Azande do as a place wired together with the causal links of witchcraft and sorcery. Whichever way you view it, there is no rational choice in favour of that way rather than another. There is no fact of the matter about who is right. Responding to this threat is the issue left undone from Chapter 3. In the last two chapters we have seen the scope for some notion of simple truth if postmodernism can accommodate the idea of universally accepted languages. Now we must see whether the idea of universally accepted languages is possible. If not, we will be forced to accept that there are no universally accepted languages because they are all, science included, equal options. Let us begin then with seeing whether science is just one among equals.

The first thing that has to be said is that on the face of it science is a universal game. The reason for saying this is that all cultures, even those that speak of witchcraft, have a grasp of the scientific understanding of the world. As the anthropological evidence makes clear, so-called primitive peoples have a firm grasp on the causal relations that obtain in the physical world. They know that if there is drought the crops will fail. They know that rotten timbers make unsafe hut supports. More basically, people with 'primitive' worldviews do not deny that if you place a ball on an inclined plane it will roll downwards. They do not believe that an object released in mid-air has anywhere else to go but downwards, quickly. They know about gravity even if they have not formulated the laws governing the general mechanics of matter in motion. Science is a game in which we are all involved. If this is so, can it really be true to say that, for example, science and witchcraft are equally valid options for making sense of our world?

Of course, the anti-rationalist will say that although the Azande know all about simple mechanics, crop propagation, the science of building, these examples are too simple to show that they share our scientific worldview. At the simple level of agreeing that balls roll when placed on an inclined plane we do not really have science, but rather a much thinner common characterisation of experience. So the anti-rationalist will say that all these examples show is that there is a thin level of description of the world that we share with the Azande but, in being such a thin level, it is insufficient to determine which of the competing theoretical descriptions – science or witchcraft – is correct. The thought, then, that underpins this anti-rationalist version of the postmodernist predicament is that science constitutes an identifiable theoretical system. It constitutes a system just like the identifiable theoretical system of the Azande. If this is right, then because of the lack of secure foundations for knowledge there is no way we can rationally choose between the two.

We have agreed that knowledge lacks secure foundations. Therefore, if there is any scope for agreeing with the main postmodernist indictment of the cosmic register without accepting anti-rationalism, it will depend on whether or not we agree that the scientific worldview constitutes an identifiable theoretical system. Our question is getting a finer focus. We started by asking if science was just another game on equal terms with other games.

In the light of the apparent shared character of science at a low level of description, the question has now become: does science constitute an identifiable framework, language or worldview at all?

The final anti-rationalist twist to postmodernism depends crucially on the idea that different worldviews form identifiable units. In order to be able to say that there is no rational choice between one way of looking at the world and another, it must be possible for the two ways in consideration to be clearly discriminated. If there is any crossover between two explanatory frameworks, then there is ground for debate about which view is correct. Of course, given that there are no foundations for knowledge, even if a debate is possible that is not to say that there is an argument that can force the correctness of either science or witchcraft. There can be no experience or argument that offers a mechanical recipe for forcing one conclusion rather than another upon us. But then, it is a peculiarly impoverished notion of rational debate that expects reason to be able to do so much. The point about the availability of crossover between science and witchcraft is not that it will show mechanically who is right. The point is the much simpler one that if there is crossover, there is some ground for thinking that there is such a thing as one of us being right, even if we have no effective decision procedure for proving conclusively which one it is.[1]

It is important then, if the anti-rationalist position is to be stable, that there be no common ground between, say, science and Azande witchcraft. We have already seen that some common ground exists, for all cultures have some grasp of simple mechanics. We have also allowed that that is an insufficient amount of common ground in determining whether it is science or witchcraft that is correct. That, however, is not the point, for knowledge is fallible and no belief can be 'determined' with certainty. The important point is that it might be protested that the thinness of this common ground fails to show that the Azande genuinely share our scientific view of the world, for science is an identifiable body of beliefs over and above this common stock of beliefs. What we need to see is whether or not it makes sense to think of science as such a body of beliefs.

THE SCIENTIFIC CATECHISM?

Try answering the following question: 'What do you have to believe in order to be a scientist?' This is a very difficult question to answer. In this respect it is a much harder question than, say, 'What do you have to believe to be a Roman Catholic?', or 'What do you have to believe to be an Azande?' or 'What do you have to believe in order to be an Islamic fundamentalist?'

In the last three cases it seems possible in principle to identify the beliefs you have to acknowledge in order to share in that particular worldview. That is to say, the last three cases are instances of belief systems that can be identified with considerable accuracy as isolatable systems. We can identify them like this because we can actually list the propositions you have to endorse to count as a Roman Catholic, an Azande or an Islamic fundamentalist. Indeed, this is such a familiar idea that in the first of these cases the Catholic Church has identified its belief system for us. The catechism is the body of beliefs that you must affirm for membership of the Church.

So, our question, 'What do you have to believe in order to be a scientist?', turns into 'Is there such a thing as the scientific catechism?' The more you think about this question the more it looks that there is no such thing as the scientific catechism. In principle, all you have to believe in order to be a scientist is that your knowledge claims should be tested rigorously against experience in repeatable experimentations. For sure, you might acknowledge that experience is never a neutral judge of a theory. You might acknowledge that any experiment you perform will only test your theory given several assumptions about the truth of other theories. You will have to acknowledge that all our experiments are larded with thick layers of interpretation and that therefore our testing of theories is necessarily hesitant and cautious. But having admitted all that, there is nothing further you have to believe that might usefully be seen as constituting the core beliefs of science.

If you try to specify core beliefs of the scientific worldview you get only anodyne beliefs, such as that the world is regulated by causal relations, or that there are general regularities governing the behaviour of matter in motion. But in so far as these are characteristic of anything distinctively scientific, they are also characteristic of that low level of understanding of the physical world that all cultures have in common. That is to say, there is nothing distinctive of the scientific worldview that is not already available from within our common understanding that the physical world continues in motion in ways independent of our observations of it. That is not a profound central claim of something usefully called 'the scientific worldview'; it is the core common-sense belief that all cultures share, and that first reveals our acceptance of simple truth.

The lack of a scientific catechism means that the scientific image of the world as a place of matter in motion governed by universal laws is an image that is continuous with and grows out of our common-sense view of the world. And 'common sense' here means a sense or experience of the world that is common to all. Once you have accepted the idea of physical objects behaving in regular lawlike ways independent of our awareness of them, that is, once you have accepted for example the idea that a ball placed on an inclined plane will roll whether you watch it or not, then you have already accepted the scientific image of the world. In certain countries there are institutions which have devoted themselves to studying the fine-grained behaviour of ever smaller and smaller physical particles. But the worldview as propounded by those institutions is continuous with the worldview of the western child, or the Azande child, who recognises that balls placed on the hillside roll away.

Science, then, is a continuation, a development, of a view of the world we have in common. Of course, since the Enlightenment we have been entranced by a particular version of this view that distorted its significance. With modernity, we came to adopt the idea that the scientific view, if developed sufficiently, would find the resources to say everything that needed to be said about the world. That now looks to have been a gross simplification of our experience. Science is no more, and no less, than a fine tuning of a common understanding that the behaviour of physical objects is regular and lawlike. Science has achieved a good deal in this fine tuning. But as long as we do not fall prey to the idea that, in doing this fine tuning, science was dialling into the world's own story; as long as we recognise that for all its achievements science is but one story we have developed about the world, then it is not an isolatable system of beliefs to be set up against others such as Azande witchcraft, Islam or Catholicism.

The fact that science does not constitute an identifiable system of beliefs can be summed up in the following way: there is no initiation ceremony, no rite of passage, that marks one's transition from ordinary citizen to scientist. In the cases of Catholicism, Islam or Azande witchcraft there are clear initiation ceremonies, rites of passage marked by the agent's affirmation of key beliefs that show that they have truly entered the community of believers. In Catholicism the convert must affirm the catechism, be baptised and taken into the Church. Similarly in the other cases. There is nothing comparable in the case of science. In so far as these cases do have clear initiation ceremonies built around the idea that the agent entering the belief system must affirm certain key beliefs, then it is fair to say that these are all cases of fundamentalism. They are all systems of belief which require the agent to accept various key foundational beliefs. Those key beliefs then become like dogmas, items that can no longer be challenged once the system has been entered. From then on, all the subject can do is work within the system. The key beliefs endorsed at initiation become untouchables; they are the authoritative guiding lights for all else.

In contrast, for the scientist there is nothing that takes on this role of dogma. For the scientist everything is, in principle, an object of potential criticism and investigation. There are no untouchables in science. That, after all, was the key idea that started Bacon off on his anti-dogmatic break with the fundamentalism of Aristotelian medieval science. The turn against dogma was a turn against a form of fundamentalism. It is the characteristic turn of science. The only core belief that the scientist needs is a belief common to us all. It is the belief in the continued existence and regular behaviour of objects. Not only is this common to us all, it is a belief that is transcendentally necessary, as argued in Chapter 5, from p. 110.

There is one sense in which the above claim that science possesses no initiation ceremonies is plainly wrong. There is a sense in which science does display fundamentalist tendencies. However, the sense in which these thoughts are wrong does not affect the claim that science offers a language that is universally spoken. Indeed, if we can clarify the sense in which there are initiation ceremonies for science, we can finally track down the source of the ambivalence that postmodernists such as Rorty show towards science.

THE AYATOLLAHS OF ACADEMIA

The claim that science has no initiation ceremonies, the claim that science is thoroughly anti-dogmatic or anti-fundamentalist in its outlook, is a prescriptive claim. It is a normative claim about how science ought to be. This normative claim is a philosophical thesis. It describes an ideal that is characteristic of science. As such, it is a claim that postmodernists recognise and value. Indeed, many postmodernists would insist that, rid of the pretensions of the cosmic register, we might be able to apply this non-fundamentalist stance in other domains and other areas of human experience.[2]

However, as a matter of sociological fact, as a matter of the observed behaviour of modern scientific institutions, there is no doubt that there are clear initiation ceremonies for science. It is clear that many scientists and their institutions practise a fundamentalist totalitarianism over their members and the community at large. That is to say, as a matter of fact, science often does not live up to its own prescription. If, as a matter of philosophical point, science is characterised as the disinterested pursuit of anti-fundamentalism in all beliefs, as a matter of fact it often does not work like that.

There are very clear initiation rites into the world of science. One of the most important is getting a degree. There is often a closed shop on scientific practice with research funds chasing laboratories and individuals for reasons that have more to do with their power within a highly bureaucratic institution, than to do with the intellectual worth of their research proposal. Now, if this is right, it does not show that there is such a thing as the scientific catechism. If the sociological observations are as supposed, this shows only that some individuals and institutions get so absorbed in their own power politics that they end up inventing catechisms to regain control.

There is then a sociological critique of some of the practices of science. It is a critique that has point whenever scientists and their institutions play at fundamentalist manoeuvres in their attempts to preserve the status quo. Many postmodernists have taken up this critique of the practice and practitioners of science. If the sociological evidence points this way, and I have no doubt that some does, then the charge of fundamentalism against parts of science and its scientists is well made. Such scientists are the ayatollahs of academia. But this failing is not a failing of science as such; it is a failing of certain scientists and their institutions. It might be argued further that it is a failing that was necessary once science entered the highly bureaucratised world of the twentieth century. That is less plausible, but even if correct it is still a failing of a particular institutional arrangement of science. It is not a failing of science.[3]

In conclusion, if there is a critique of science in terms of its fundamentalist tendencies under certain institutional arrangements, that is not a criticism that dilutes the central prescriptive claim that the value of science lies in its core anti-fundamentalism. Indeed, it is only because of the hope of regaining that disinterested anti-fundamentalism that the charge that the practice has been debased has any point. When postmodernists criticise the fundamentalism of science they are not denying the philosophical point that, as a matter of prescription, science should be a disinterested pursuit of anti-fundamentalist belief. Rather, they are saying that science has fallen from grace. Further, in so far as science is not the only language or explanatory framework that we might employ in making sense of the world, the anti-fundamentalist stance is something that could be transplanted into other languages, other frameworks.

WHOSE RATIONALITY?

Some postmodernists might still insist that there is a distinctive rationality due to science and a separate distinctive rationality due to, for example, the Azande. If that is the case then there is no common belief system, that of science, which could provide a bridge between the Azande and the scientist. Given what has been argued so far, it seems unlikely that this is the case.

Given that science does not constitute a clearly defined set of beliefs with an initiation ceremony, and given that it is characterised most basically in terms of an anti-fundamentalist pursuit of simple truth, then it simply is not true that we can set up a system called scientific rationality and say that the Azande do not share in it. What is characteristic of science is so minimal it turns out to be something we all share. Its basis is the common observation of the regular behaviour of the physical world plus a thoroughly anti-dogmatic or anti-fundamentalist investigation of that behaviour.

It is true that various peoples, like the Azande, have not developed this investigation in the way that the developed nations have. It is also true that they have established a worldview that offers alternative explanations of some phenomena to those provided by science. But it is not true that they operate with a wholly different notion of what it is rational to believe. They simply start from different basic assumptions. Starting from the assumption that there are such things as witches and that these things can affect what happens in the physical world, on certain matters they come, via rational means, to answers different from ours.

None of this shows that there are alternative kinds of rationality. The Azande, like us, argue about their beliefs in just the way we do. They use the same logic. Where they differ is in the premises of their arguments. Rationality is the procedure of assessing our beliefs given various starting points. If you change the starting point you will invariably change the finishing line too. But that does not show that you employed a different kind of rationality.

Rationality, then, in so far as we mean by that the reasoned assessment of our beliefs, is something we share with the Azande. It seems then that, contrary to the anti-rationalist version of things, we share an awful lot with the Azande. This should not be surprising, for we have managed to translate their beliefs and talk about them. Besides, we have so much in common. In many respects the human predicament looks very different in the southern Sudan from the way it looks in urban Britain, but for all that we have many central human preoccupations in common, like making sense of our lives, our loves, our births, deaths and place in the world. What makes the Azande stand apart and have a novelty value for philosophers is the highly distinctive starting point they adopt in making sense of the world. They start with the idea of witchcraft.

However, given the enormous amount we have in common, does this mean that we can now settle the matter of who is right, the scientist or the Azande witchdoctor? Of course we cannot. Given the lack of foundations for knowledge no issue can ever be conclusively settled. There is no matter on which we could expect to find settlement via a knock-down argument. Do not expect philosophy to do your dirty work for you and tell you, by pure reason alone, whether you should believe the Azande or the scientist (although in the next chapter I shall sketch the argument that suggests that the Azande are mistaken about the existence of witches). We have lost secure foundations for knowledge, and nothing can be known for certain. That means that every explanatory scheme on offer in the world is an option. But it does not mean that we have to view these schemes as equals and it does not mean we should deny the possibility that some of them might be right and some wrong. What it does mean is that, as we try to figure out who is right and who is wrong, we shall have to be extremely cautious, but we do not have to give up on the idea that one of us might be right and one wrong.

However, even if philosophy cannot settle definitively such first-order issues as 'Are there witches?', it can raise some pertinent questions that we can begin to ask. It can raise questions that offer a liberating vision of knowledge in the postmodernist era. There are questions we can ask that, in building upon the humble and simple common beliefs we all share, take us forward to consider which other beliefs we ought to add to this common stock.

There is a common stock of beliefs that constitute a universal bridge between different cultures. It is a small common stock. It comprises only beliefs about the regular lawlike behaviour of physical objects plus a common method of assessing reasons for beliefs in terms of a common concept of rationality. It is not much to go on, but it is not nothing either. It is, however, perhaps sufficient to take the simple human quest for simple truth and simple knowledge forward. If it does achieve this, it will do so falteringly and with many mistakes. It will take our beliefs forward in the pursuit of an anti-fundamentalist or anti-dogmatic stance about simple truth. Simple truth is not revealed by fundamentalist dogma. It is revealed, if at all, by seeing what beliefs can be made to square with our broadening conception of our common sense as we transplant the anti-dogmatism of science in its good moments to other areas of human experience – consciousness, the arts, morality, religion, and so on.

Before we look to see how postmodernism can offer a liberating vision of the many-faceted options for knowledge in a world that no longer thinks that knowledge must speak the language of mathematical physics, it would be well to note the conclusions we have tentatively reached so far. We have come a long way in learning to live without the cosmic register. Before we set off without that standard to guide us ever again, we need to be absolutely clear about where we are and where we are going.

Chapter 7

The fragility of knowledge

REPRISE

What have we discovered so far? The simple answer to this is that we have discovered the end of modernity. We have seen the sense in which we are all postmodernists now. However, we have also seen that the very idea of postmodernism is vague and covers a number of different ideas and positions. At its most general, though, we seem to have reached the following position.

The Enlightenment taught us to think of knowledge and the world at which we aimed in knowledge in a very restricted way. It taught us to think of the world as it is in itself, conceived independently of the effects it has upon us humans and conceived independently of our perspectives and points of view. With the advance of the physical sciences, modernity's attempt to write the world's own story from scratch developed into a physicalism in which the only thing that could be spoken of in this manner was a world stripped bare of the things that matter to us. It became a world stripped of values, colours, human emotions and relationships. We acquired a vision of a world that consisted of various bits of matter in motion. In this world there is little room for the human subject, the thing with a point of view, with ideas of value, colour, a sense of religious wonder, and so on. What the end of modernity amounts to at the most general is the realisation that this vision is an error. It is an erroneous philosophical image. There is no such thing as the world's own language. The only world there is, is the empirical world as described by our common sense. That thought is liberating, for it allows that there may be many dimensions to common sense, there may be many different explanatory frameworks that we will need to employ in order to make a common sense of the world. Before we proceed to examine the scope for this liberation as we try to build a richer and more diverse notion of common sense, a notion that might find room for finding values and God within our common sense, it would be helpful to summarise the conclusions reached so far.

THE END OF MODERNITY

The end of modernity and the arrival of postmodernism comprises a number of different ideas. It also offers some scope for different versions of postmodernism. What I want to do now is to list the ideas that we have reviewed and place them in order one to another. I want to show which postmodernist claims are compatible with a liberating notion of objective knowledge and which are incompatible and herald anti-rationalism. There are eight theses that I want to highlight from our discussion so far. The first four provide the core to the postmodernist critique of the end of modernity; the second four characterise the version of postmodernism that still allows space for the idea of objective knowledge.

The first thesis that lies at the heart of postmodernism is this:

I All experience is based on interpretation.

In the modern worldview that developed out of the Enlightenment, it was assumed that there were experiences that provided certain foundations for knowledge. It was assumed that it was possible to have an experience that was a direct contact with the world and that would reveal the world as it is in itself. That is to say, it was assumed that there could be an experience that transparently read the world, an experience that was not larded with interpretation. There is no such thing. All experiences are thick with interpretation. What experiences you have is not simply a function of how things are in the world; it is in part a function of the theories or explanatory frameworks that you bring to bear upon experience. Experience is a two-way interaction and it is impossible to filter out all of that which we contribute to the generation of experience.

Accepting Thesis I commits us to accepting:

II There are no secure foundations for knowledge.

Thesis II means that because all experience is interpretative it is always possible to challenge any knowledge claim that is made. There are no knowledge claims that are impervious to challenge. Therefore, there are no knowledge claims that can provide a certain base for the rest of our claims. However, to accept Thesis II is not to accept that there is no knowledge. It is only to accept that there can be no mechanical recipe for uncovering knowledge.

Given that Thesis I is correct we also have to accept:

III There is no such thing as the world's own language.

Given that we cannot peel away the assumptions and theoretical presuppositions that make up our contribution to experience, then we cannot aspire to speak the world's own language. Indeed, it makes no sense to suppose that there is such a thing. Thesis III is the rejection of the idea of the cosmic register. It is the rejection of the idea that knowledge could only be encoded in the world's own language. There is no such thing.

If Thesis III is correct it follows that:

IV All languages are human languages.

If there is no such thing as the world's own story, all the languages or explanatory frameworks that we employ in making sense of experience are our languages. The only perspective we have on the world is a human perspective. Furthermore, there is a potential plurality of such perspectives. The idea of the world's own story always looked to be the idea of a view upon the world from just over the horizon of human experience. In rejecting that idea, we have to accept that the only views of the world we have are views of and from the middle distance and foreground. We have to shake off the urge to peer over the horizon of human experience and try for something impossible. We have to learn to live with a view of the world from just where we are.

Theses I–IV constitute the core postmodernist critique. If we accept these theses we are postmodernists. The vast majority of philosophers now accept Theses I and II. As we have reviewed the development of the postmodernist arguments it is difficult to see how, having accepted Theses I and II, one could deny Theses III and IV. It is certainly true that there is less consensus amongst the philosophical community about whether we should accept Theses III and IV, but nevertheless there is strong support for the idea that, having accepted the first two, we have to accept the next two. I think that is right.

What is important to note is that if Theses I–IV constitute postmodernism, postmodernism is not such a radical position as it is sometimes presented.[1] In particular, postmodernism as defined by Theses I–IV does not involve anti-rationalism. Theses I–IV are compatible with the idea of objective knowledge and objective truth although not, of course, with the cosmic register version of those ideas.

Some postmodernist thinkers are inclined to say that because all languages are human languages then truth must be human truth. That connection is not valid. As we saw in Chapter 5, the fact that talk about colours is a peculiarly human language is still compatible with the naïve idea that colours are objective real properties of the world. All that is required is the acknowledgement that colours are properties that it takes a peculiar sort of mind to detect. Indeed, if colours are such properties of the world, it is no wonder that evolution has provided us with minds to key into these properties. Of course, the world of which colours are a part cannot be the world as conceived in the image of the cosmic register. It is rather the simple idea of the world constituted by the simple truth, like tomatoes are red; bank balances go up and down independently of our thought about them; cricket balls when dropped fall to earth whether we like it or not.

So, if we accept Theses I–IV we can still be postmodernists and accept:

V There is such a thing as simple truth and simple knowledge.

Thesis V is the admission of the common-sense idea that the world continues on its way whether we are taking notice of it or not. Of course, given Theses III and IV, there are potentially many ways in which the world might be going on independently of our noticing it. There may be many different languages and explanatory frameworks we would need to employ to capture all that is going on independently of our noticing it. But in all those languages it still makes sense to speak of things being true or false. That is the point of Thesis V. And if it still makes sense to speak of simple truth, then knowledge of simple truth is still possible.

The compatibility of Theses IV and V can be made vivid with the following image. Thesis IV says that all languages are human

languages. Let us capture that by saying that the way we conceptualise the world in experience is due to categories and concepts
that we invent. Think of a set of categories as a grid or net that
we place upon the world. This grid of categories is contingent. It
is shaped by human interests, by human history, by peculiarities
of the human brain. There may even be a matter of convention
regarding what this grid of categories is like. For example, if
asked to count the number of objects on a desk, it is a matter of
convention whether we choose to count books, or count by pages,
or count molecules, include sugar grains, etc. Nevertheless, despite
the contingency of the conceptual grid with which we form experience, it is the world that fills in the gaps and provides the answers,
true or false, to the questions we pose with these grids. It is up
to us whether we count the objects on the desk as 2 books or
650 pages. But it is up to the world that those are the right
answers, if they are.

Why then are so many postmodernist thinkers – Rorty and
Lyotard for example – reluctant to acknowledge Thesis V? The
reason is that they are inclined to think of the different languages
that are now in play in the postmodern world as separate isolated
points of view with nothing in common. They think of them as
conceptual grids with no overlap. They are inclined to think that
with the loss of the cosmic register and the world's own language,
there is only a plurality of distinct languages available. If the
different languages now available are genuinely distinct, then,
given that there is no neutral non-interpretative experience and
no foundations for knowledge (Theses I and II), there can be no
objective knowledge at all. All that we can do is measure our
claims from within one language or another. In a peculiar way,
such postmodernists are not really postmodernist enough, for
they still hanker after the idea that unless knowledge can be
founded upon certain foundations it cannot exist at all. But that
is simply one of the key beliefs of the modernist programme and
it is false.

More importantly, I suspect that the reason why some postmodernists are reluctant to acknowledge Thesis V is because they
do not admit:

VI There is a common language or point of view.

It is acceptance of Thesis VI that provides a bridge between
different cultures and different points of view on the world. With-

out Thesis VI we could not hold on to Thesis V, the idea that objective knowledge is still possible. It is only if there is some common agreement that there remains the hope that our disagreements are not the sign of an intransigent relativism. Thesis V is the point at which postmodernism can break with antirationalism. Thesis VI is the reason why we can, as postmodernists, avoid anti-rationalism.

In the last two chapters I have shown why we are still entitled to accept Theses V and VI from within the postmodernist critique of the meta-narratives of modernity. I have argued that if we are careful to pay attention to what we mean when we say that all our languages are human languages, this does not stop us saying that when we speak these languages we are speaking about the world and trying to say things that are objectively true. Of course, we have lost a faulty and distorting philosophical image of truth – the cosmic register – but we have not lost truth. If thinkers like Rorty cannot see the scope for endorsing Theses V and VI this is only because they fail to clarify accurately what it means to endorse Theses I–IV. In the previous chapters I have tried to clarify the key postmodernist insights. If that clarification is correct, postmodernism offers not anti-rationalism but the liberating vision that simple knowledge is to be found in many domains other than the natural sciences. It offers the vision that knowledge may be available within many of the languages that we speak; the languages of colour, consciousness, morality, religion, and so on.

However, if knowledge is still available, then if we have accepted Theses I–VI we must also accept:

VII Knowledge is fragile.

Given that knowledge is still possible, but given also that there are no secure foundations for knowledge (Thesis II), we must accept that the process of gathering knowledge is a fallible and fragile affair. There is no certainty. There is no mechanical recipe for arriving at knowledge. Indeed, there must be much confusion and hesitation. We will undoubtedly get a lot of things wrong. We will make mistakes and we will continue making them because we cannot fashion a mechanical recipe that would make us avoid the mistakes. But despite all this, given Theses I–VI, it is still worth continuing to probe the world through our interpretations and experience, for there is still a simple notion of truth to aim for.

We can have no secure way of telling when our aim is good, but we should not give up trying. Knowledge is fragile, but it can be had.

Of course, given the fragility of knowledge one might think that there are no rules whatsoever about knowledge-gathering. However, that is not right. There are no mechanical rules that will churn out knowledge when applied to our experiences, but there are some general methodological prescriptions that we should take. Furthermore, they are prescriptions that are universally acknowledged. Quite what these prescriptions are is contentious but a minimal start is noted when we agree that:

VIII Objective knowledge is anti-fundamentalist.

As we saw in the last chapter, there is a common sense that fundamentalism about our beliefs is contrary to the spirit of a genuine enquiry. Rorty accepts the spirit of gathering our beliefs in an anti-fundamentalist manner. But this, of course, is simply the anti-dogmatism which was characteristic of the birth of science in early medieval Europe. As we saw in Chapter 1, Bacon's insight regarding the methodology of knowledge-gathering was an insight against the dogmatism of the Aristotelian science of his time. Bacon endorsed Thesis VIII. Postmodernists can also endorse Thesis VIII.

The methodological consequences of Thesis VIII are limited but they are not without point. Indeed, there is no reason why a postmodernist should not reinstate Bacon's idea of critical empiricism provided we acknowledge that in testing our claims against experience we are not testing them against a neutral standard. That proviso is important, for it comes from accepting the lack of foundations for knowledge. It means that it is impossible to test all our dogmas at once. We can only try to disinherit our beliefs and assess their validity one at a time. And, once again, that means that we can never be sure that our answers are true. But that lack of certainty is not a good reason for not testing our beliefs at all. Furthermore, in so far as the common ground of beliefs that we all share is a common-sense view that includes Thesis VIII, there is nothing really contentious about this thesis.

Accepting Thesis VIII amounts to reinstating critical empiricism with the proviso that experience is not a mechanical judge of our theories. Also, and more importantly, having accepted the plurality of different explanatory frameworks, in accepting Thesis

VIII we are accepting the idea that critical empiricism can be applied from within different languages or points of view. That is to say, we no longer have to think of critical empiricism as a peculiarly scientific method. Critical empiricism is not the method of science, but simply the beginnings of a method for gathering knowledge from within whatever language or explanatory framework we are employing. And that was precisely what we said in Chapter 1. Bacon's idea of a general methodology for gathering knowledge was not distinctive enough to capture the scientific view of the world. In order to get that we needed also the later idea that there is such a thing as a special language for gathering knowledge, a transparent language, often taken to be the materialistic language of the natural sciences. That is the idea that really informed the Enlightenment dream and shaped the modern world. That is the idea that postmodernism properly challenges. The whole point of the possibility of postmodernism accepting all of Theses I–VIII is just the point that what is really lost with the end of modernity is the idea that there is only one proper way of speaking when gathering knowledge, the way that physics teaches us to speak. The end of modernity signals the end of the idea that the language of physics is the language of the world, for there is no such thing as the language of the world. That does not mean that we should stop talking the language of physics. It means only that in our attempts to gather knowledge, we should not restrict ourselves to talking in just that way. Postmodernism, understood as Theses I–VIII, liberates us from that restriction.

This liberation introduces its own methodological problems. We have seen that the proliferation of languages or explanatory frameworks does not threaten knowledge as long as there is some common language that we all speak. However, when we are confronted with a clash of perspectives it is not clear how the existence of common agreement helps. That is to say, when we are confronted with a situation where different explanatory frameworks offer competing accounts of what is going on and what we should do, how do we settle the matter? In particular, if the Azande witchdoctor advises us to perform a sacrifice to avert the spread of an infection and the medical doctor advises us to take some drugs, how are we to decide who is right? So far we have seen that the lack of a mechanical recipe for deciding such issues does not show there is no right answer. But what we have not got is much idea of how to obtain that right answer.

The methodological issue that we are still left with is this: it is one thing to accept extra explanatory frameworks to that of the natural sciences in order to make sense of the world and ourselves if those frameworks complement the scientific. That is to say, it looks a good idea to accept extra frameworks that give us a fuller picture and further complementary insights into the world. However, when these further frameworks no longer complement but contradict our common understanding, how are we meant to decide which account is best? As in any instance of knowledge-gathering there can be no mechanical rules here, but we need at least some idea of the appropriate questions to ask. If we can get some sense of the appropriate question to ask in such cases, we can then proceed with the liberating expansion of explanatory frameworks offered by postmodernism.

THE NECESSARY COMPLEMENTS

What we have seen is that when we are careful to specify exactly what the key postmodernist claims are, we can still make sense of our search for knowledge. The novelty is that there are now many more places to look, or, better, many more ways of looking. Instead of trying to attain a semi-divine vision of something just out of sight and over the horizon, we have seen that there is nothing wrong with concentrating our enquiries in the middle distance and foreground and looking at the world in distinctively human terms. That can still be a way of gathering knowledge.

That is to say, when we forgo the philosophical imagery that made us try to look for something that did not exist, an ordinary common-sense confrontation with the world can be seen to be just fine. As long as we have some common sense we can proceed with the knowledge-gathering. The proliferation of explanatory frameworks that comes about from rejecting the idea of the world's own language, offers the idea that we may be able to find knowledge that complements the restricted scientific knowledge with which we have become so obsessed. The first question we need to attempt is that of what complementary languages or explanatory frameworks are permissible. Are there any limits to the range and diversity of complementary forms of knowledge?

Clearly there must be some restriction on what can be allowed as a complementary form of knowledge. The following seems to be a restriction that has some point: we should employ only those complementary explanatory frameworks that are necessary in order to make sense of our experience and world. That, I suggest, is a plausible methodological constraint on the proliferation of explanatory frameworks. In applying this restriction, in effect, we are asking which explanatory frameworks we have to accept in order to make sense of our lives and which are mere optional extras. The former we have every good reason to adopt, for without them we could not make proper sense of our lives. That is to say, they are transcendentally necessary. The latter are optional extras because there is no good reason why we should adopt them, even if it turns out that some people have.

Let us see how this restriction works in practice. Consider the first extra explanatory framework we considered back in Chapter 2 – the world as described from the point of view of human consciousness. Surely, we cannot help but include this explanatory framework, for otherwise we would not be able to make sense of ourselves as conscious subjects. That is just the thought that if we try to work with only the physical scientific description of the world we will not be able to make sense of consciousness; indeed we will not be able to locate consciousness at all. In summary, that was the argument of Chapter 2, pp. 56–62.

Consider another example. Some people have argued that, in addition to the frameworks of physical science and of human consciousness, we need to include the framework of religious experience. If we work with the above constraint on the prolifer-ation of explanatory frameworks that amounts to the claim that unless we include religious discourse amongst the tools employed in understanding ourselves and our world, we will not make proper sense of it all. And that claim looks to be just the sort of claim one would expect from a religious believer. Of course, if we now try to decide whether or not it is necessary to employ religious language in the general enterprise of making sense of ourselves, we will find that it is extremely difficult to settle this matter. But that is only a reflection of the fact that we now accept that there are no foundations for knowledge. Knowledge is fragile. Nevertheless, the question whether or not religion is necessary in order to make sense of ourselves and our world seems to be the right sort of question.

This suggests that the proposed methodological filter on the proliferation of explanatory frameworks is correct. As we work to complement our understanding of the world and ourselves by proliferating the languages which we employ, we must always ask whether any given language is an optional extra or whether it is something necessary in order to do justice to the fullness and complexity of human experience. Of course, with no Archimedean point of leverage on what is available in human experience we are still highly fallible, but we are at least asking the right sort of question. It is also a question about which we could try to have some sort of reasoned discussion.

The fallibility of our attempts to work out what is available in human experience is highlighted by the following thought. Suppose atheists say that the proposed test shows that religion is unnecessary because, they say, religious language is an optional extra. We have to acknowledge that matters cannot be as easy as all that. Atheists must acknowledge that their conception of what is available in experience may have been distorted by the materialist culture in which they live. It is possible that their ability to find God in their experience has been clouded by the materialist upbringing they have had. That reveals, once more, that no methodological test can give us a mechanical recipe for knowledge. We are impressed once again by the fragility of the whole affair. Nevertheless, we are not debarred from argument about the possibility of seeing religious discourse as a necessary and complementary component to the overall project of making sense of our lives.

This means that the atheist and the religious believer can have a rational argument about what to believe. They can argue about whether religious beliefs are necessary in order to make sense of human life. They have a common project of conceptualising and understanding human life. The atheist says nothing is lost if we forgo religious discourse within this common enterprise. The believer says everything is lost. In the absence of a general criterion for truth and a mechanical recipe for belief, the issue of who is right can only be settled on the basis of a detailed analysis and account of the particularities of human life. This is not a task especially for philosophers. It is not a task that demands a general philosophical criterion of truth, although it is clearly a task that can be greatly assisted by careful philosophical reflection upon the two cases. But, to a certain extent, I believe that the special skills of philosophy are exhausted with the legitimation of the whole enterprise. The process of legitimation is the process that shows that the project of knowledge-seeking is viable; it is not concerned with the execution of this project. The philosopher can certainly speak to the issue of legitimation. How much the philosopher can add beyond that is a matter I leave for now. However, I would note just this: I am inclined to side with the atheist in this case, for the following reason. When considering what explanatory frameworks we have to employ in making sense of human life, it seems a reasonable method to insist that we start with as few as possible and see what we need to add. In that way, we stand to be more honest and rigorous in our attempt to unearth the frameworks that are truly necessary. But that methodology stacks the odds against the religious believer. The onus of proof seems to lie with them to reveal what is missed out by the atheist refusal to employ religious discourse.

Two further examples will help to highlight the significance of this sort of methodological test. Consider once again the Azande. Does the proposed test give us any leverage on the question of whether there are witches or not? I think that it does. I think that we are finally in a position to see some reason for doubting the existence of witches. The reason turns on whether the witchcraft beliefs of the Azande complement our shared common understanding of the world in a way that is a necessary component of a full understanding of human experience. That is to say, is the Azande witchcraft system of beliefs a necessary complement or an optional extra? It looks to me as if their belief system is not a necessary complement for the very simple reason that it provides no further explanation or understanding that would not be provided without it. Of course, this view may be wrong. Perhaps my inability to find witches in my experience and to see what extra explanatory role they could provide has been distorted by my western upbringing? Of course, that is possible and it cannot be ruled out. But at least if we ask these sorts of questions we are offering reasons for whether or not to believe in witchcraft. We are not contemplating a leap of blind faith between science and witchcraft. The challenge to the Azande is for them to show that their magic beliefs are not cogs turning in a void, disengaged from our common world. Specifically, the challenge asks whether we can account for all operations of the chicken oracle without assuming the existence of witches? If we can, the onus lies on believers in witches to support their beliefs, for they then seem to be mere optional extras. I believe that we can do this. That is why I do not believe in witches. Of course, this belief may be a reflection of my upbringing. But, if so, that does not show it to be wrong. Only detailed case study will do that.

Consider another example which, I think, probably goes in the other direction. Take the case of complementary medicine. Consider the case of acupuncture in particular. Here we have a system of practices and beliefs that do not currently fit within the normal physiological understanding of human illness. Suppose further that these practices cannot be modelled within the physiological framework. Even so, that is not sufficient reason to discount such practices. For if these practices genuinely complement our understanding of illness in such a way that they offer understanding that simply would not be available without employing them, then they will pass the proposed test. Of course, in so far as these practices do offer such understanding we will expect them to follow the prescriptions of critical empiricism, but only within their own account of experience and the world. That is to say we would not allow the complementary practice to divert in its rationality from our common core notions of the rational assessment of belief. However, it is not necessary that the complementary practice offer understanding that can be expressed in the physiological view of the world. What is necessary is that the complementary practice offer understanding by the lights of critical empiricism and that this understanding not be available by other means. By such a test, although I suspect witchcraft is out, acupuncture may well be in.[2]

The judgements of which practices are out and which are in are, of course, hesitant and fallible. But then, so is everything. And recognising that is not cause for despair, but cause for humility and caution.

THE ESSENTIAL DEMOCRACY

In the final three chapters we are going to explore what postmodernists say, and what they could say, in opening up the range of options available to us in making sense of the world, ourselves and our place within it. There is one further point that needs elaborating first. The idea that knowledge-gathering is an anti-fundamentalist or anti-dogmatic activity seems to amount to the idea that the community of knowledge-gatherers is essentially a democratic community. Is this true and, if so, why?

The connection between knowledge and anti-authoritarianism is extremely plausible, although it generates all sorts of difficulties. In the first instance I think it is true that the community of knowledge-gatherers must be democratic. The reason for this is not hard to see. If, in gathering knowledge, we are trying to catch hold of the simple truth, we are trying to catch hold of something that is independent of us. But if what we are after is independent of us, then it ought in principle to be independent of anyone. If it is simple truth we are after, it cannot depend on any particular person. In principle, we are equal before the truth.

It is the recognition of this that is characteristic of the spirit of the scientific and academic communities in our society, even if it is not always characteristic of their actual working practices. Indeed, when scientists or academics operate in a totalitarian manner, their fault is not political but philosophical. There are no high priests of the simple truth. If what we are after is the simple truth, it must, in principle, be available to all.

Despite this, the history of western thought is full of examples of thinkers connecting the idea of knowledge with the idea of elites and, therefore, the threat of totalitarianism. The most obvious example is Plato, who believed that in order for society to be ruled wisely it would need to be ruled by an elite sect of philosopher kings. The deep connection that we seem prone to draw between thinking that there is knowledge to be had and thinking that the knowledge can only be possessed by an elite is false. The existence of knowledge, whether in politics or science, does not require an elite to possess and guard the knowledge.[3]

Chapter 8

Who are we?

INTRODUCTION

So far we have concentrated on issues concerned with the nature of our knowledge of the world. We have seen that if we forgo the idea of knowledge-possession as possession of an absolute conception of the world, we can still retain a concept of objective knowledge. Possession of objective knowledge amounts to possession of the simple truth. The simple truth may be found in all sorts of perspectival accounts of reality but, for all that, it is still truth. We do not need the idea of the world's own story in order to give substance to the idea of objective knowledge. What we now need to investigate is how this leaves our conception of ourselves.

In this chapter I shall sketch some key features of the modern idea of the self. I shall then sketch the moral and political consequences of this view and the way that it has constrained the dominant moral and political philosophies of the twentieth century. The important point to bear in mind throughout this discussion concerns the way that our modern conception of the self has been shaped by the metaphysics of modernity. Modernity centres on the claim that truth, reason and the self can be understood in an ahistorical manner; this is the claim that these ideas stand for timeless universals. We have seen how the concept of truth survives a rejection of this claim. We now need to see what survives of the self.

THE MODERN SELF

Suppose modernity had been right; suppose we could conceptualise the self in an ahistorical manner. What would such a concept of the self look like? First, if we are to conceive of ourselves as entities that can be understood this way, we must be committed to the idea that there is such a thing as the true self. This will be an account of the self that latches on to its essential characteristics. The true self will be the self understood in a way that abstracts from the particularities and contingencies of history and circumstance. It will be the self described as it is in itself independently of features that are possessed contingently, features that might not have been true of the self had historical circumstances been different. What can figure in such a conception of the self?

If we try to understand ourselves in this manner then most of the features that characterise us will turn out to be extrinsic to our true selves. I have red hair, but surely I might equally have had dark hair. Similarly, my height, weight and other bodily characteristics are all features it seems to make sense to suppose that I might have lacked. Any feature I might have lacked cannot be part of my essence and even gender would appear to be something that is extrinsic to my essence.[1] If gender is inessential to our conception of self, so too must be all those features that we pick up as a function of the particular historical path we take through life. So, class, education, skills, beliefs, tastes and values are all things that we can imagine could be different for us. That means that none of these things can be part of our true self on the modernist picture. None of these features would be constitutive of our selves, but contingent features that the self might or might not possess depending on the vagaries of historical circumstance.

The modern self is a highly abstract entity. The conception of the self that modernity provides is a conception of a self stripped bare of its history, gender, class, achievements, values, passions and beliefs. Such things are the mere possessions of the self, extrinsic to it and not constitutive of it. There are many reasons why such an abstract notion of the self has acquired the dominance it now has in current moral and political thought. I want to concentrate on the central philosophical motivation for this notion of the self. The motivation concerns the way we theorise truth.

Suppose we had retained the image of the cosmic register; that is, suppose we had retained the identification of the truth with the absolute truth of the world's own story. On such a modernist concept of truth, the truth is that which can be conceptualised independently of the particularities of contingent human history and the contingencies of the human condition. On this scenario, for a proposition to be a candidate for truth it would have to be possible to frame that proposition in the transparent language of the world's own story. This is an image that we have now rejected, but it is important to see the concept of the self that it supports before we move to investigate the grounds for an alternative conception of the self.

If truth is limited to the transparent truths of the world's own story, then the true self must be an account of the self that strips off all features of the self that are a function of its contingent historical perspectives. The true modern self is not then a self that occupies any particular historical, social or cultural milieu. It is not a self that could be identified with any particular religious, political or moral background. It must be a self that stands beyond all such characteristics, a self that can be theorised independently of all such ideas. The modern self is a holder or possessor of religious, political and cultural properties, but it is not constituted by them. Such a conception of the self flows directly from the modernist image of truth as the world's own story. Of course, it might be objected that such a modernist conception of the self is, in turn, merely the construct of a particular moment in history – modernity. That is a fair criticism but the modernist reply will be that in so far as the project of modernity is done properly, in so far as the modernist enterprise of writing the world's own story from scratch with history and tradition thoroughly disinherited is observed, then the modernist self is a self that can be understood independently of tradition. The modern abstract concept of self is not offered as just another variant in a shifting play of historically contingent ways of thinking of ourselves; it is offered as an account of the truth about ourselves. If we theorise truth in the modernist way, we end up theorising ourselves as the abstract inhabitants of no particular place or time, of no particular culture or society.

From the perspective of modernity we are citizens not of the here and now; our true selves are not subjects of the historically real and contingent conditions of real culture and society. From the perspective of modernity, we are subjects of an abstract ahistorical realm from which we must then select our culture, our morals, politics and social institutions. Central of all the characteristics of the modern self is its individualism. In the first instance, the modern self stands alone.

If my attachments to culture and history are extrinsic possessions of mine rather than constitutive of me, so too are those attachments and relationships in which I stand to others. I am a husband, father and son, but even these fundamental facts about who I am are, from the point of view of modernity, mere contingencies. I might have been none of these things. They are not of my essence. Being a father is something true of me; it is not a truth that defines me. My essence is given independently of my acquisition of that particular relationship. The key feature of this individualism is the idea that relationships to others are not constitutive of self. What constitutes the self is something that can be described independently of how the self is related to other selves. The metaphysical image of the self in modernity is essentially a metaphysics of loneliness. For the modern self, personal relationships, let alone moral and political associations, stand in need of construction and formation. They play no role in the making of the self, for the modern self is not made, it is a given. What are made are the relationships, the culture, the morals, politics and social institutions in which the self may find itself but from which the self can, in principle, always disengage.

The ability of the self to disengage from relationships, from culture, and so on, is central to the individualism of modernity's image of the self. The individualism is a metaphysical individualism, for it is an individualism that holds that the self can be conceived and described independently of it having attachments to others. This does not mean that the modern self is essentially selfish, but given that attachments to others are not constitutive of self it does mean that it is an open question whether the modern self has any good reason to form such attachments, let alone to embrace a concern for the well-being of others. To say that the individualism of modernity's view of the self is metaphysical is to say that the formation of attachments to others and the concern for the well-being of others is something that has to be achieved and justified. It is not something that is discovered as part of the nature of the self.

It is the metaphysical individualism of the self in modernity that has created a legitimation crisis for our morals and politics.

Contrast modernity's conception of the self with an older, pre-modern concept. Consider a notion of the self that is not disengaged from its historical circumstances. The serf/master relationship of medieval Europe provides a simple example of this kind of embedded conception of the self. The serf's notion of selfhood is a notion of a self bound to the feudal lord and his estate. Similarly, the feudal lord is a person whose self-conception is tied to the land he has inherited and which he holds temporarily before bequeathing it to his heirs. For such selves, bound to a strict historical hierarchy and sense of destiny, the rules of conduct for life are not optional. The rules of life are part and parcel of the self-conception. If you conceive of yourself as a serf or a lord your life's plan is already set out for you within that self-conception.

Of course, this is only to say that for such embedded selves there was little sense of a question about how one ought to live one's life. For such embedded selves knowing one's station is to know what one ought to do. However, once we arrive at a conception of self abstracted from the notion of one's station in life, the question of how that life should be lived becomes inherently problematic. Stripped of the rich resources of culture and history, stripped bare of all contingent circumstances, the modern self is left with no firm guidance on how to live a life. Indeed, the modern self is so bare it even has space to ask the question whether it need make any attachments to others at all; it even has space to ask whether it should concern itself with the well-being of others. Having been defined in a way that makes disengagement from history an option, the modern self now finds that disengaging from morality, in general other-regarding values, is an option to be considered. With the rise of modernity the question 'Why be moral?' becomes a real issue. Furthermore, the legitimation of morality becomes inherently problematic, for the metaphysical individualism of the self means that when the self asks why it should have a concern for others, the only resources to hand are a description of itself conceived as something completely detached from others.

Metaphysically, the self stands alone. If it is to have reason to endorse altruism that reason will have to be grounded from within its own self-conception, for anything else is mere contingency and can have no bearing upon the self and its projects. The self's projects in life are radically its own projects and its alone. But given the metaphysical detachment of the self it is wholly unclear how there could by anything within such a self that would give it reason to endorse altruism. The modern world postulates selves so detached from one another that they are threatened with the prospect of finding no reason for altruism. At that point the individualism of the metaphysical isolation of modernity turns into a selfish individualism of egoism.

The modern self is a familiar figure, as is its crisis of legitimation with regard to attitudes to others. With the metaphysical individualism in place, the key moral and political issues of modernity are set and find their home in a general sense of the fracturing of our moral and political sensibilities. There are two key features of the metaphysical individualism of the modern self that are worth recording. First:

Modernity's constitution of the self: The self is constituted by an essence that can be characterised independently of contingent historical circumstances; history, culture, social, moral and political relationships are all extrinsic possessions of the self, not constitutive of the self.

Second:

The legitimation problem: If moral and political relationships are possessions of the self, any reason for the self to possess such things must be found from within an account of the self's essence, an account which, *ex hypothesi*, makes no mention of moral and political relationships. If the self can be characterised independently of moral engagements then, by definition, it would lack nothing if it did not enter such engagements.

The legitimation problem has shaped most modern accounts of morals and politics. Altruism, the concern for the well-being of others, is inherently problematic for selves whose constitution is complete regardless of whether they have such a concern. Modernity leaves us threatened with a moral and political isolation that flows from the central metaphysical isolation.

The metaphysical individualism of the modern self is central to the modernist conception. However, it might be thought that if it generates the legitimation problem that is reason alone to call into question the modernist conception of the self. That would be too hasty a response, for it fails to take note of the central pull towards the modernist conception. The central attraction of the modernist conception concerns the concept of rationality.

THE RATIONAL SELF

I have said that the pull towards the metaphysical individualism of the modernist conception of the self flows from the concept of truth and the idea that there is such a thing as the true self. This pull is mirrored in a related set of concerns to do with the rationality of the self. The point concerns the idea that the self should have reasons for its moral and political options.

The modernist idea that our moral and political engagements are possessions of ours and not constitutive of our selves captures an important point. If such engagements are possessions that are, in principle, detachable, such a model vividly captures the idea that we need to ask questions such as: 'What reason have I to keep a promise?' 'Why should I help others in distress?' 'Is it right to pay taxes in support of the state/monarch/feudal lord?' 'Is euthanasia ever permissible?' 'Is censorship a legitimate constraint on artistic expression?' The point is that if we think our moral and political views are subject to reason then we need some notion of how they may be subject to assessment and, should they fail that assessment, be abandoned. That is to say, if our moral beliefs are subject to rationality it seems that they should, in principle, be detachable, for reason may decide that some of them are false.

The idea that our moral beliefs are subject to rationality is a further development of the idea that truth applies to our conception of ourselves. If there is such a thing as a true self, and if truth is to apply to our moral beliefs, then such beliefs must be subject to the demands of rational assessment and critical reflection. However, once a belief is subject to rational assessment the possibility of its being false must be acknowledged. If a belief is a possible candidate for being false, then it must in principle be capable of being detached from our sense of self. The metaphysical individualism of the modern self gives a ready model in which the detachability of our moral beliefs is realised.

So, starting with the assumption that our moral and political beliefs are potentially subject to truth, we are led from the requirement that they are subject to reason to the thought that they must, in principle, be items that are detachable from our sense of self. At the least, this means that we must acknowledge the fallibility of our self-conception. The issue concerns what model we employ in acknowledging this fallibility. Metaphysical individualism provides a simple although extreme model of what this fallibility consists in. It is a moot point whether any alternative situated concept of self could make proper sense of such fallibility. This is an issue that we will not settle until Chapter 9, pp. 184–9. In the absence of an alternative model for the fallibility of our self-conception, we are led back to the metaphysical individualism of modernity.

The above considerations should not be underestimated. The same point can be made with a simple example. In the last section I suggested the case of the medieval serf/lord relationship as an example of an embedded self – a self whose sense of station left no option in its choice of life plan. However, a self with no options about its life plan, a self bound to the station that history bequeathes it, is not a self that is subjecting its actions to rational control. We are inclined to think that both the serf and his master are the victims of historical forces. They are not deliberating and choosing rationally about how to live their lives, but are acquiescing in an inherited framework of life plans. Being rational about our life options is to question our inheritance and subject it to critical scrutiny. That means that there must be scope for some distance between what tradition and history teach us and what we rationally ought to select as our moral and political options. If our life plans are subject to the demands of rationality and truth they cannot be thought of as no more than the unquestioned inheritances of history.

The same point is of obvious contemporary significance. In a number of contemporary conflicts protagonists are pursuing courses of action that they feel history and tradition demand of them. If there is an issue of whether it is right or wrong for the Bosnian Serbs to pursue their ethnic cleansing; if there is an issue of whether it is right or wrong for the factions in Northern Ireland to pursue their sectarian interests; if there is an issue of whether it is right or wrong for Islamic fundamentalists to pursue the *fatwa* against Rushdie; or for the Rwanda Hutus to pursue the Tutsis, then it must be possible for the protagonists in these cases to step back from their history and culture and consider the question whether their traditions comprise elements that they might do better to abandon. The metaphysical individualism of modernity provides a ready model in which such stepping back and questioning of tradition is made possible. The demand that we be able to achieve some such distance from our traditions is not a negligible demand. It is a demand that flows directly from the idea that our moral and political choices are subject to rational scrutiny.

There is then a profound and important point that the metaphysical individualism of modernity tries to meet. It is the point that our moral and political options are subject to reason; rationality and the pursuit of truth apply to our moral and political dilemmas. Of course, we may come to believe that the thought that rationality applies to morals is no more than a comforting illusion. We should not, at this stage, simply assume that our moral and political lives are subject to reason. The present point is that if we think they are subject to reason then we are committed to giving some account of how a moral self can distance itself from its inherited traditions of history and culture. If we think that rationality can operate in the moral and political domain we must give some model of the detachability of history and culture. The metaphysical individualism of modernity's conception of the self gives a simple and attractive model of this detachability. The issue we need to settle is whether this detachability can be accommodated without appeal to the extreme model of it found in the modernist conception of the self. Before we can approach that issue we need to say a bit more about why this detachability of history and culture was ever theorised in the modernist fashion. I shall then proceed to give one example of the difficulties facing the modern self in the attempted reconstruction of moral and political life.

THE RATIONAL SELF – FROM PATHOS TO LOGOS

The idea that our traditions should be detachable flows from the idea that reason operates in the domain of our moral and political beliefs. If those beliefs are subject to rational evaluation, it must be possible for us to jettison some of them; it must be possible for the serf to break free of his inherited life plan and replace it with something better. But why should this detachability get modelled in the extreme modernist picture in which all historical and cultural traditions become mere possessions, extrinsic to the identity of the self? If our moral beliefs are as detachable as modernity conceives of the matter, then they cannot be part of our conception of our true selves. Therefore, by making moral beliefs detachable possessions, we threaten the idea that they are subject to questions of truth and reason, at least as those concepts apply to the self, for our moral beliefs are taken to be detachable from the true self. In short, although the pull towards the demand for the detachability of moral beliefs flows from a legitimate demand that such beliefs be subject to rational assessment, there is a danger that the modernist model of detachability leaves such beliefs outside the domain of rational evaluation. That danger is, I believe, realised in the modern concept of the self. To understand why this is so we need to probe further the dominant model of rationality.

In Chapter 1 I introduced the idea of a transparent language. This is the idea of a language the meaning of which is fully expressible in the language's symbolic system so that there is no interpretation required in order to understand sentences of the language. The idea of such a language was shown to lie at the basis of the modernist image of the cosmic register and the idea of absolute truth. This model of truth supports what is now the dominant model of rationality. It is this connection that underpins the continuing appeal of the metaphysical individualism of modernity's concept of self.

Rationality concerns the systematic connectedness between one belief and another. If you believe that today is Wednesday, you cannot rationally believe that yesterday was Sunday. Holding one belief to be true forces you to hold various other beliefs true because of the very meaning of the beliefs in question. You cannot mean what is normally meant by 'Today is Wednesday' and 'Yesterday was Sunday', and hold that both are true. Given what these sentences mean, something has to give in such a situation. Either you give up one of the beliefs or you give up being rational. The connections between such beliefs are the connections that characterise our rationality, the systematic way in which we adjust our beliefs in the light of other beliefs, experiences and the beliefs that experience forces upon us. The systematic connections between beliefs are connections that hold because of the meaning of the beliefs.

Now, once more, suppose the cosmic register model was right; that is, suppose the world's own story model of absolute truth was attainable. If that were so, then the truth about the world would be fully representable in a set of sentences formulated in the transparent language of the world's own story. But a transparent language is one in which meaning is fully expressible in the language's symbolic system. Therefore, in a transparent language the connections of meaning that define our rationality would be fully representable in the symbolic power of the language. That is to say, whether or not a belief represented in one sentence entailed a belief represented in a second sentence would be marked in the way those beliefs were encoded in the language, for, *ex hypothesi*, a transparent language encodes everything without loss or remainder. Therefore, in a transparent language, not only is meaning fully represented in the symbolic resources of the language, but the connections of meaning that define our rationality are also fully represented in the symbols. What this amounts to is the idea that rationality can be defined in terms of purely formal or syntactic operations upon symbols. The paradigm of a rational action is the sort of symbol manipulation which occurs in making a formal logical deduction. It is the sort of thing that a digital computer can do. Rationality is a form of symbol juggling.

However, rationality is the route to truth. Therefore, the route to truth is a route that can be mapped in terms of formal operations upon symbols. The way of truth is the way definable in terms of formal operations upon symbolic systems. This is what is sometimes called the logocentric view of man, or at least of our rationality. It is a view that flows naturally from the pretensions of the cosmic register. If truth is what is expressible in the transparent language of the world's own story, then rationality is no more than the formal manipulation of the symbol strings found within that language. The idea that rationality can be modelled in terms of formal operations upon symbols is still powerful. Until very recently it dominated most research programmes in cognitive science and philosophy. It threatens to obliterate our sense of moral worth and purpose.

On a symbolic model of rationality how are we to assess the rationality of moral beliefs? Consider simple platitudes such as 'Kindness is a virtue' or 'Murder is a vice'. What can we say about the rationality of such beliefs? On the face of it such beliefs cannot be candidates for truth or rational evaluation. The reason for this can be seen by considering an analogy between moral beliefs and beliefs about the colour of objects. This is an analogy that has perhaps been overemployed in recent philosophy, but some points of contact are still useful.[2]

In Chapter 1 I argued that beliefs about the colour of objects could not be represented in a transparent language. The reason was that in order to understand a sentence such as (1) 'Ripe tomatoes are red', it is not sufficient just to understand the formal relationships that sentence has with other sentences in the language. In addition, in order to understand (1), one needs to be able to enjoy certain sorts of experiences. In particular, one needs to be equipped to have the sort of visual experience normal-sighted humans have when confronted with a ripe tomato in ordinary daylight. This means that (1) is a perspectival claim about the world. As we have seen (Chapter 5), the fact that (1) is a perspectival claim is still compatible with it being a report upon an objective fact, for it is still possible that (1) is a candidate for simple truth. For the moment I shall disregard that point, for I want to make use of the perspectival nature of (1) in order to make a point about the rationality of morals for the modern self.

Moral beliefs are clear examples of perspectival beliefs for much the same reason that (1) is a perspectival belief. The meaning of (2) 'Kindness is a virtue', and (3) 'Murder is a vice', is not something that is fully representable in the language, nor in the formal relationships such sentences have with others. In the case of colours, the perspectival character of (1) consists in the fact that understanding (1) requires that one have the capacity to have certain sorts of experiences, experiences the availability of which depends on the possession of perceptual apparatus that is not universally enjoyed. In a similar way, it seems plausible to say that understanding (2) and (3) requires possession of capacities that are not necessarily enjoyed by all life-forms. However, in the moral case, the capacities at issue are not perceptual capacities but what we might call capacities of sensibility, of our emotions. The idea that (2) and (3) are perspectival is captured by the thought that only creatures with the appropriate sort of emotional make-up will understand fully what is meant by (2) and (3). Creatures lacking such a make-up (like Mr Spock from *Star Trek*) will suffer a deficiency of understanding not dissimilar to the deficiency of understanding that a colour-blind subject would experience with regard to (1).

Now, if we continue to acquiesce in the cosmic register imagery of truth and its accompanying formal model of rationality we will be forced to conclude that moral judgements are not candidates for truth. That being so, moral judgements will not be susceptible to rational evaluation either. The metaphysics of modernity will require that the true self, the rational essence of being human, amounts to no more than the capacity to manipulate symbols according to formally specifiable syntactic rules. Our moral lives will be completely detachable from our rational truth-seeking essence which is defined to contemplate the abstract absolute truths of logic and mathematics, but not of culture, morals, art and politics. If we think of rationality in the formal manner dictated by the metaphysics of modernity, then our true self will be the rational self, the symbol juggler and not the emotional moral agent. This means that the detachability of our moral beliefs will not then be the detachability required by the possibility of being false (as advocated in the previous section); it will be a much more radical notion of detachability.

It is the formal model of rationality that forces a distinction between logos and pathos, between our rationality and our sensibility. It is a moot point when these facets of our characters first became conceptually separated but modernity thrust them apart.[3] The response to this separation of truth and sensibility is twofold.

First, the separation of truth and sensibility means that moral beliefs come to be seen more properly as a function of our passionate emotional faculties rather than our cognitive faculties. Moral beliefs are things we feel rather than know. Hume is usually taken as providing the classic statement of this view of morality, which has become known as emotivism.[4] Emotivism appears to be a profoundly unsatisfactory account of our morality, for it means that there can be no genuine argument about moral issues. If emotivism is correct, moral judgements are not objects of cognition and they are not things to be assessed as true or false. They are simply the results of emotional responses that we have to the world; they are not responses subject to the demands of rational assessment as true or false.

We are inclined to feel threatened by emotivism because it takes away the point of moral argument and disagreement. Ordinarily, we take it that moral disagreements are genuine disagreements, matters that need to be resolved by some kind of cognitive-cum-rational procedure. If emotivism is true, moral disagreements ultimately amount to no more than the fact that we are emotionally wired up differently; things that upset you do not upset me and vice versa. This is a profoundly unsatisfactory account of moral disagreement. It makes morals simply a function of taste, more like aesthetic disagreement. Our ordinary usage suggests that even if we were content to view aesthetic disagreement as simply a matter of difference in taste, we ordinarily assume that moral disagreements are not like this.[5]

Of course, if it could be shown that the whole of our species had the same emotional responses, emotivism would not threaten our sense of moral purpose. If our emotions were all wired up in the same way, emotivism would not leave us with the threat of intractable disagreement in morals. However, it would only achieve this result at the expense of denying that there is such a thing as real moral disagreement; if our sensibilities are emotionally wired up in the same way then we cannot really disagree. Therefore, the possibility of saving emotivism by assuming that we all have the same set of emotional responses is simply refuted by the ordinary fact that real moral disagreements abound.

The second response to the separation of truth and sensibility is more central to our current interests. Suppose we identify the true self with its rational core. We still could not deny that selves had emotions and desires, but would simply have to deny that these came within the province of reason. Our desires for things, people and situations, and the emotional strength of these desires, would be basic facts about ourselves, but they would not be subject to reason. This produces a model of the self as a possessor of reason and desire. The former is modelled formally; the latter is conceived as basic drives for things that are not subject to rational control. Action comes about when we move so as to satisfy our desires. What then, given the separation of reason and desire, is the role of rationality in the genesis of action? The only answer left seems to be this. First, we accept as bare simple fact that we have certain desires, things that require satisfaction. Rationality cannot select our desires for us, nor can it evaluate them as true or false. However, what it can do is rank our desires in order of satisfaction achievement. That is to say, our rationality can select for satisfaction those desires that will maximise our satisfaction and produce the greatest pay-off between resources expended in undertaking the action and benefit achieved in the action.

What we have here is the familiar model of economic man, a possessor of basic desires and drives whose rationality is restricted to the weighing and measuring of the satisfaction achieved in selecting one desire rather than another as the one to act upon. The concept of rationality is an instrumental one, for it is a rationality that evaluates outcomes relative to satisfying one desire rather than another. Given an end, such as the maximisation of desire satisfaction, rationality will evaluate the means to that end; it will not address the rationality of the end itself. The end is taken as a primitive fact, a fact concerned with the nature of our emotional sensibility and that is isolated from evaluation by rationality. So, the rational self turns out, on this model, to be the calculating satisfier of desires governed only by an instrumental rationality that measures the means–end relationship. The rational self is not governed by a substantive rationality that can adjudicate between different ends. Our ends are given in our desires and they are not subject to rational evaluation. The only thing that rationality can measure is the choice of means to meet our ends.

For the modern self there is no moral knowledge as such. The only knowledge relevant to the determination of action is knowledge of the satisfaction to be achieved by different courses of action and the relative weighting of these satisfactions. This model of the rational self is ubiquitous in modern moral and political thought. Combined with metaphysical individualism it motivates most of the central problems of contemporary moral and political philosophy and fundamentally colours the way we currently view our moral and political predicaments. It is a model of the self that is anchored in the metaphysics of modernity and the imagery of the cosmic register model of truth. These are ideas that we have seen good reason to jettison. If they go, so too will the above concept of the rational self have to go. Before we see why it must go and before we explore what goes in its place, I want to conclude this chapter with a brief account of Rawls's influential theory of justice. Rawls' theory captures all the central features of the modernist concept of self, from its metaphysical individualism to its instrumental rationality. It will also provide us with a starting point for the critique of modernity's concept of self in the next chapter.

JUSTICE AND THE LONE STRANGER

The modern concept of the self supports the following theses:

1 Metaphysical individualism: The self is not constituted by culture, history or its relationship with others.

Hence:

2 Culture, relationships, social position are all possessions of the self.

Also:

3 Any legitimation of moral and political relationships must come from within the resources of the rational self, a self that would, by definition, lack nothing of its essential true character if it engaged in no such relationships.

Hence:

4 There is in principle a problem whether any moral/political relationships founded on altruism can be seen as legitimate.

Further:

5 The principles of disengagement from or attachment to moral views, relationships, political affiliation, etc., are the principles of instrumental rationality; that is, a cost-benefit analysis of the satisfaction accruing to any particular disengagement/attachment.

And so:

6 Relationships and associations stand in need of construction by metaphysically isolated selves and the terms of this construction are concerned not with those selves coming to acquire moral knowledge, but with them coming to acquire the conditions under which they achieve the greatest choice of options for satisfying their desires.

I shall sum these up by saying that modernity leaves selves isolated as lone strangers struck by the profound problem of legitimising whether, let alone how, they should come together and engage in moral and political relationships. Furthermore, these lone strangers possess only an instrumental rationality to solve this problem of legitimation – a rationality in which the basic issue concerns the trading of our possessions, where these include relationships.

With all this in place it should be apparent that the legitimation problem posed for these lone strangers looks insoluble. Modernity starts with such a fractured sense of our social world that there is a real issue whether anything resembling our ordinary sense of moral and political concerns can be rebuilt from these resources. Rawls's theory of justice attempts just such a reconstruction. All the above characteristics are to be found in Rawls's theory, which I now want to sketch.

Rawls's concern was to produce a theory that, starting with the lone strangers of modernity, provided a legitimation of the construction of social and political institutions governed by a sense of justice that embodies redistributivist and welfarist concerns for the well-being of others. He wanted to show why it is rational for lone strangers to agree to a conception of justice as fairness that would institutionalise an altruistic concern for the less well-off in society. In short, Rawls set out to show how, from the lone stranger starting point, we have good reason to construct a familiar model of a liberal democratic state that embodies a welfare concern for the disadvantaged in society. Rawls's conception of justice has strong egalitarian tendencies although, as we shall see, it does not support equal distributions of goods and services. Rawls's theory is a paradigmatic example of the attempt to overcome the fracturing of the sense of self that modernity created.

Rawls's fundamental task was to uncover the principles governing the distribution of goods in society, the principles of justice. The key principle he sought to justify is called the 'difference principle'. This principle states the following:

Difference principle: Inequalities in distribution of goods are only permitted if they leave the worst-off better off than they would have been under any other distribution.

The effect of this is to guarantee that inequalities are to everyone's advantage. The difference principle requires that deviation from an equal share of goods is permitted only as long as it improves the lot of the worst off beyond an equal share, in addition to whatever benefits accrue to others.

The difference principle is not an egalitarian principle, but the distribution of goods that it entails is defined relative to an equal distribution. The difference principle imposes restrictions on distributions that ensure that inequalities cannot diverge from a range of holdings defined by the equal distribution. The difference principle captures many central intuitions of liberal democratic welfare states. It captures the idea of welfare provision as a safety net of holdings in goods and services below which no one should be allowed to fall. Clearly, it defines this safety net at a higher level than is currently found in most democracies, for it says that this safety net must constitute the level of goods that would be achieved under an equal distribution. The difference principle then offers to do real work. By what argument does Rawls arrive at this as his fundamental principle of justice as fairness?

Rawls's is a contractualist argument. Rawls invites us to consider what kind of contract we would accept for arranging society and its institutions with regard to the distribution of goods in what he calls the 'original position'. The original position is a device that is supposed to take us from the starting point of metaphysical individualism to a rationally justified concern for the well-being of others, especially the worst-off in society. In the original position we are to conceive of ourselves stripped of knowledge of our social position and intellectual and social equipment. In the original position we stand behind a veil of ignorance about our capacities and our advantages and disadvantages. We are then asked, from behind this veil of ignorance, to contract social arrangements in the light of our rational self-interest. The key idea is that by pursuing rational self-interest in the conditions of ignorance of the original position we will be led to choose social arrangements that support the difference principle. It is our ignorance in the original position that diverts rational self-interest into an altruistic concern for the well-being of others. So, Rawls's claim is that if we were ignorant of our advantages and disadvantages, the pursuit of rational self-interest would lead to the pursuit of altruism, the welfarist concern for others.

There are a number of key features of this argument strategy. First, the way Rawls asks us to conceive of ourselves in the original position is as metaphysical individuals. The self in the original position is detached from history, culture, relationships and its achievements. These are all theorised as possessions that have been discarded for the purposes of the thought experiment of the original position (Theses 1 and 2 above). Second, the only

resources the self has left in the original position are the resources
of rational self-interest; that is to say, the principles of choice
and of whether or not to engage in one kind of institutional
structure or another are principles of instrumental rationality as
defined above. The only sorts of consideration that are open to
selves in the original position are considerations of the costs and
benefits to itself of whatever social arrangements it chooses
(Thesis 5 above). This means that the legitimation of Rawls's
distributive theory of justice based on the difference principle
arises out of the resources of the rational self bounded only by
this instrumental economic concept of rationality (Thesis 3
above). Therefore, the construction of a just society is, for Rawls,
driven by a rational consideration of the conditions governing
the choice of options, possessions, etc. The construction of a just
society is driven by the rational constraints on the way we structure our choices for satisfying our desires. It is not driven by the
search for moral knowledge (Thesis 6 above). But if Rawls
embodies these central theses of the modern concept of the self,
how does he overcome the seemingly inescapable legitimation
problem of deriving moral and political relationships and altruism
in particular from such an individualistic starting point? How
does he overcome Thesis 4 above?

Many philosophers doubt that Rawls can overcome the legitimation problem, but let us be clear how Rawls thinks he overcomes
it, before we consider whether he is successful. The difference
principle is a maximin strategy; it is a strategy that enjoins us to
maximise the worst case scenario. Rawls's central claim is that,
under the circumstances of the original position, the only rational
option is to select social arrangements that ensure that the worst
case scenario is as good as it can be. The worst case scenario is
one in which goods are allowed to be distributed unequally and
you end up among the worst-off. To maximise that worst case
scenario is then to ensure that if there is any inequality of distribution it only occurs if the worst-off are as well-off as they would
be under equality. That is the difference principle. It encodes a
cautious hedging-your-bets approach in the selection of social
arrangements. Rawls's central claim is then that such an approach
is a requirement of rational self-interest from within the confines
of the original position. Of course, Rawls does not think that
such a principle would be a requirement of rationality from a
position of self-knowledge; all he requires is that under the veil

of ignorance that defines the original position, the rational thing to do is to opt for caution and the difference principle.

I do not want to discuss Rawls's argument in detail, for I am using it only as an example of the sort of state our moral and political philosophy finds itself in under the modernist conception of the self. But I shall now sketch the two main lines of criticism of Rawls's theory. The second line will be developed in the next chapter when we turn to look at alternative conceptions of the self.

There are two basic lines of criticism of Rawls's theory. The first line challenges the validity of the argument. This asks, 'Is Rawls correct to think that under the conditions of the original position it is rational to select the maximin strategy of the difference principle?' The second line challenges the point of the argument. This asks, 'Why accept Rawls's premisses? Why start with the original position?' I shall sketch each line of criticism in turn.

The key problem with the validity of the argument lies in the assumption about what it would be rational to do within the constraints of the original position. Rawls thinks that the maximin strategy is a requirement of rationality, but this is contentious. Consider for a moment the original position and suppose that, ignorant of your intellectual and social standing, you are choosing contracts for the distribution of goods and services within society. Is it really irrational to be prepared to dispense with the maximin strategy and gamble on an unequal distribution in the hope that you will turn out to be one of the favoured well-off? It is simply not apparent what the argument can be with someone who is prepared to adopt such a strategy. Of course, quite how much we will be prepared to gamble will depend on the odds in any given situation. But economic life is full of people who gamble their life and home for the prospect of great riches. Whether or not you find yourself able to concur with such risk-taking, it is simply not convincing to charge such gamblers with irrationality. And that is the charge that Rawls needs to be able to make stick.

Rawls tries to avoid this problem by a number of manoeuvres all of which are problematic. For example, he argues that because the choice in the original position is a choice about a 'whole life' the stakes are so high that his cautious maximin strategy is the only rational one. This is too weak, as also is his appeal to the value of self-respect and the idea that agents will face loss of self-respect if, in dispensing with the maximin strategy, they end up among the worse-off. Both these points throw up a more substantial worry with Rawls's argument that leads us into the second criticism, that the argument is not compelling. The worry is that both the point about choosing for a 'whole life' and the point about self-respect introduce into Rawls's argument assumptions about what the good life is like to which he is not entitled. If we are to consider the choices in the original position from behind a veil of ignorance, from where do these substantial ideas of the good come from? This points to a more serious worry. Even if Rawls were right in his presumption of the maximin strategy as the rational requirement in the original position, why should we share his premisses and find the argument compelling as well as valid?

The point now is that even if the argument was valid, why should it be compelling, for why should the choices that we would make from behind the veil of ignorance have any bearing on what we do and should do from our position of knowledge both of our own situation and that of others? This is a major problem that afflicts all theories that, like Rawls's, attempt to derive substantive moral conclusions from principles of pure rationality alone. One way of expressing the depth of this problem is as follows. The question that Rawls's argument is meant to answer is something like this: 'Why should I endorse distributions which treat myself and others equally?' The argument, if it works at all, works by so dissolving the notion of myself behind the veil of ignorance that differences between myself and others are lost. Then, from the thinness of the ensuing conception, it might look rational to endorse welfare distributions according to the difference principle. But that is irrelevant to the original question, which was why I – me, the self with current dispositions to treat my self as more important than the selves of others – should treat others as equals. The original question, essentially that of how to justify altruism, is ignored by the assumption of the veil of ignorance which effectively blurs the distinctions that make the need for an argument here so pressing.

Another way of putting this point is to ask how I am meant to know what I would choose to contract if I were so radically different from the way that I am to the point of being ignorant of my own intellectual and social standing? Further, what sense can there be in considering myself divested of knowledge of my desires, intellectual and social standing, etc.? If I am divested of all that information, surely it is hardly me that I am considering in the original position; it is someone wholly unlike me, as unlike me as it is possible to get. But then, if the argument was an argument to get me to treat others as equal, does it not beg the question by making me consider myself so unlike myself as to make the intra-self comparison nothing more than the inter-personal comparison for which, so the original problem has it, there is need of supporting argument? In short, the whole argument scheme looks to derive concern for equal treatment of others only by reducing concern for others to the model of concern for self, in working with a concern for self that is stripped of all that makes me the person I am. And that just short-circuits the whole problem situation. Concern for others is different from concern for self – that is why there is a problem of justifying altruism from the starting point of metaphysical individualism.

The above sketch serves as an illustration of the predicament in which modernity leaves our selves. Starting from modernity's conception of the self there is a profound question whether such selves have any good reason for behaving decently with respect to one another. There are, of course, other sources for the same sceptical idea; for example, Nietzsche. The interest in Rawls's theory is that it plugs directly into the logic of modernity's model of the self.

I have represented Rawls as offering an argument that starts with an assumption of metaphysical individualism. In his more recent writings he has denied that his theory has a metaphysical basis and insisted that his argument is a political one, not a metaphysical one.[6] The political basis for Rawls's argument is, he claims, the plurality of conceptions of the good that are to be found in modern democracies. For a society in which there is a plurality of competing conceptions of the good life, of what makes life worth living, the primary concern must be for institutions that acknowledge the rights and freedoms of all to choose their ends and goods and not have them foisted upon them. It is, so Rawls now says, the political imperative of learning to live with pluralism that makes justice the primary virtue and that places the concern for justice over the concern to achieve any particular conception of the good. That is why the just society is a society shaped to provide the conditions for choice of conceptions of the good and not to provide the conditions under which knowledge of the good is to be achieved.

The political defence of Rawls's liberalism makes an important point and one to which we shall return in the next chapter. Notwithstanding Rawls's disavowal of a metaphysical basis for his theory it still remains the case that the conception of the self at the heart of his theory is a self that has three central characteristics. The self is conceived prior to its ends; the self is the possessor of its ends and not constituted by them; and finally, the self is a chooser, not a discoverer, of its ends. Whether or not this conception serves a metaphysical or political purpose, it is still the conception of the self that lies at the heart of Rawls's liberalism. In the next chapter, we shall examine the options for a conception of the self which breaks with this modernist self-image.

Chapter 9

Citizens of the here and now

INTRODUCTION

At the heart of the modernist conception of the self is a profound loneliness. The modern self belongs to nowhere and no time in particular. It is a citizen of an abstract kingdom of ends. Any attachments or relationships that such a self has, it has only as contingent possessions. Such possessions are items that can, if the price is right, be detached and exchanged for replacements. At the extreme, such an abstract self is so dislocated from its traditions of history and culture that it becomes an inveterate trader; all its attachments and relationships become commodities to be exchanged should the market offer the right price and the option of a bargain elsewhere. The concept of a bargain amounts to no more than the thought that by exchanging one relationship in favour of another the self can enjoy a higher return of desire satisfaction for its investment of time and energy.

The isolation of such a self becomes apparent when we realise that, as described, the modern self has no real grasp on the concepts of loyalty and betrayal. The attachments of the modern self are never constitutive; they do not constitute its character, for the self is conceived prior to the possessions that it may detach or not, depending on price. As such, the modern self loses nothing intrinsic to itself if it trades one attachment for another, for the modern self never really belongs in any one relationship or situation as opposed to any other. The modern self is the ultimate displaced person who stays only long enough to satisfy his or her desires. Once satiated, and once a better offer is available elsewhere, the modern self moves on without a trace of betrayal to those others, or those situations, organisations or groupings, that it leaves behind. For the modern self, betrayal can be, at best, no more than a worry that one miscalculated the benefits accruing to a particular relationship.

Let us contrast the modernist lone stranger with a self constituted by its sense of belonging. It is only in so far as a self belongs to a relationship or a social group that it has the scope for loyalty and betrayal. It is because one belongs to a group that loyalty is required and betrayal a possibility. I shall take the possibility of betrayal as a mark of the situated self, a self whose self-conception is characterised by its sense of belonging to a time, a culture, a race, a social group or whatever. It is problematic how we are to conceive of this sense of belonging, but some such sense must be accommodated if we are to replace modernity's lone stranger conception of self. In this chapter I shall explore what such a situated self might look like and what problems need to be overcome in order to make a sense of belonging do any work for our self-conception and our morals and politics in general.

The issues before us now are highly complex and will require considerable unravelling. The very idea of a situated self is of questionable coherence. I believe that it can be made to do real work for us, but it is no easy matter to get the concept into a fit shape. Much of this chapter will be concerned with clarification and the removal of conceptual obstacles to the coherence of the concept of a situated self. This is sometimes painstaking, but it is necessary. Most of this chapter is also highly exploratory. Although the idea of a situated self has become fashionable in recent years, the concept is still in very rough shape. In trying to clarify the issues we are now entering poorly charted territory.

BELONGING TO A TRADITION

Set against the loneliness of the modernist conception of the self, the idea of a situated self has immediate attractions. The concept of a situated self has figured in a number of recent works in moral and political philosophy. It is an idea that many writers have tried to theorise lately, even if none have to date overcome the obvious difficulties that such a conception faces. First, let us note the attractions of the idea of a situated self.

The concept of a situated self offers the prospect of a conception of self concretely realisable in real historical circumstances.

It offers a conception of self in which the contours of self are found in real social and historical traditions rather than shaped by abstract demands of rationality. This looks to offer a notion of self that would be recognisable, a notion that fits the realities of our ordinary daily lives and that acknowledges the potency of contingent circumstances in shaping our notion of our self-being. Most important of all, such a conception of the self places the self in direct contact with ideas of human goods.

The Rawlsian self sketched at the end of the previous chapter is a self for which claims of rights have priority over conceptions of human goods. The Rawlsian self is deliberately conceived independently of ideas of the good life. Such ideas are lost behind the veil of ignorance. For the Rawlsian self, unattached to real history and tradition, the primary objective is to achieve the conditions for choice in which one would have maximum freedom to choose a conception of the good life. As such, the primary objective is the securing of the freedoms and rights necessary to provide one with the capability of making such choices, but what constitutes the good life is a matter left to the self.

In the Rawlsian conception the self has sovereignty over the good. The self has a unity prior to its selection of goods. It has a unity, a being, defined by the rights and freedoms that single it out from others. Notions of goods and ends are then, on such a conception, never constitutive of the self – they are extrinsic possessions. The self is prior to its ends; it can be conceived unattached to any particular conception of what makes a life worth living and unattached to its relationships with other selves. That is the metaphysical loneliness of the modernist self as theorised by Rawls.

However, a conception of the self as situated and partly constituted by its belonging to a tradition, history or set of relationships is a conception of a self constituted in part by some conception of ends, a conception of the good life. What immersion in a tradition provides for the situated self is a notion of what makes life worth living. The abstract modernist self encapsulated in Rawls's theory is a self that is complete prior to its having any conception of what makes life worth living. The ends and goods of human life are things that the unattached self must choose for itself. In contrast, the situated self, bound by its membership of a tradition, is a self that is formed by notions of the good inherited from its tradition. The situated self does not choose its ends, but comes to discover its ends by coming to know its traditions.

The contrast between these two conceptions is deep and covers a number of distinct points, but the idea of a situated self negates the three features of the Rawlsian self that we noted at the end of the last chapter. In contrast to the modernist unattached self, the situated self is not prior to its ends. It is, therefore, not merely a possessor of ends but, partly at least, it is constituted by its ends. Third, as constituted by its ends, the situated self is not a chooser of ends but its ends are things that it discovers about itself and its situation. Its ends are not items subject to its will, but are items of cognition.

Among the various difficulties we face in trying to make sense of the idea of a situated self there is one very basic apparent incoherence in the idea. The central attraction of the idea of a situated self is that we might conceive of the self as embedded in real history. The situated self is constituted by being an agent with a particular history, culture and tradition. But these things are clearly contingent properties, for we can conceive of these things having been different. However, if history constitutes the self then it must be part of what makes the self the thing that it is; that is, history is part of the self's essence. But if that is so, how can mere contingencies contribute to the essence of the self? That, surely, is incoherent?

If there is anything which constitutes the self it will be something that contributes to the essence of the self, that which gives it its identity. However, all that is on offer to constitute the identity of the self is something which is intrinsically contingent – the vagaries of history and circumstance. This is either flatly incoherent or else it heralds the collapse of any notion of the identity of the self. If the self is situated in history then, because of the contingent character of history, the self will lack any underlying identity, that which makes it the thing it is by its passage through contingent circumstances. The self will then be in constant flux. But if it is in flux there is no such thing as a real self, for it changes constantly with the changes in contingent circumstances. The attempt to situate the self in history leads to the dissolution of the self and the loss of any coherent notion of its identity.

The difficulties raised in the previous two paragraphs are important and are not satisfactorily addressed in the current literature on the situated self. I believe that they can be answered, but doing so requires more resources than we currently have to hand. I shall sketch how the above problems can be resolved on pp. 184–9. For the moment, whatever other difficulties the concept of the situated self faces, we must bear in mind that we are owed an account of how, given our historical embedding, it is even so much as possible to construct an account of self-identity and stop the self being dissolved before the flux of historical circumstance.[1]

Within the literature on these issues in political philosophy, the idea of a situated self has been identified with what has become known as a communitarian account of the self. The label seems appropriate and captures the obvious point that what a situated self is primarily situated in is a community of selves with a common purpose and sense of what makes life worth living. However, the very label also makes vivid the obvious challenges that any notion of a situated self must meet. In particular, if the situated self is located in a community, which community is to be preferred?

One of the most striking features of contemporary political life is the frequency with which our problems are the problems caused when one community, confidently assured of its notion of what makes life worth living, confronts a community with a different and incompatible conception. Whether we think of the Hutu massacre of Tutsis in Rwanda, the Serbian ethnic cleansing in Bosnia, or the sectarian violence that Protestants have inflicted upon Catholics and Catholics upon Protestants in Northern Ireland, we know too clearly of the destruction that is done in the name of common goals that bind individuals in one community or another. There is a difficulty here that any account of a situated self must face. However, the difficulty can look insurmountable, in part because of the way we are prone to describe the problem. There is an issue about whether the notion of a situated self is best theorised in communitarian terms. It is an issue that we need to address before we can proceed to sketch what a situated self might look like. Accordingly, before we can do any more with the notion of belonging, we need to consider first whether it is correct to think of the situated self as something that belongs in a community. So, next, a detour on the concept of a community.

BELONGING AND COMMUNITIES

Communitarians are usually characterised as occupying a position defined in contrast to liberals. The distinction is between a collectivist concept of the self and an individualist conception. In addition, the distinction between communitarian and liberal is often allied to a separate distinction between theories that prioritise the good over the right and theories that prioritise the right over the good. Both these distinctions require clarification before we examine the question of whether either of these distinctions is required in making sense of the idea of a situated self. First, the distinction between theories that prioritise the right over the good or vice versa.

The distinction between prioritising the right over the good, or the good over the right is a distinction between different approaches in political theory. A theory which gives priority to the right is a theory which prioritises claims of rights, such as freedom and justice, over issues about the good life. Rawls's theory is a theory in which the right has priority over the good. For Rawls, justice is a claim that takes precedence over theories about the good life. A theory that gives priority to the good over the right is a theory in which political institutions and policies are primarily shaped by notions of the good rather than by claims of rights and claims of justice. Classical utilitarianism is an example of theory that prioritises the good over the right. For utilitarians, the best political institutions and policies are those that achieve the greatest good for the greatest number. It is because of this that utilitarians have usually been charged with failing to observe adequately notions of individual rights, for the greatest good for the greatest number may sometimes be achievable only by overriding the concerns of individuals and minorities.[2]

The distinction between liberals and communitarians as it figures in contemporary literature has to be understood as referring only to modern liberal theorists, such as Rawls, and not to the classical nineteenth-century liberals such as Bentham and Mill. Although Mill was, for example, a staunch defender of individual liberty, his moral theory was nevertheless a theory of the good, not a theory of the right. In contrast, a modern liberal like Rawls not only has a highly individualistic conception of the self, but also prioritises the right over the good. The clearest expo-

sition of a communitarian position which also advocates the
priority of the good over the right is to be found in M. Sandel's
Liberalism and the Limits of Justice. It is by reference to Sandel's communitarianism that I shall address the issue of the role
of the community in giving an account of a situated self.[3]

WITHOUT THE GOOD COMMUNITIES

There are a pair of related questions that we need to consider
in opposing the metaphysical individualism of modernity's lone
stranger conception of the self. Do we need to propose a collectivist communitarian conception of the self if we oppose the individualistic one? In addition, do we need to prioritise the good
over the right if we challenge the modern liberal prioritising of
the right over the good? On the face of it, Sandel's communitarianism appears to answer both these questions in the affirmative.

Like many contemporary theorists, Sandel criticises the individualism and the emphasis upon rights in the Rawlsian conception of the self. Sandel claims that 'to imagine a person incapable
of constitutive attachments ... is not to imagine an ideally free
and rational agent, but to imagine a person wholly without
character, without moral depth'.[4] If this means that in order to
imagine a person with moral depth we must conceive of him or
her as capable of constitutive attachments, this suggests that a
moral self will be a self constituted by its attachment to its
community. I take it also that the contrast Sandel is making in the
above passage is a contrast between a self without a conception of
the good (ideally free) and one with a conception of the good
founded in its constitutive attachments.

However, we should be cautious in drawing such conclusions
and in assuming that we are presented with a clear-cut dichotomy
between individualism and communitarianism, theories of the
right and theories of the good. First, Sandel's critique is aimed
at theories that postulate a self incapable of constitutive attachment. The opposite to this is to have a theory of self that holds
that it is capable of constitutive attachment, but does not mean
that it actually has such attachments. The distinction here is a
fine one, but important. Clearly, the lone stranger of modernity
is incapable of constitutive attachments, for it is a self that is fully
constituted independently of whatever attachments it may have
or lack. Let us agree that that is a conception we need to oppose.

However, the opposition to that is not necessarily to posit a conception of self that is constituted by attachments to one particular community or another. The opposition we need is a conception of self that is capable of making constitutive attachments even if, at any one point, it lacks such attachments. Similarly, we might say that the conception of self that we need is one in which the self is capable of being constituted by its orientation to the good, not that it is constituted by the particular conception of the good it currently possesses.[5]

We can express the same point in another way. Suppose we think that any credible account of the self will be an account of a self that is situated via constitutive attachments. Now, what matters in this theory of constitutive attachments? Is it what the self is attached to that matters? Or is it the way in which it is attached that matters? If we think that it is what the self is attached to that matters then we will be in danger of providing a conception of self that has selves immersed in real historical communities with no resources for escaping from those communities or for evaluating the conceptions of good embodied in the beliefs of those communities. However, if we think that it is the nature of the attachment that matters in our account of a situated self then it will be possible for a self to adjust its attachments to move from one community to another, for it is the kind of attachment that matters, not what the attachment relates the self to. Let us reserve the label 'communitarianism' for the thesis that the important element in an account of a situated self is the account of what the self is attached to. If that is communitarianism, then it faces obvious and perhaps insuperable difficulties. Four problems with communitarianism are immediately obvious.

First, under communitarianism the self is constituted by its attachments to real historical communities. If that is so, the self can never exit such communities; it can never make a rational decision to abandon the beliefs of its current community in favour of those of another. On such an account, the Bosnian Serb would never be able to disinherit the prevailing beliefs of his or her community, for on this account it is by being attached to this community and its beliefs that the self gains its identity. But this is simply false. We know that individuals can ask questions of the communities and of the beliefs characteristic of those communities in which they live. We know that individuals can disinherit their traditions and we tend to believe that this is possible by an act of rational deliberation. On the communitarian account of attachment, all this becomes impossible. It might be countered that this objection works only by assuming that communities have a unity that defies the possibility that a community might encompass a range of beliefs and opinions. But of course, if the notion of a community is not that of something with a dominant set of unifying beliefs, immersion in the community could not provide the orientation to the good that it is supposed to offer. If a community encompassed a collection of varying points of view, it would provide no more than a display of options not unlike that faced by the lone stranger on waking up in the original position. If belonging to a real community is to offer orientation to the good, the community must present some unified set of beliefs. Hence the original objection to this conception stands.

Second, on the communitarian account of attachment, we are faced with the threat of relativism. If the identity of a self is constituted by its attachment to a community, then where communities are in conflict there will be no vantage point from which the members of these communities can rationally deliberate about how to resolve their disagreements. Indeed, in true relativistic fashion, it is not clear that there will even be genuine disagreement.

Third, I argued in the previous chapter (pp. 156–8) that one of the main motivations for the modernist theory of the lone stranger self was the need to give selves the ability to detach from their traditions and their history. It is only if we are able to detach that we can think of our traditions, and also communities, as offering opinions that are ripe for assessment as true or false. If there is any objective content to the deliverances of tradition, they must be susceptible to such detachment. It must be possible for us to conceive how we could disinherit our traditional beliefs because we think them false. However, on the communitarian model of constitutive attachment this is not possible. It is not possible because on the communitarian model what matters in the theory of constitutive attachment is the thing to which the self is attached, namely, the community and its traditional beliefs. Accordingly, the communitarian model of attachment fails to capture the requirement that we see our moral beliefs as subject to rational evaluation. The communitarian model of attachment has us unquestioningly immersed in our traditions.[6]

Fourth, the communitarian account of constitutive attachments may capture something of the close emotional ties that we are prone to feel towards small-scale social groups like families. However, it is totally unclear that it is appropriate to model moral relationships on analogy with the cloying familiarity of family life. Many would argue that the moral point of view is a perspective that we owe to everyone, regardless of how well we know them, let alone whether we feel able to offer them the sort of love we might feel for our families. I exhibit a moral point of view when I treat a stranger with due respect, equal concern, etc. It is no great surprise or achievement to behave decently with respect to one's family. The task of morality is to behave decently with respect to the rest of the world. Helping a brother in distress is not necessarily a moral act; the good samaritan helping the total stranger is. Further, it is grossly unrealistic to expect that we might be able to generate the sorts of attachments we feel for family to the extent that they apply to the whole of humanity. Our moral and political world is not then a replica of the family and it is a naïve romanticism to suppose that it ever could be.[7]

The way to avoid these problems and yet still achieve an alternative to the unattached self of modernity's lone stranger is to provide a theory of constitutive attachment in which what matters is the character of the relation of attachment rather than the relatum, the thing to which one is related. That is to say, if there is to be a credible conception of a situated self, it is the manner of its situatedness that will matter, not what it is situated in. It is how we belong, not to what we belong, that provides a conception of a situated self that contrasts with the lone stranger of modernity. If this is right, we do not need a collectivist conception of the self immersed in a community (small or large) in order to oppose the metaphysical individualism of the lone stranger.

So, we do not necessarily need the community in order to oppose the individualism of modernity, but what about the priority of the good over the right? That was the second question that I posed at the beginning of this section. Similar difficulties to the ones just addressed arise when we try to answer this question.

If a situated self is to be constituted by its ends then, as with the problem with a community, unless those ends exhibit the potential for being detached, they will not be items of cognition. Part of the appeal of the concept of a situated self is that it captures the idea that the self's ends – its notion of what makes life worth living – are items of knowledge. However, the dilemma we now face is simple. If the self's ends are genuine items of cognition it must be possible in principle for the self to detach those ends. The requirement of detachability is once more the requirement that flows from seeing human ends as subject to rational deliberative scrutiny. Where knowledge and rational deliberation are involved we must find space for the idea that we might have got things wrong. Therefore we must find space for the idea that our ends are things we might find reason to jettison. Once again, this is the point from pp. 158–9 in the previous chapter.

Of course, if we were to abandon the idea that reason, deliberation and knowledge applied to our notions of what makes life worth living we could avoid the present difficulty. However, if we did that, we would then be left with the issue of what ends we pursue as no more than a sociological matter concerned with what social groups we happen to find solidarity with. The purpose of the present chapter is to investigate what options there are for preserving a cognitivist account of human ends and purposes along with a concept of a situated self. The fact that we could situate the self in terms of its solidarity with a group, where that solidarity was precisely not a matter of rational scrutiny and control but mere historical/social pressure, is neither here nor there with respect to our present concerns.[8]

So, the need to find our ends as potentially detachable once more threatens the coherence of the concept of a situated self. Without the in-principle detachability of our ends we are threatened with either a non-cognitivism about ends or a relativism about ends, or with both. Relativism is threatened, for if our ends are not detachable we become stuck with whatever ends our community provides for us. Where communities and ends differ, there will be no rational means for adjudicating between opposing accounts of what makes life worth living. Our notions of the ends of human conduct would then be relative to where we were brought up and nothing more could be said.[9]

As before, I suspect that the answer to these difficulties lies in refusing to accept a sharp dichotomy between prioritising the right over the good or the good over the right. If we challenge the modernist lone stranger conception of the self we will challenge the priority of the right over the good. That is to say, we will need to see the self as, in some way, constituted by its conception of ends. However, this does not mean that we need to be able to give an account of human ends that we will then prioritise over rights and employ in giving an account of the self. Instead, what we will need is an account of the characteristics of the self that render it capable of acquiring ends that shape its self-conception. As with the rejection of communitarianism above, what matters for the situated self is that it is capable of finding ends and purposes to life that are more than temporary attachments. What matters for the situated self is that it be the kind of thing that is capable of constitutive attachments to others that give us the scope for finding life the sort of thing that is worth living.

We do not then need to prioritise the good over the right. To do that would oblige us to come up with a general theory of the good. What we need, for the concept of a situated self to be coherent, is the idea that selves can be constituted by their ends and attachments. It is the mode of belonging to a tradition and to a notion of what makes life worth living that matters, not what tradition one belongs to. Once again, the central idea to the notion of the situated self is that it is a self with a capacity for modes of belonging, attachment and engagement with ends that is not available to the modernist lone stranger self. It is the way in which we belong, not to what we belong, that makes us situated selves. This means that the central task in shaping a concept of a situated self must be to give an account of the concept of belonging. It is the nature of that relation that makes us situated, not the nature of that to which, at any particular point in time, we take ourselves to belong.[10]

THE LOGIC OF BEING SITUATED

We are now in a position to pursue a concept of a situated self without losing the self in the relativistic and non-cognitivist notion of solidarity. We are also now able to resolve a central problem with the idea of situatedness that was left unresolved on pp. 174–77. In that section I noted an apparent central incoherence in the idea of a situated self. The incoherence was this. The situated self is located in history. But history is contingent. Therefore, history cannot provide the resources to define the identity of the self – that which makes it a continuing item. Therefore, if we situate the self in history we run the risk of dissolving the self altogether. The problem here is a straightforward logical difficulty in rendering the concept of a situated self coherent. In the light of the above clarifications of how we can proceed without communitarianism, I think the difficulty can be overcome.

I have argued that in order to make sense of the concept of the situated self we need to concentrate on the nature of the relations of attachment rather than what the self is attached to. This means that we will need a theory of the nature of belonging that does not reduce to economic possession. In addition, if this belonging is to be subject to rational deliberation, the rationality of belonging will not be reducible to the economic rationality of the lone stranger. These points help us to understand the present problem concerned with the threatened loss of self-identity.

The loss of self-identity is threatened because if we situated the self in real historical circumstances, we would situate it in things that are contingent and constantly changing. Therefore, the self would also be constantly changing. It would be in flux and would have no continuing identity. It is not enough to respond to this by appealing to moderately stable and long-term historical contingencies, for this misses the central point. The problem is not simply that even long-term and stable historical conditions can change quite suddenly and almost overnight (witness the break-up of Yugoslavia, Rwanda, etc.); the problem concerns the means that the self has for navigating such break-ups if and when they occur.

Modernity's lone stranger navigates such changes in historical circumstances by the application of economic rationality. The lone stranger buys and sells his possessions as circumstances change. The communitarian model of a situated self looks to amend this scenario by attempting, as it were, to plaster some of the possessions acquired through history on to the self and call them constitutive possessions. However, by bundling some of history's circumstances into a conception of self, this makes the self in flux and subject to loss of identity should any of these circumstances, which have been stuck on to the lone stranger in an effort to give it depth, change. The model we are tempted to deal in here is one in which we still essentially have the lone stranger self, bounded only by abstract principles of economic rationality plus the laws of logic, on to which we try and stick the accretions of history in an effort to make the self more substantial. However, none of these accretions sticks properly, for they are all contingent historical circumstances. Hence, either we revert to the identity of the lone stranger, or the self becomes subject to such radical flux that it loses all notion of identity.

Clearly, as a model this will not do, but it is only a model if we employ the communitarian notion of situatedness in which it is what we are attached to that matters and not the mode of attachment. Put another way, the communitarian model, by concentrating on the historical features that get stuck on to the self in order to give it situation, can give no account of the principles of self-navigation when some of those elements come unstuck as history changes. In contrast, if we can make something out of the idea that there are modes of attachment that are not reducible to mere possession, and ways of rationally deliberating about such attachments that are not reducible to the principles of economic rationality, we can perhaps make sense of what it is for a self to possess an identity and a rationality that allows it to navigate the changes of real historical circumstances. Furthermore, we might then make sense of the idea that it navigates these changes while still acknowledging its embeddedness in a real narrative structure.

The issues here are complex. A simple image may help. Think of the lone stranger as a naked human being standing before a wardrobe full of uniforms signifying different social roles. For a lone stranger, the question of what uniform to wear is simply a matter of economic rationality – which uniform will give the greatest satisfaction, allowing for whatever costs are involved in hiring one suit or another? Prior to wearing any one uniform or another, the lone stranger's nakedness is exemplified in his possession of nothing other than his logical ability and the ability to calculate desire satisfaction according to the principles of economic rationality. When the lone stranger changes clothes, his continuing identity consists in no more than the continuance of this abstract rational nature.

According to the communitarian model of situatedness, the lone stranger before the wardrobe is little more than a tailor's dummy; it has no real identity prior to its adoption of one uniform or another from the wardrobe. However, this model cannot cope with the scenario when we change our uniforms. If I am a soldier and that is constitutive of my self-identity, then, if I give up wearing that uniform and take on that of a priest, I do not survive the change. I have changed identities or, more accurately, one version of something I call 'me' has gone and has been replaced with something else that I now call 'me' although the 'I' that does this calling is not something that persists through the change. This makes the whole business of real change in time utterly mysterious and not subject to rational scrutiny. From the point of view of the soldier, there can be good reason for killing another man. From the point of view of the priest, there is perhaps no reason for killing another. All that can be said is that at one point I was a soldier with whatever notions of good reasons there were to my actions and then, all of a sudden, I became a priest with a different set of reasons that governed my actions. There is nothing to explain or bridge this change unless we revert to the economic rationality of the lone stranger.

Of course, the above imagery simplifies real life considerably, but that is precisely the point. The point is that in real life the reasons that lead us to amend our roles, to drop some and take up new ones, are complex and can involve our deepest sense of what makes life worth living, what sorts of things count as flourishing, and so on. My suggestion is that if we are to make something more of ourselves than the abstract lone stranger self of modernity, we need to see our situatedness not in terms of the uniforms we acquire, but in terms of the kinds of reasonings we employ as we engage in such deliberations about what to wear, what role to play.

The image that the choice before the wardrobe threatens is once more a false dichotomy. It suggests that we identify the self either with the economic rationality of the naked lone stranger or with the thickly constituted self defined by the clothes it has inherited from history. The alternative to this choice is to identify the self with the creature who deliberates on what clothes to wear where there is a long and complex story to be told about the nature of the deliberation involved. Whatever is said about this deliberation, it is a deliberation employing principles of substantive rationality which do not reduce to the mere calculation of economic worth. The alternative notion of situatedness comes about when we recognise that the issue of what clothes to wear can amount to far more than merely the calculation of desire satisfaction. It involves making overall narrative sense of our self-conception and self-worth judged against a variety of criteria, only a few of which reduce to economic calculation. There are criteria concerned with affirming one's membership of a group, tribe or circle of friends, that involve codes of decency, what is fit or not for certain circumstances.

We become situated selves when we acknowledge the existence of principles of substantive rationality. The principles of substantive rationality are principles which themselves have a history and can gradually shift over time. They are not principles that hold true a priori for all time. On a large enough timescale, we might find instances of peoples who were separated by their principles of selection before the wardrobe, although nothing guarantees that that will be the case. However, if we can make out the case for principles of rationality that do not reduce to the economic rationality of the lone stranger, the case for a situated self looks promising. I suggest our formula for the situated self be that it is that item that has a need and responsibility to make overall narrative sense of its life and purposes, where this process of making sense is bound by the thicker norms of substantive rationality. What makes this a 'situated' self is that, because its principles of rationality are not the abstract principles of modernity's lone stranger, it is not a self that can be made sense of outside real historical time.

Such a situated self would not figure in our defunct cosmic register, for from the point of view of the world's own story such a self does not figure at all. It is a self whose ongoing projects, purposes and ends, whose sense of what makes life worth living, are the essentially perspectival conceptions of creatures with a history, a range of sentiments and emotions. Such a self is not in flux, although it is a dynamic conception of self.

Let us reserve the charge of being in flux for the tailor's dummy conception of self which one day is a soldier and another day is a priest. There is nothing constant for the dummy, unless we revert to the abstract lone stranger. The dynamism of the situated self is the dynamism that comes from acknowledging two things. First, the situated self governed by substantive rationality concerning our modes of attachment is a self that grows and diminishes as it makes better and worse decisions about what it will do and what it will be. Second, the very principles by which it deliberates these decisions are subject to review and emendation. The principles of substantive rationality are not fixed for eternity. As with the selves who construct their own self-narratives by these principles, the principles of substantive rationality are themselves being adjusted through time. In principle, this means that

over a long enough timescale we could reinstall the drama of the
soldier who suddenly and inexplicably becomes a priest. But it is
an empirical question whether dramatic and inexplicable breaks
could ever happen overnight. History suggests that they do not
and that some sense and continuing narrative thread can usually
be found in our self-evolutions. But, if we can make something
of the existence of the principles of substantive rationality, we
can avoid the charge of being constantly in flux.

Everything turns on our discovering modes of constructing a
self-narrative that do not reduce to the principles of economic
rationality. If that cannot be achieved, I see no real option for
the concept of a situated self. The communitarian model is subject to the criticisms discussed in the previous section. The lone
stranger I also take to be untenable. This leaves us only with the
refashioned concept of a situated self that I have now sketched
in the abstract. In order to start the investigation of this conception, I propose to return to the point made in the introduction
to this chapter. I claimed that the modernist lone stranger could
have no real sense of belonging because he could have no sense
of betrayal. I want to investigate the idea of a situated self further
by looking at what we have to say about the concept of belonging.
It is the existence of the idea of belonging, as something that
invokes the possibility of betrayal, that reveals the possibility of
the existence of the principles of substantive rationality.[11]

BETRAYAL AND BELONGING

One cannot betray a country, club or relationship to which one
does not belong. One can betray one's friends, but not a total
stranger. How important are these facts and what do they amount
to? Instead of being detached from history, culture and relationships, can we conceive of a self that has a sense of belonging to
a history, to a culture, to a set of relationships where this belonging is constitutive of the self? We need to begin with a simple
and rather crude distinction of the options before us in order
that we may then see what our acknowledgment of the concept
of betrayal commits us to.

Let us begin with a crude distinction between two notions of
belonging that polarise the extremes of the idea we need to
articulate. Contrast what I shall call mercantile belonging and
obsessive belonging. We can contrast these by thinking about a

very simple example, the case of belonging to a sports club, say a tennis club. How are we to theorise our belonging to such a club?

I shall say that our belonging is a mercantile belonging if the sense of membership is an attachment conditional on that membership providing benefits in the sense of desire satisfaction. In the case of mercantile belonging, our belonging to the club continues only so long as the club benefits us; the attachment is as temporary or longstanding as the benefits of membership. Mercantile belonging ceases just as soon as the benefits of membership cease. The benefits of membership cease just as soon as they fall below the level of desire satisfaction that could be achieved by investing one's time and energies elsewhere. So, for example, in the sense of mercantile belonging, one's membership of the tennis club would be conditional on the club providing greater benefits than any neighbouring club. Indeed, were a competing tennis club to set up business and offer higher benefits for the same subscription, mercantile belonging to the former club would not stand in the way of exchanging membership to the new club.

Mercantile belonging is a tradeable commodity. As such, it may be doubted whether it really captures the notion of belonging at all. If we assume that belonging requires the possibility of betrayal, then mercantile belonging is not genuine belonging, for it does not provide the space for betrayal. If your membership of the tennis club is the membership of mercantile belonging you do not betray that club or its members if you trade your membership for that of the new club down the road with the attractive new membership deal. Mercantile belonging only provides an attachment until a better return is available elsewhere.[12]

It might be objected that I have made the attachments of mercantile belonging too tenuous and have merely assumed that mercantile belonging must always be fickle. However, this misses the central point. First, it is true that if we assume that your membership of the tennis club is the attachment of mercantile belonging, this does not entail that you will leave the club and trade your membership for a slightly cheaper club as soon as it becomes available. One can accommodate something like the notion of one's loyalty to the first club simply by assuming that amongst all the other desires one has, one has a desire for a degree of stability in one's relationships. If we assume such a desire and provide it with a high ranking above other desires, such as gaining a profitable return for your club subscriptions, then the advocate of mercantile belonging can make sense of the fact that most people are not so fickle as to change their attachments at the first fluctuation in market prices. It is important then that my account of mercantile belonging should not depend upon a portrayal of the attachments formed by such a notion as being essentially short-term and fickle.

The central charge against mercantile belonging is not that it cannot accommodate the patent fact that many of the relationships in which we engage are long-term ones that we are prone to stick with through thick and thin. That fact is easily accommodated by supposing that we have a desire for stability. This is a second-order desire that shapes our first-order desires for pleasure, tennis, good club facilities, etc. However, this does not answer the point that such a model of relationships does not and cannot capture the concept of betrayal.

The model of relationships provided by mercantile belonging operates with at least a two-level conception of desires, including now a desire for such things as stability in our engagements. However, as this is a model of mercantile belonging, this desire for stability is still a desire the satisfaction of which can, in principle, be measured. On the mercantile model there must still be a point at which the costs of meeting all our desires, including the desire for stability, outweigh the benefits of switching our membership to the new club. The introduction of the desire for stability prolongs our attachment to the first tennis club. Nevertheless, once the costs of staying outweigh the benefits of switching membership, the only rational thing to do is to switch membership. But at that point, precisely because the original belonging is conditional upon satisfaction of desires, there is no sense to the idea that switching membership might involve betrayal. Once the benefits of joining the new club are greater than those of sticking with the original (however complex the calculation of that point may be), then the original attachment of mercantile belonging is erased. It is the in-principle erasure of attachment once a more profitable relationship is on offer that explains why, on the model of mercantile belonging, there is no such thing as betrayal.

Just suppose that you decide to leave one tennis club and join another because in some sense the facilities on offer at the second are greater. From the point of view of mercantile belonging there are only two possible analyses of this situation. Either you have miscalculated the costs and benefits and you are moving to a set of attachments which will produce less satisfaction, or you have made a move towards greater satisfaction. Suppose the latter is the case. In this scenario you have moved to maximise your benefits. By hypothesis, you only belong to the first tennis club to the extent that it offers the better matrix of desire satisfaction and so, in this scenario, when the second club offers a better deal your belonging to the first club lapses; you no longer belong.

What about the first scenario, when you miscalculate and move to a club which turns out to provide fewer benefits? In this case you are in error, but the error has nothing to do with questions of loyalty and betrayal. The error is solely to do with a failure to yourself. The only error concerns your failure to secure the rational optimum solution to the satisfaction of your desires.

The above two scenarios exhaust the range of possible outcomes on what to do with respect to the two tennis clubs on the model of mercantile belonging. On neither scenario is there room for the concepts of betrayal and loyalty. The idea that one might, in transferring one's allegiance, be betraying the former club and its members simply does not figure in the descriptions of the situation that the model of mercantile belonging provides. The concept of mercantile belonging fails to capture aspects of our relationships as we experience them. It fails to capture our concept of belonging.[13]

As I have defined it, mercantile belonging is the notion of belonging that the lone strangers of modernity might achieve. It is a limiting case of belonging that fails to capture the ideas of betrayal and loyalty. We can contrast it with an opposing limiting concept that I shall call obsessive belonging. Obsessive belonging is the belonging to a group, relationship, club, etc. that holds regardless of the costs or benefits of attachment. Obsessive belonging amounts to a submersion of the self in a group relationship regardless of the costs of attachment.

On the face of it, there are few cases of obsessive belonging in real life. The nearest example of this extreme case of belonging is membership of a family. The attachment that family members have to one another and to the family group is an attachment that can defy the rationale of economic reason. Family members can exhibit a commitment to the well-being of their fellow members that cannot be accommodated by the notion of mercantile belonging and that seems to defy all notions of costs and benefits.

Once again, this is still an extreme concept of belonging, for it indicates a level of attachment that extends beyond the demands of loyalty. For sure, if, under conditions of moderate hardship, one abandoned one's family in order to secure benefits for oneself, one would probably be accused of betrayal, of lack of loyalty. Such a person would, in their betrayal, be ignoring the sense in which their fate belonged alongside that of their family. However, obsessive belonging is a much more extreme notion of belonging; it is a belonging to the family, for example, regardless of the costs/ benefits. Obsessive belonging is characterised by the person who sacrifices his or her own life to tend to, say, a dying parent. Such attachments may strike us as noble and deserving of admiration and praise, but it is still a supererogatory act, one that is over and above what one would ordinarily expect to be required to under-take. In such extreme circumstances, where there is no hope of saving a relative and the effort would almost certainly entail one's own death, it is hardly an act of betrayal to save yourself.

Of course, this is not to say that it is rational to save oneself in extreme circumstances because the benefits of so doing out-weigh the costs of one's own death. To say that would be to cede to the rationality of mercantile belonging. The present point is simply that if there are forms of belonging that shape attachments that do not figure in the rational calculations of mercantile belonging, that is not to say that there is no point at which it would be rational to break such attachments. Indeed, the central issue that concerns us in this chapter is precisely the issue of whether any sense can be made of the rationality of our attach-ments if we think of them as more than the attachments of mercantile belonging.

The task before us is then to make sense of a notion of belong-ing which falls between the above two extremes. Mercantile belonging does not really capture our pre-theoretic notions of attachment and belonging; it does not really capture the concept of belonging at all. Obsessive belonging provides a model of attachments in which we stand to submerge ourselves in our relationships. However, it does so in such an extreme way that it leaves our attachment beyond rational evaluation. It has us stuck with our attachments, come what may. If we were to try to fashion a concept of a situated self out of the concept of obsessive belonging it would be a concept of a self with no rational control and evaluation of its attachments; it would leave such a self as the mere plaything of its inherited attachments. Such a self has solidarity with its inherited attachments but no rational evaluation of those attachments. This is the image of the postmodern fragmented self with various overlapping attachments of solidarity but with no overall sense of control and rational evaluation. So, if mercantile belonging is the form of attachment that lone strangers possess, obsessive belonging is the form of attachment that communitarian selves possess and that the fractured selves of postmodern theory possess. We need a concept of belonging between these two.

There are two basic constraints on how we develop a concept of a situated self that have been in operation repeatedly throughout this chapter. First, the concept must provide an account of the self that is guided by more than the economic rationality of the modernist lone stranger. This will be a concept of rationality that provides for a notion of belonging that does not reduce to mercantile belonging. Second, the concept of a situated self must nevertheless be a concept of a self with scope for rational deliberation and evaluation of its attachments; it cannot be a self that is submerged in its traditions and attachments so that no distance can ever be opened up between how it conceives itself and its surroundings. The ability to step back and distance oneself from one's history, culture and attachments must always be available. These two constraints look to be incompatible.

The former constraint pushes us towards a conception of self submerged and lost in its traditions; the latter constraint pushes us towards the lone stranger conception of modernity. I am convinced that the simple dichotomy that has us oscillate between these two extremes is misconceived. Nevertheless, our central problem is to provide a description of ourselves that shows that we can cut through the rigid simplicities of modernity and the scientific outlook and find more options for theorising our concept of self than the two extremes of modernity's lone stranger and postmodernity's solidarity of selves.

It is important to note that what is lacking here is an adequate sense of how to describe ourselves. The problems we have in theorising the concept of self are problems that arise from our acceptance of the categories of modernity. We have become enamoured of the notion that rationality can amount to no more

than the concept of economic rationality because we have swal-
lowed the story about the possibility of a transparent language
to codify truth and our rational manoeuvres towards truth. We
have been complicit witnesses to the unmaking of the self as
we have accepted ever more meagre resources with which to
construct our self-description. We are not used to describing ourselves other than in the rarefied language of economic rationality
and the simplistic utilitarian calculus of desire satisfaction. Our
difficulties here are difficulties that arise from our limited sense
of the horizons of possibility in how we might conceive of what
it is to be a human being. It is time to broaden our horizons.

What then does the existence of belonging reveal? It reveals
that if we are to understand our sense of betrayal and the notion
of belonging that makes this possible, we must acknowledge that
there are modes of living other than the economic and the
unquestioned submersion in history. Between these two extremes
we need to rediscover our sensibilities, our shared feel for what
makes life worth living. Such sensibilities involve more than the
rational calculation of economic worth, for they introduce a mode
of talking about human life that falls outside the province of
logos. However, I am not merely reintroducing the province
of pathos, for by our sensibilities I mean our capacities not just
for feeling, but for knowing what must be done and how to
deliberate about it. I am talking about sensibilities that provide
perspectives on human goods, purposes and our sense of what
makes life worth living. We need to stop thinking that sensibility
is a wholly non-cognitive and non-truth-oriented faculty. We are
short of words to classify ourselves and our faculties, but 'sensibilities' is as good as any for picking out those features of our selves
that instruct us on our loyalties and betrayals, our belongings to
and our exclusions from others.

CONCLUSION

The central conclusion of this chapter is that the concept of a
situated self is not empty. However, in order to fill out this
concept we need an account of substantive rationality or, as I
have now called it, the operation of our truth-oriented sensibilities. The existence of our concept of belonging and the notions
of betrayal and loyalty reveals that there are modes of sensibility
that provide perspectives on human goods and conceptions of

what makes life worth living. These generate highly perspectival claims about the ends and purposes of human life. The mere fact that our sensibilities provide us with perspectival claims is not, of itself, a reason for denying truth to the deliverances of our sensibilities. At best it merely repeats the point that we are not inhabitants of a world described by the transparent language of the cosmic register. We are inhabitants of the here and now. We can make the here and now a place subject to truth and reason, and a place peopled with situated selves subject to substantive rationality, if we can give a model for the knowledge generated by what I am calling our sensibilities. I shall provide a sketch of what such a model might look like in the next and final chapter.

Chapter 10

The making of our selves

> I sing with my fingers, so to speak ... It is a singing body and
> this I (here, too, so to speak) sings.
>
> D. Sudnow, *Ways of the Hand*

INTRODUCTION

The concepts of truth, reason and the self and its moral perspective on life can survive the loss of the cosmic register. However, a condition of this being possible is that we supply an account of the principles of substantive rationality. We need to show how the sensibilities that inform and shape our moral outlooks can be seen to be subject to truth. We need to be able to make sense of the idea that our moral judgements are candidates for simple truth. To a certain extent, we have already done much of the work required to accomplish this.

The reference to sensibility reveals that the model of moral judgements in play is an account that accepts that moral judgements are not judgements of pure reason. In addition, moral judgements are not simply judgements recording empirical facts, where we conceive of empirical facts as things that can be described independently of human perspectival concerns. Empirical facts, as thus characterised, amount to no more than the facts revealed by the physical sciences. However, we have already seen in earlier chapters that we can broaden the range of truth-oriented judgements to let in a concept of facts that accommodates things like the facts of colour. We can make sense of the idea that colour is an empirical fact; we need only remind ourselves that it is a fact that only certain sorts of minds are equipped to detect. For all that, there can be facts and truths about colour.

In like fashion, it is open to us to insist that moral judgements are perspectival judgements open to assessment for the simple truth. They are perspectival, for they are judgements the sense of which is graspable only by creatures with the appropriate sensibility. This is analogous to the idea that colour judgements are perspectival because their sense is graspable only by creatures with the appropriate sensory systems. Although the possibility of proliferating our explanatory schemes further to include the language of morals is available, there are a number of points that must be addressed in order to make this option viable.

In particular, not only do we need to make sense of the idea that the perspectival judgements of morals are candidates for simple truth, we need also an account of the principles by which they are evaluated for simple truth. We need an account of substantive rationality, the historically embedded principles of assessment by which we locate ourselves in real history. In addition, we need a model of moral knowledge. If moral judgements are perspectival, and the principles of moral rationality are substantive historically embedded principles, we cannot think of moral knowledge as mere possession of propositions. A propositional model of knowledge will not apply for moral judgements, for moral judgements are embedded in our historically real sensibilities; they cannot be abstracted from the context of sensibility. Therefore, we require some outline of what moral knowledge might amount to.

In this final chapter I shall sketch in how the above points can be met. I shall examine the consequences for our politics and our self-image of the answers I propose. I shall also briefly examine the issue of what further explanatory frameworks, if any, we should accept in the completion of our self-description. In particular, in addition to the framework of moral sensibility, should we employ the framework of religious discourse in the ongoing process of the making of our selves?[1]

THE RATIONALITY OF SENSIBILITY

We need to know what is at stake if we claim that moral judgements are susceptible to simple truth. Moral judgements are judgements shaped by our sensibilities, our capacities for engaging distinctively human feelings in our responses to the world and to each other. If such judgements are to be candidates for simple

truth, what must they be like? There are a number of basic
requirements that we need to impose on moral judgements in
order that their candidature for truth be coherent. I shall note
three requirements, one of which is basic.

The basic requirement is that we be able to make sense of the
independence of truth from judgement. This is the point of
the basic constraint of Chapter 1, p. 28. If a judgement is a
potential candidate for truth, we must have some account of
a truth/judgement distinction. We must have some conception
of how our judging something to be the case does not make it
true. We must have a conception of what it would be for the
judgement to be true independently of whether we judged it or
not. At the very least, this means that we must have some sense
of what it means to make a mistake with the judgement. The
importance of the idea of a mistake is that an error, unlike a
change of mind, involves the idea of something independent of us.

Two further requirements that we can make of moral judgements flow from the basic constraint. The second of our requirements is that moral judgements have a systematic structure. The
third requirement is more complicated to state, but goes like this.
If we have a conception of what it would be for a moral judgement to be true independent of our judging it (the basic
constraint), then we have a conception of a state of affairs that
makes the judgement true. The third requirement is that this
state of affairs be just the sort of thing that can be appealed to
in the standard explanation of why someone makes the judgement. That is to say, our understanding of the nature of moral
judgements should provide us with a conception of states of the
world that normally explain why we make the judgements that
we do. In other words, the most obvious and straightforward
explanation of why someone believes that helping an old person
across the road is kind may be no more than the explanation
that cites the fact that helping an old person across the road is
kind.[2]

Our three requirements on moral judgements are then: (i)
there must be a truth/judgement distinction for moral judgements;
(ii) moral judgements must be systematically structured; and (iii)
our making of the moral judgement that p, must be susceptible
to explanation that cites the fact that p. I want to discuss (i) and
(iii) briefly before explaining (ii), which is the requirement that
will turn out to be hardest to meet.

Requirements (i) and (iii) are in principle already met, for these are requirements that are in principle met once we acknowledge the idea of the applicability of simple truth to perspectival judgements. Ever since Chapter 2 we have been exploring the scope for extending truth to perspectival judgements. Clearly, if the judgements of colour and judgements about consciousness and its states are candidates for simple truth, then our model of the truth/judgement distinction cannot be a model founded on a purely physicalist metaphysics. If a judgement such as 'Tomatoes are red' is a candidate for simple truth, then our grasp of a truth/judgement distinction for this (our grasp of the possibility of it being true independently of our judging it to be true) will require our grasp of the tomato possessing the property of redness. The world will have to be the sort of place that can, at points, be red independently of our thinking about it. This is, of course, no more than the common-sense view that objects remain coloured whether or not we look at them and whether or not light shines upon them. The tomato in the coal cellar is red; it is simply that no one can see it if the lights are off. The account of colour defended in Chapter 5 was an account that allowed that the world is straightforwardly a coloured place.

By the same token, the simplest and normal explanation of why someone makes a judgement such as 'The tomato is red' intrinsically makes reference to the fact that the tomato is red. Normally, it is such facts that explain why we make such a judgement. There is nothing mysterious about any of this unless, of course, you have already decided to commit yourself to a prior metaphysical prejudice in favour of physicalism – the thesis that the properties of the world are exhausted by the properties captured by physics. But why adopt that prejudice? It is not enough to respond that the prejudice in favour of physics is grounded in the explanatory work that physical properties do, for colour properties may also do explanatory work. In particular, as just claimed, they explain in the simplest way possible why we are prone to make judgements about the colour of objects. It is, once more, a metaphysical prejudice in favour of physicalism to think that any decent explanation must be one that deals only in physical properties.[3]

However, having accepted such a proliferation of frameworks for characterising the world and for framing explanations of our judgements and our doings, what reason is there to resist the further move of accepting that the world contains, in addition to objects with physical properties and colour properties, objects, people and situations with valuational properties? Of course, the world that contains such a variety of properties is not the physical world. Neither is it the world as described by the language of the cosmic register. But so what? The cosmic register is a pretension that we have given up. We have accepted that the only world we have is the world as described in the contours of our human perspectival judgements. It is the world as we find it, but it is something we find; that is, the way it is is independent of the way we judge it to be.

What matters in our account of the world is that we be able to make sense of the idea of truth independent of judgement. That amounts to the requirement that we be able to make sense of a notion of objective truth, of things being thus and so independently of whether or not we think that they are thus and so. The objectivity of truth is a separate matter to whether or not we can conceive of the world independently of how it affects us, or independently of how it is perceived by us, or independently of how it strikes our minds as opposed to other kinds of minds. If we could conceive of the world independently of how it strikes our minds then we could aspire to understand the world's own story. That, however, is something that we have seen reason to doubt. We cannot conceive of the world independently of how it strikes the particular sorts of minds that we happen to possess. We can only conceive of the world, therefore, in terms that shape our perspective on the world.

However, it does not follow from this that we cannot conceive of the world perspectivally described as being just that way independently of whether we think it is that way. Our conception of the world is not independent of the kind of creatures we are and the kind of minds that we have. But that does not mean that there cannot be truths about the world as conceived by us that are true independently of our judging them to be true. To think otherwise is merely to confuse the independence of truth (the basic constraint) with the independence of conception. The latter is the key to the cosmic register and transparent language of the world's own story. The two are distinct.[4]

So why not accept the picture of the world as a place with valuational properties that match the responses of our sensibility? The world at issue is the world that we have evolved with and helped to construct. It is the social world that we inhabit, that has grown with us over time and that has affected us and been moulded by us, by our passions and interests. Is it not reasonable to expect that this mutual dependence between the social world and its occupants should bring forth connections of property and response pairings? We have built for ourselves a world of value. That is the world that we have colonised. It is fashioned in our image and we in its. Furthermore, we have developed rich practices of talking about and arguing about the valuational properties of our world. We have longstanding practices of interpretation and discursive enquiry about whether we should keep our promises, pay our debts, help those in distress, and so on.

On the face of it, there is an enormous amount of truth-oriented talking, arguing and discussing about values going on in our world. Of course, judged against the standards of the cosmic register we cannot take this at face value. Judged against such standards, the discourses of value fail to meet the requirements of a transparent language of the cosmic register. But again and again we come to the conclusion that we do not need to judge ourselves and our discourses by the illusory standards of the cosmic register. Despair is not the appropriate response when we see that we cannot aspire to talk the language of the world's own story. The appropriate response is to carry on talking our languages, including the language of valuation.

This is not to say that we can complacently carry on talking about values as if there is no task of legitimation required for this discourse. But I suspect that the task of legitimation is completed in two broad parts. The first part is that which diagnoses the false standards that have so often been used to call our valuational discourse into question. That we have done, many times over. The second part consists in noting, if indeed it is the case, that our valuational discourse has all the properties one expects of a truth-oriented discourse. Again, much of this relies on the observation that the properties that constitute a truth-oriented discourse are less demanding than modernity conceived them. But it is more than that. What is also required is a recognition of the inescapable role our valuational discourse plays in providing a full and accurate picture of ourselves and our world.

It is not as if, shorn of the pretensions of the cosmic register, we can immediately and unproblematically make sense of the independence of truth from judgement. It is rather that our valuational discourse provides complex patterns of explanation, prediction and of self and other interpretation and, in the absence of a general scepticism, this points to the whole discourse being a practice aimed at truth. Our valuational judgements are not isolated offerings, nor abnormal or aberrant fragments of a behaviour that otherwise makes tolerably good sense if they are disregarded as exceptions or marginal jottings. Our valuational judgements are central to our self-conception and they exhibit the structural complexity that is typical of truth-oriented judgements. Our valuational judgements are systematically related one to another and are systematically implicated in our self-narratives and ongoing projects of self and other understanding. That is, the key second claim in the legitimation of valuational discourse is that these judgements are an inescapable part of our self-conception. If that is right, and if they have the structural properties of other truth-oriented judgements, then it seems to me that there is no more that we can ask of the process of legitimation.

The claim that our valuational judgements are central to our self-conception is the claim that I am taking from the previous chapter. I argued there that if we were to make sense of a concept of self with real historical shape, we would need to acknowledge the substantive rationality of our sensibilities. Or, to put the point in the way in which Charles Taylor expresses it, any credible account of the self will have that self as possessing an orientation to the good.[5] Our sensibilities, our principles of substantive rationality, are not optional extras; they are the things that give us our being as selves inhabiting the real historical world.

The claim that moral judgements are structured is requirement (ii) noted above, and I shall have more to say about that shortly. However, on the general issue of what constitutes a legitimation of valuational discourse we ultimately have to accept that in philosophy, as in all other fields of human enquiry, there are no knock-down arguments. Often, the central task is to assemble a picture of how a bundle of claims, hypotheses and theoretical presuppositions fit together. You are then invited to stand back and take in the overall picture at the same time as you ask yourself the question, 'Does this picture make the best overall sense of how we find ourselves and our world?'

Much of the point of this book has been to show that there is an overall picture available that lacks the pretensions of older visions and, precisely because of its humbler perspective, it is a picture that does not invite a scepticism of despair. Measured against the vision of the cosmic register it is perhaps rather middlebrow and tame. Measured against the impoverished metaphysical vision of a positivistic view of the world it is perhaps stunningly bold and exotic. But I suspect no great applause is required for reminding ourselves of the contours of a common sense that positivistic philosophy had systematically by-passed and modernity had discarded.

The legitimation of our valuational discourse turns on the same point that was made in defence of our ordinary reports of psychological states in Chapter 2. In both cases, we are dealing with discourses that have an ineliminable role to play in self-understanding. They are essential to our ongoing project of describing and explaining ourselves. The various reductionisms that try to do without these modes of description fail to fit the facts of life as it is currently lived by our species at this point in our evolution. Further, it is inconceivable how we might learn to live without the facts of life as conceived in these discourses. As David Wiggins has put the point:

> That such mental and valuational properties as the cognitivist finds in our ordinary thinking should enter into the explanation of that thinking and the explanation of actions that that thinking can rationalize – this can seem like common sense, or if you already have a certain prejudice, like outrageous metaphysics. But whichever it is, this is the claim that shows what it is for consciousness to take on a life of its own in the world. . . . [W]hen such a moment comes . . . the point has been reached where what happens in the world cannot be properly understood for what it is by explanations that dwell exclusively upon mechanisms.[6]

What happens in the world – our world, not the mystical visionary thing of the cosmic register – what happens in our world cannot be made sense of without the discourse of valuation.

What about requirement (ii), the requirement that moral judgements be structured? This requirement is made because it is of the nature of a judgement suited for aiming at truth that it exhibit a systematic structure. Our truth-oriented judgements are items that are systematically related to one another in terms of a common component structure. This is important, for it is because judgements have a common component structure that they can figure in rational arguments. Arguments are valid because of the structure they exhibit. Judgements are built up out of component parts that can occur in other judgements. It is the common occurrence of components in judgements that makes our judgements systematically related to one another in ways that bear upon the truth of them all. The point is abstract but very simple.

For example, consider the argument:

(1) All good basketball players are taller than 6 foot 6 inches
(2) John is a good basketball player

therefore,

(3) John is taller than 6 foot 6 inches.

The argument is valid, and its validity turns on the recurrence of a number of repeatable components of judgements. There are the predicates '. . . is a good basketball player' and '. . . is taller than 6 foot 6 inches'; there is the name 'John'. We can represent the form of the argument as:

All Fs are G
a is an F

therefore,

a is a G

where F and G are variables for predicates and a stands for a name. We can then see that as long as each of F, G and a are replaced on each occurrence by the same item, we can generate any number of valid arguments with the same structure. What matters is that the same repeatable component of judgement occurs for each replacement of a. The same applies for the predicates too.

It is the availability of this component structure of judgements that makes them systematically related one to another in ways that figure in logical arguments. The possession of this component structure is called compositionality. The ways that judgements relate to one another in logical arguments are the ways in which we rationally assess one judgement in the light of others. The requirement that our judgements exhibit compositionality is then simply the requirement that they be susceptible to rational scrutiny.

For example, we can subject to critical scrutiny the claim that all good basketball players are taller that 6 foot 6 inches by observing the existence of Charles Barkley, who is less than 6 foot 6 inches. The argument at (1)–(3) is valid. Therefore, if there exists a star basketball player of less that 6 foot 6 inches, the opening judgement at (1) must be false. The example is trivial but the general point is important. If our moral judgements are to be subject to rational assessment, which they must be if they are to be candidates for truth, then they must exhibit the sort of compositionality that explains the systematicity of truth-oriented judgements.

I have drawn heavily upon Wiggins's work in supporting the legitimation of our valuational discourse as a discourse aimed at truth. However, a central requirement of this legitimation is that the discourse provide scope for the rational assessment of our valuational judgements. This requires compositionality of our moral judgements. However, I have also stressed the idea that our moral judgements are the judgements of sensibility and this threatens to conflict with the requirement of compositionality. The threat can be summarised as follows. Rationality requires that our moral judgements exhibit compositionality. Compositionality requires that judgements be modelled as arrangements of repeatable symbolic components. The historical embeddedness of our sensibility means that moral judgements cannot be modelled as arrangements of symbolic components. We have a problem!

Let me explain this problem a little further before I attempt to resolve it in the next section. The main conclusion of the last chapter was that in order to make the concept of the situated self viable we would need to make sense of the idea of our sensibility providing us with principles of substantive rationality. But these are principles governing our embeddedness in real historical practices. They are principles governing our essentially perspectival sense of value. It is the perspectivity of our moral judgements that stands to conflict with the rational requirement of compositionality. Because they are essentially perspectival and embedded in real historical sensibilities, our moral judgements cannot be characterised independently of their context. This means that we cannot provide a propositional model of moral knowledge in which moral knowledge is represented in terms of arrangements of propositional symbols abstracted from their context. However, the model of compositionality that we possess is precisely that of arrangements of symbols. As I have noted on a number of occasions, the dominant model of rationality in modernity is that of symbol manipulation – sentence juggling. If rationality is something that can be formally modelled in terms of syntactic operations upon symbol strings – like sentences – then we have a problem in applying the requirements of rationality to moral judgements. As Wiggins says in the above passage, valuational properties must figure in the rationalisation of our thought and action. It is not enough that they are merely posited as properties that explain the making of our moral judgements; they are properties at which we rationally aim when we make judgement. We must have some account of rationality that accommodates the existence of judgements that cannot be modelled formally as arrangements of symbol strings.

Rationality requires that our moral judgements exhibit compositionality. Compositionality is normally thought to require that judgements be modelled as arrangements of repeatable symbolic components. The historical embeddedness of our sensibility means that moral judgements cannot be modelled as arrangements of symbolic components. We have a problem. Something has to give. In the next section I shall suggest that the villain of the piece is the idea that rationality is best modelled as the manipulation of symbol strings. That should not be surprising, for the work left undone from the last chapter is precisely the task of providing a model of substantive rationality – the rational truth-oriented structure of our sensibility.

PRAXIS – A SENSIBLE MODEL OF KNOWLEDGE

What we require at this stage of the argument is a novel picture or image to help us conceive of moral knowledge. The picture needs to satisfy a pair of apparently incompatible demands. First, it needs to show how moral judgements can be truth-oriented and this entails that they be subject to compositionality. Any given moral judgement will be systematically related to a whole field of judgements by inferential connections. These inferential connections will hold in virtue of a common compositional structure. Second, our picture must accommodate the historical embeddedness of moral judgements in our evolving sensibilities. The first demand seems to require that judgements be conceived as arrangements of symbols, characterisable independently of context; the second demand says that they cannot be conceived in such a way. What we need is a picture that shows how the first demand can be met without treating judgements as formal arrangements of symbols characterisable independently of context.

We need an image that captures the nature of moral knowledge. I suggest that we look, in the first instance, at the nature of practical belief and practical knowledge. Two examples that are pertinent are knowing how to play the piano and knowing how to play tennis. I want to suggest that such examples provide the beginnings of the general picture we need. However, on the face of it, these examples fail to capture the essential ingredient of compositionality required of truth-oriented belief.

Gilbert Ryle famously drew a distinction between 'knowing how' and 'knowing that'. The former is exemplified in behavioural skills like knowing how to ride a bike or knowing how to swim. Such behavioural skills lack the truth-directed character of propositional knowledge, 'knowledge that'. Therefore, if knowing how to play the piano and knowing how to play tennis are cases of knowing how, then they will not meet our first demand that our picture of moral judgements captures the compositionality of judgements aimed at truth. However, Ryle's distinction is, I believe, too crude. Although knowing how to ride a bike is clearly a historically conditioned piece of behavioural repertoire, to suggest a sharp dichotomy between propositional knowledge and such skills is to miss the phenomena that lie in between, such as knowing how to play the piano. My suggestion is that the cases of piano-playing and tennis lie instructively between the cases of raw behavioural skills (bike-riding) and fully abstracted propositional knowledge (knowing that $2 + 2 = 4$). That is to say, these examples indicate the existence of forms of skills-based judgements that are historically conditioned and that at the same time exhibit the kind of compositionality that rationality requires of our judgements.

Suppose we conceive of moral knowledge as a form of practical wisdom, a knowledge that is in principle not fully codifiable sententially. In the first instance, think of moral knowledge as more akin to knowing how to play a musical instrument. Such a model of knowledge provides a better purchase on the idea that there might be a worthwhile story to tell about the real historical conditions for the possibility of knowledge; this would be a story that reveals the historical and cultural embeddedness of moral judgements. Consider the following scenario.[7]

Suppose musicians and music teachers end up taking the rap for a series of political and natural disasters. For example, suppose that a series of key political assassinations led to widespread political and economic collapse and that, each time, the assassin was the piano player! Music teaching and recordings get banished from our culture. Attempts are made to erase the whole practice of music-making. However, suppose that after several generations, people recovered some pianos and tutorial books on piano-playing. It does not seem at all unreasonable to think that, in such circumstances, a condition for the possibility of a recovery of knowing how to play the piano would require the recovery of a whole culture of music playing, interpretation and performance. The rudiments of the mechanics of playing the instrument might be recovered quite quickly, although even that could involve all sorts of confusion. But knowing how to play in a romantic style as opposed to the classical, like Chopin or like Liszt, like Rachmaninov or like Schoenberg, these would be elements in musical knowledge that would not be recovered quickly, if at all, precisely because they are not items of theoretical knowledge.

Practical knowledge, like knowing how to play the piano, is a good example of knowledge for which there could be a substantial issue about the historical conditions for the possibility of the knowledge. What we need to know is whether such knowledge can meet the demands of rationality. Propositional knowledge is subject to the demands of rationality – if you believe that P and you believe that P entails Q, you must believe that Q, etc. Truth, rationality and the terms of cognitive evaluation apply to propositional knowledge. Do they also apply to the kind of 'knowing how' exemplified in knowing how to play the piano?

We want to make sense of the idea that the existence of cultural and historical contingencies is a condition of the possibility of moral knowledge where the latter is conceived cognitively, as some thing fit for cognitive evaluation. We need a conception of practical knowledge that, like knowing how to play the piano, is dependent on certain contingent conditions obtaining, and that also has the property of being a form of knowledge that is subject to the normal terms of cognitive evaluation – truth and rationality.

This sounds like a tall order. We need a notion of practical belief that possesses the characteristics of ordinary propositional belief – compositionality and systematicity of conceptual repertoire, the ingredients that make beliefs suitable for evaluation as true or false. But we also need these beliefs to be items that are not fully expressible sententially so that, in part at least, they share some of the features of practical knowledge, a dependency on the availability of contingent conditions.

I believe that the ingredients for our solution are already to hand. For a long time, the paradigm for cognition has been the manipulation of symbolic strings. Cognitive psychology took a great leap forward when it latched on to the image of our cognitive abilities as things to be modelled symbolically. This has led to the metaphor of the mind as a digital computer. Digital computers manipulate symbol strings. If that is a good model of human cognitive skills, then in essence we are just like digital computers. However, a growing tide of research from different fields now suggests that the rush to treat cognition as symbol manipulation has been too simplistic and unrealistic. New developmental paradigms are arising in the core study of our cognition. These are paradigms that emphasise the role that experience and training play in the development of our core cognitive skills. These are paradigms that see our core cognitive machinery as much more than abstract symbol manipulation; rather, the central image becomes that of systems embedded in the world and with the ability to move and manipulate the objects found in the world. The key shift in image is between the idea that sees the creation of an intelligent robot as the making of a system that manipulates symbols, and the idea that sees an intelligent robot as fundamentally a system with the ability to experience the world, move around in it and manipulate the objects in its environment. The shift is from the manipulation of symbols to the manipulation of the world.

We are perhaps at a new watershed in our understanding of our core cognitive machinery. These are revolutionary times. If the revolution proceeds in the direction I am indicating, then our current problems with moral judgements are premised on a false image of rationality. Even in our core cognitive functions, our rationality may not be the abstract manipulation of symbols but the embedded manipulation of the world.[8]

To return to the point in hand. Can we provide a general

picture that accommodates the idea that our cognitive functions are worldly operations rather than operations upon symbols? I believe we can make a start on this by concentrating on the concept of a habit. Habits are things that we acquire in so far as we immerse ourselves in various historically situated forms of training. In the first instance, habits are things we acquire by mimicry. At the same time, however, habits are often susceptible to an ongoing critique, a reflective adjustment in the light of good practice. Good examples of the right kind of habit here are: habitual actions of a skilled tennis player, habitual actions of a pianist, habitual actions of a teacher. I want to concentrate on the habits of a jazz pianist.

The concept of habit needs to do two things. It needs to pick out an engagement with the world that is only available for a subject thoroughly embedded in a contingent framework. Having the right habits *qua* tennis player comes from an immersion in and mimicry of the traditions that shape the sport. Having the right habits *qua* jazz pianist comes from an immersion in the cultural traditions of that form of music. Second, the concept of habit needs to offer a mode of being in the world that is more than mere mimicry; it is a mode of being that is susceptible to critical evaluation. As such, the concept of habit must accommodate the ideas of systematicity and combinatorial structure in order that this critical evaluation bears the hallmarks of truth. The point of the example of good habits at playing jazz piano is that, if it works, this shows that we should not succumb to models of rationality that focus upon pure reflexive reason and forget the kind of sense of immanence in the world that only comes with a developed and educated sensibility of what must be done under certain concrete circumstances.

Let us take as an example here the kind of habits that mark out the successful jazz musician from the rest and denote them with the elusive notion of a 'feel for the music'.[9] The concept of a feel for the music captures the refusal of our practical belief to bend to the demands of intellectualisation and codification. At the same time, the feel for the music that the experienced pianist has is not simply a matter of brute mimicry. There is considerable training that has to be undergone in order to acquire a competent player's feel for the music.

The idea of a feel for the music does service on two fronts. First, it captures the notion of involvement with a practice and tradition which makes one's belief about which note or chord to play next distanced from a sentential model of belief that is subject only to a cool engagement of pure reason. Believing that the chord to play next is a C major seventh is not a belief that appears as a sentence before the mind's eye of the experienced pianist. It is a belief that appears as a sense of what they must do, in their sense of the appropriateness of responding in just that manner.

Second, the concept of a feel for the music gives some content to the notion of an immanence in the world by which the world can impose a sense of things to be done or said, or played or sung. This is important. For players with a developed feel for the music, the music is read in such a way that their embeddedness in the flow of the music means that they are left in no doubt about what has to be done next. Determining the course of the next chord is not a matter of ratiocination, indeed it is not really a 'determining' at all if we stick with the sentential model of reason. It is the kind of creative response that comes from having precisely that embedding in a situation that is captured by the phrase 'feel for the music'. When we are playing a piece and improvising successfully we live in the music; it is at our fingertips. In such cases I might say that I am

> doing singings with my fingers ... a single voice at the tips of my fingers, going for each next note in sayings just now and just then, just this soft and just this hard, just here and just there, with definiteness of aim throughout, taking my fingers to places, so to speak, and being guided, so to speak. I sing with my fingers, so to speak, and only so to speak, for there is a new 'I' that the speaking I gestures toward with a pointing at the music that says: It is a singing body and this I (here, too, so to speak) sings.[10]

However, we must not let this concept run away, for although I want to stress the embeddedness which comes from having a feel for the music, I want also to stress that this engagement with the world is an engagement which is subject to something akin to the norm of truth. The concept of a feel for the music must exhibit sufficient systematicity and compositionality to capture truth.

First of all, note that the habits of a musician need training. This training typically involves not only a rich embedding in music-making, but also concentrated practice upon component elements in playing music. Interminable wet afternoons will be devoted to practising scales and arpeggios; you will learn the classics and learn standards by heart; you will exercise different styles and repertoires. You will learn through this training a whole musical landscape and the various ways of navigating your way around it.

This training involves not only this specialised practice on components of music-making; it also involves a practice of evaluation and criticism. The development of musical habits includes also the development of musical judgement; judgement about how softly to play certain pieces, judgements about rhythm, texture and tonality. The capacity for making these judgements depends on the capacity to make discriminations where the untrained ear hears only an undifferentiated wall of sound. It is an education that the skilled performer undertakes and it is an education that not only provides them with a behavioural repertoire that is used systematically to produce quality music; it is a repertoire that underpins their growing faculty of judgement. The novice plays a bum note and is criticised by the tutor. They learn to avoid bum notes, but they also learn how to pass judgements on what constitutes a bum note.

The judgements that an educated musical sensibility comes to make bear the marks of truth. It is not the case that thinking that x is the right note to play makes it the case that x is the right note to play. Whether or not x is the right note to play is independent of the musician thinking that it is the right note. Furthermore, given the open-endedness of the activity, whether or not x is the right note to play is potentially independent of what any current musician thinks. Therein lies the room for creative adjustment and the possibility for music to evolve. It does so when musicians of ability learn most of what is available in terms of (a) the underlying components of play – the scales, arpeggios, snapshots of standard melodies and standard melodic developments; (b) current good habits of play, that is predominant styles of harmonic and melodic structure; and then, (c) in the light of a critical assessment of these habits they devise novel strategies of musical expression.

All this sounds like something that observes the independence of truth. There is a dimension of assessment of our musical skills and judgements that allows space for the thought that what constitutes pleasing play is independent of our own and others' judgement. Of course, the notion of 'good play' is dependent on the existence of traditions of playing music. But saying that is just to acknowledge that our sense of what is going on in music is conditioned by contingencies, for example, by the fact that our ears respond to a limited range of frequencies. That does not stop it being the case that it is true that the right harmonic development at such-and-such a moment is variation x and that, therefore, this fact gives the player a reason to play variation x even though that is a reason only within the contingencies of this particular game.

One aspect of the objectivity of truth – its independence of judgement – is the idea that under favourable circumstances truth commands convergence. Truth is what we will converge on, providing the circumstances are favourable. This also applies to the music example. Judgements about good play at jazz do not concern good play just for you, or for me. Rather, if an E flat is the right note for me then it is, other things being equal, the right note for anyone. Of course, 'other things being equal' here covers things like our having similar reach, mobility around the instrument, grasp of the tradition and familiarity with the standards, etc. Notoriously these things are not equal. That is what makes jazz a dynamic activity as we try to adjust for our inequalities and find sites of musical conversation. Nevertheless, under favourable circumstances where such things are equal, if E flat is right for me, it would be for you similarly positioned.

The lack of sentential codifiability of musical knowledge is evident in the terminology that gets employed as the tutor trains the student. Metaphor abounds as the teacher says the student played a phrase too harshly, too sweetly, or suggests that the student 'lean' on a note, 'attack' a note. And, more often than not, the tutor simply says 'Try playing it like this' and proceeds to show the student how the phrase should be played.

I think that the notion of a feel for the music and the habits of playing jazz show the availability of a concept of habit that serves the dual function of providing us with a concept of rational action that is also essentially conditioned by contingencies. The conditioning is obvious. The rationality is also obvious in so far as there exists a practice of critique and ongoing amendment of habits that matches the marks of truth. This latter point is what ensures that the concept of habit is not concerned with an engagement with the world that is untouchable by reflection. It is subject to reflection and, furthermore, it is a reflection that reveals the combinatorial structure of good play at jazz. It is a reflection that employs this structure in making available critiques of what you have done in shaping a musical phrase. The point to the concept of habit is simply that it signals an engagement with the world that is not necessarily mediated by ratiocination, reason modelled on juggling with sentences.

The account of habit I am trying to characterise claims that there are engagements with the world that are not constituted by reason and reflection; they are engagements constituted by body, position, a feel for one's bearing, posture and perspective in the context of a culture. To try to represent sententially the bearing and feel for the action that is typical of a skilled pianist would not only be impossibly tedious and probably pointless; it would fail altogether to represent properly the engagement the pianist has with his or her surroundings. However, although this is important, endorsing this concept of habit is compatible with insisting that when a human agent enjoys such an engagement with the world, that engagement is, like the engagement of rational reflection, subject to evaluation, refinement and critical adjustment. There is a normative dimension to such an engagement not unlike the normativeness of aiming for truth when we engage the world in a more reflective spirit, for the pianist's engagement is one that underpins a faculty of judgement about the music-making. This normative critique operates via a detection of the repeatable components of playing the piano that make up the combinatorial structure of play.

A 'feel for the music' is something that can be critically adjusted in the light of an ongoing assessment, in much the same way that a belief can be adjusted in the light of an evidenced argument. If this characteristic of practical sense is not accommodated, then the bodily involvement with the world referred to by 'habit' fails to be the bodily engagement of an agent as opposed to the mere material engagement of a body. To claim this is not to take sides between positivism and rationalism. It is to insist that those two familiar options are mere extremes of the real middle ground.

Note that the musician, although contingently conditioned, is not a self in flux, continually changing as contingencies alter. The musician is a dynamic self that evolves over time around a set of core skills. There are principles of navigation that such a dynamic self may employ in its passage through the changing circumstances of the world. A pianist confronted with a new piece, or a new improvisation, does not expect to be given a set of propositions determining what to do. There is an important element of creativity in how the pianist shapes the new piece, especially if the pianist is engaged in improvisation. But that creativity is not random. It draws upon a number of structural impositions. Most basic of all, it draws upon the fact that the player is a pianist. That is to say, there is a core of skills that constitute being a pianist and that get employed time and again in confronting new pieces and new melodic structures and harmonic patterns. These skills are not necessarily sententially coded. The same, I suspect, is true of the moral self and our moral skills. Despite the attempts by utilitarians and others to codify propositionally our moral knowledge, I suspect that most of the time in our moral lives we are playing by ear – and none the worse for it.

The pianist is not a self in flux, changing radically from one piece to another. The pianist is a dynamic self who is constituted by the core skills and practices that are called upon in the new pieces. Once a pianist, a pianist for life. You will still need your scales, your sense of melodic and harmonic development, whatever styles you choose to play, however you develop musically.

It is these core skills, core components of musical knowledge, that provide the normative structure to the principles of navigation by which the dynamic self adapts to and adopts new musical ideas. The core can evolve. There can be aspects of that core that you only come to know about quite late in your instrumental development. There can be practitioners who add radical new elements to the core that define whole new musical styles – think of Charlie Parker and the emergence of be-bop. Despite that, Parker was still a saxophonist and had elements of his core skills in common with all others who have mastered the instrument. If you change from playing classical sax pieces to jazz you will change your mouthpiece from a narrow lay piece to a wide lay piece. The articulation of notes will change; the phrasing and rhythms will change. But you are still a saxophonist whether playing Ravel or Parker, Bach or Getz.

THE CONTINGENT CONDITIONS OF SELF AND MORALS

If we think of moral knowledge as a kind of praxis modelled on the above example, it is a kind of knowledge that is intrinsically conditioned by contingent circumstances. This is what we wanted, for the contingent conditioning of moral knowledge reveals the real historical embedding of this knowledge. I said at the outset that what we needed was a sense of how our normative pursuit of truth and knowledge could be preserved while accepting that it was not dislocated out of real historical time and circumstance. That possibility is now, I suggest, wide open. If we are to take it up and make something of it, we will need to abandon the symbol-manipulating models of rationality that have dominated our reflections through modernity. As indicated, the rejection of such a symbolic model is now on the cards for a number of different reasons. Modernity's idea of a uniform symbolic form of representation of all that counts in human life is fracturing under pressure from a number of sources. I am merely suggesting that we take advantage of this to fashion new ways in which to make sense of our cognitive purpose in morality.

To acknowledge the contingent conditions of the self and morals is to turn away from deep-rooted assumptions that have shaped the dominant strands of moral philosophy. The option that I am suggesting we explore is a radical option that barely fits within the accepted purview of the domain of moral and political philosophy. On the account that I am suggesting, the self and its values are not givens. The self is not a metaphysical given, an absolute starting point for moral enquiry. On the account that I am promoting it is something that is achieved within the fragile contingencies of our history and culture.

If this is a correct account of our selves and our moral purposes a number of conclusions follow. First, we can have no guarantee that the moral point of view will be a universal point of view that will apply to all people at all times and in all places. In so far as the moral point of view is an engagement with the world that is aimed at truth then, in so far as the pursuit of truth is a pursuit that commands convergence, the moral point of view cannot accommodate contradictory moral judgements. That is to say, it will be a point of view that aims towards universal applicability. However, we can have no guarantee at the outset that such applicability currently obtains or will be attained in the future. Quite what becomes of our moral outlook will turn on the vagaries of what we have done and what we do next. We cannot assume the universality of the moral point of view as a priori truth; it is something we have to work for.

Second, given the contingency of our self-conception and of our values we cannot fail to be struck by the sense of responsibility with which we act. If our moral selves are not metaphysical givens, then neither are they divine givens. We cannot fall back on the support of divine intervention or inspiration to make our moral world work. Given the contingency of the moral it is up to us, and no one else, what we make of our morals. It is on us, no one and nothing else, that the responsibility falls for how we make and how we conceive our moral lives. The moral world is ours. It is not leased by a divine landlord who will bale us out if we mess it up. We alone bear the responsibility for holding it in being. We alone bear the responsibility if we fail to colonise our world and make of it a place of value. The moral world does not rest upon an absolute framework of timeless abstract truths derived from pure metaphysics or the mysticism of religion. The moral world has its being in, it rests upon, what we do and how we act. It is in our actions and the way we treat one another that values come into being and are preserved in being. Not unlike the Australasian aboriginals who go 'walkabout' in order to renew their songlines and preserve the being of the world, we renew our moral world only in so far as we continue to use it, to inhabit it and find our homes built within it.[11] If we fail to go moral 'walkabout' we can literally unmake ourselves and our values.

This brings us to the third and most dramatic departure from traditional ways of conceiving of the moral. Given the contingency of the self and its values, morality and moral selves are things we can fail to achieve. The world and our selves have to be made moral and this is a task in which we can fail. Accepting the contingency of the self and its values means that there is no thing or person to underwrite the achievement of morality, the achievement of moral selfhood. This is an achievement and it is an ongoing achievement. Not only is it our achievement; it is also, potentially, our failure.

In these three respects, the picture of morality that I have sketched is in sharp contrast to most traditional models. There are, of course, a number of contemporary writers who challenge the traditional models, but the position so far is unclear. As I have sketched the alternative contingent conception of morality, it is only a beginning. It does, however, point to some interesting possibilities that I want briefly to explore.

THE MAKING OF OUR SELVES ...

If our values and sense of self are things that we make, there is space to investigate what conditions are required for this making to take place. It might be that there is no general answer to the question 'What are the conditions for the possibility of making moral selves?', but on the conception outlined the question is one that invites investigation. Whatever answers we give to this question, some points must be observed.

First, the conditions for the possibility of making moral selves must be conditions that provide for more than the mere mimicry of traditions. If the self to be made is a self with the apparatus to subject its inheritance to critical scrutiny, the conditions for the possibility of self-making must give priority to this facet of the moral self. This means that however much we may identify our selves with inherited traditions there is a point at which we must acknowledge the responsibility we each of us bear for our self-creation. We fashion ourselves in the thick context of inherited historical, cultural and social traditions; we draw our self-images against a rich backdrop of idols and ideas; but we only fashion ourselves as moral agents in so far as we seize the day and, in the light of a critical assessment of history's lessons, we make something new, something appropriate to the conditions of the present.

In his final interview, broadcast shortly before his death, the playwright Dennis Potter captured this point:

> We tend to forget that life can only be defined in the present tense, it is and it is now only. As much as we would like to call back yesterday and indeed ache to, sometimes, we can't. . . . And however predictable tomorrow is – and unfortunately for most people, most of the time, it's too predictable, they're locked into whatever situation they're locked into – no matter how predictable it is, there's the element of the un-predictable. . . . The only thing you know for sure is the present

tense . . . if you see the present tense, boy do you see it, and boy can you celebrate it![12]

The celebration of the present that Potter speaks of comes from an immersion in the task of creatively adjusting to circumstance rather than timidly mimicking words and actions provided by others. To extend the analogy of pp. 207–16, the celebration of the present is the attitude of the jazz soloist who, thickly immersed in a tradition of harmonic and melodic parameters and surrounded by fellow musicians, nevertheless finds the space to create out of their inheritance a response to the present that is new. It is a moment that is both response to what went before – the soloist being constrained by the preceding harmonies – and an acceptance of responsibility for laying down some of the parameters for what will come next. The jazz soloist lives in the present, but it is not the unattached present of the metaphysical loneliness of the liberal individual. The jazz soloist lives in a present that acknowledges its inherent shaping by the past and yet also seizes and shapes the future. It is a dynamic present.

What bearing does this have upon the issue of the conditions for the possibility of making moral selves? First, it means that the making of the self is not achieved by instruction. The making of the self is an educative process, not a training. It is a process that needs to produce selves with the capacity to improvise upon life and not merely mimic the past. Our model of moral education cannot then be a model based on any simplistic notion of teaching young people the difference between right and wrong. Such a model is too suggestive of an image of moral knowledge as possession of a set of instructions how to live. That is too restrictive. We need to know how others have, in the past, solved their dilemmas about how to live, but most of all we need to acquire the capacity to take responsibility for framing new responses to what will often be new situations. We need to become the moral equivalents of the jazz soloist.

The achievement of self-making is no mean feat. Jazz soloists do not spring unnurtured from a vacuum. To achieve such musical skills requires lengthy immersion in a rich culture of music practice. The same applies to the making of moral selves. The making of moral selves requires immersion in culture. No one would be surprised if a seventeen-year-old with no previous experience of music could not play the saxophone like Charlie Parker. So why should we be surprised if people with little experience of a culture of care and compassion, with little experience of critically reflecting upon their relationships with others, should fail to engage the values and virtues of moral life? If moral knowledge really is a form of practical knowledge, a skill that requires training and nurturing in contingent frameworks, then if we strip away the frameworks that provide the exercise ground for morality, we will fail to make our morals.

The indications are that when such failure occurs part of the explanation lies in our collective failure to provide the conditions necessary for the making of the self. That is to say, the provision of the conditions necessary for self-making is, in part, a political enterprise. This is an option that becomes available on the model I am outlining. Moral education, on my model, is much more than the rote learning of pious sentiments about the distinction between right and wrong. It is not a matter of internalising a code, a set of sentences that articulate what is right and what is wrong. Rather, moral education is an extraordinarily fragile process that requires an immersion in a variety of experiences and opportunities by which we learn the sensitive deployment of the process of intelligent selection among the options that shape modern life. Critical informed choices from among the lessons that history presents us is the key to moral behaviour, not the dumb incantations of one set of self-proclaimed wise men or another.

Instruction in morality is complex, fragile and requires considerable resources, not least of which is a couple of decades of careful parenting. Strip away the resources and we are prone to make a very bad job of it. Provide young people with limited vistas for future employment, with wretched housing, dilapidated schools and hospitals and absent parents who work ever longer hours in order to remain solvent and it is no surprise if their grip on morality is more fragile than most.

I am not suggesting that social deprivation is a universal explanation for moral delinquency, let alone an excuse for it. It is no excuse at all. However, on the general model of moral knowledge that I have suggested, there is room for the idea that the provision of empirical conditions is a contingent factor in the achievement of moral selfhood. The failure to provide those conditions is then a contingent factor in the failure to achieve moral selfhood. And where those conditions are items that we take to be the proper task of collective political action, there is scope for the thought that the achievement of selfhood is a political task and that its failure is a political failure.

There are two points that I am making here. First, there is a conceptual point that the notion of moral knowledge that I am defending is one that has moral knowledge grounded in contingent circumstances. The second point is that the relevant circumstances are often circumstances the management of which fall within the domain of the political. It does not follow from this that all failures of selfhood are explained by political failure; nor does it follow that all political failure to alleviate wretched circumstances of living lead to failures of selfhood. That there is scope for a connection between the making of selves and the realm of politics is the conceptual point. Quite what that connection is and how it operates is an empirical point and, as such, there is no reason to suppose that the connection operates with a universal regularity in all cases.

An analogy is helpful here. Conceptually we accept that various conditions, such as lung cancer, can be caused by noxious substances irritating the body. What the connections are between such irritations and the onset of disease is not, however, something that can be settled conceptually – it is a subject of empirical study. That smoking causes lung cancer is a claim that requires empirical support, and it is a claim that is not diminished by noting that the correlation between disease and smoking is statistical and not deterministic. We have all heard of the octogenarian who still smokes forty a day. That does not diminish the importance of the empirical findings that warrant governmental action to curb cigarette advertising.

A similar point applies in the moral case. Admitting the possibility that our self-achievements can be affected by matters that are subject to collective political control does not give us the right to plot connections between political circumstance and moral self-achievement by armchair conceptual investigation. The philosophical conceptual point that I want to press is simply that on the model of moral knowledge I propose, we cannot ignore and would do well to investigate the political conditionings of the making of our selves. Further, I suspect that, despite the fact that we all probably know of the moral saint surviving in our urban decay, there is an accumulation of evidence to suggest a statistical (not deterministic) correlation between criminality and social deprivation. On the philosophical model I have proposed this is a matter for urgent further investigation.[13]

In the musical example, when we make a new self there is 'a new "I" that the speaking I gestures toward with a pointing at the music that says: It is a singing body and this I (here, too, so to speak) sings.' If it is true that we are creating a society that is slowly forgetting how to sing, whose music is being diminished to a karaoke mimicry in which we literally lose ourselves, then we need to address the question of why we are failing to make the new 'I' that sings.

... IN WHOSE IMAGE?

To the question 'In whose image should we make ourselves?' there can be only one answer – 'Our own'. It cannot be the task of philosophy to provide at this point anything more than this banal platitude. Given the contingency of our self-making, it would be presumptuous to expect a philosophical recipe for self-making. The claim that the moral self is an achievement to be made is a philosophical claim. Quite how that achievement is undertaken and what, at any given moment in time, looks to be the best way of accomplishing it, must be left to the circumstances of life. Philosophy will not tell us how to live; it can, however, tell us that the resources for living are more various, subtle and complex than modernity had us suppose.

The images we employ in self-making are drawn from our history and culture, but that does not mean that we should indulge the past and expect the future to comply with the lazy comforts of our nostalgia. On both sides of the Atlantic there has, of late, been a nostalgic appeal to the values of family life by politicians and writers alike. The appeal is double edged and potentially deeply conservative in a problematic way. On the model of moral knowledge that I have sketched there is a central role for the family in the business of moral education. However, to say that is not to prescribe any one particular model of what constitutes a family. There is no a priori reason why a family has to be built around a male/female pairing. The appeal to family that is inescapable on my model is the appeal to the security of a nucleus of close relationships sustained by care and compassion. Whether or not such a nucleus can be sustained by a pair of adults of the same gender, the same sexuality, or by a single parent is an empirical matter than cannot be ruled on in advance. It should be no surprise if conceptions of the family evolve to suit the changing socio-economic circumstances in which child-rearing takes place. Indeed, in the context of rapidly shifting economic structures, the achievements of, for example, single-parent families should be applauded as an example of an avant-garde attempt to adapt the central businesses of self-making to changed circumstance.

The philosophical point about self-making in a postmodern world is that, in the light of the preceding argument, we have the right to appeal to a wide range of explanatory frameworks as we build ourselves and our world. We should not make do with the reductionisms and limited instrumental rationality of modernity. We can, instead, acknowledge the reality of our evaluative and aesthetic points of view. We should not acquiesce in the silence that comes from failing to talk the discourses of value, from thinking that we can capture the purpose of human life in modernity's calculi of desire satisfaction. Dennis Potter again: 'in politics certain statements become derisible. We're destroying ourselves by not making those statements.' Just so, and what we can learn from philosophy is that the discourses that modernity called into question are, once again, legitimate devices in the ongoing dynamic of understanding ourselves. Once we have seen how to legitimise reason, truth and self without the extravagant images of modernity, we have seen how to make ourselves impervious to derision.

Of the explanatory frameworks that we employ in our self-making there will, however, be no room for a religious framework that grounds moral values in the divine. The contingently framed self is a self of the here and now, in real history and real culture. Its values are part of the ongoing contingently evolving world. They do not arise from or get their grounding in some hidden region just over the horizon of human experience. This does not mean that we should not celebrate our sense of wonder – why we sing and dance, why we make art, why we care and feel for others. It does not mean that we should ignore all those things that separate us from the purely animal responses to the world. It means only that there is no reason to locate such things in a grand metaphysical narrative. We locate them in the thick context of the earth we daily inhabit, not in a heaven located just out of our sight.

Glossary

The glossary defines a number of key terms and gives chapter and page number in the main text where the term is first introduced.

absolute conception
A conception of the world as it is in itself, as opposed to how we experience and conceive it (Introduction, pp. 10f.). See also **world's own story**.

basic constraint
The idea that there is such a thing as a distinction between truth and judgement, that judging something to be true does not make it true (Chapter 1, pp. 28f.).

communitarianism
The thesis that our sense of self and moral purpose can only be retrieved if we conceive of ourselves as intrinsically situated in communities of agents (Chapter 9, pp. 178f.).

cosmic register
The model for absolute knowledge, the record of absolute truths (Chapter 1, pp. 25f.).

critical empiricism
The thesis that scientific knowledge involves making hypotheses about entities and events beyond the realm of evidence supplied by our senses and that all such claims must be subject to experimental testing (Chapter 1, pp. 38f.).

difference principle
Rawls's principle that inequalities in distribution of goods can only be permitted where they leave everyone better off than they would have been under an equal distribution (Chapter 8, pp. 166f.).

dualism
The thesis, originating with Descartes, that the world is made out of two basic kinds of stuff: mind and matter (Chapter 2, pp. 53f.).

embedded self
Also 'situated self': a conception of self that, like **communitarian** conceptions, denies that the self can be made sense of in isolation

from the real historical situations in which it lives. But the embedded self is not necessarily embedded in particular communities (Chapter 8, pp. 151f. and Chapter 9, pp. 184f.).

indexicals
Expressions such as 'I', 'now' 'here', 'there', 'you', etc., whose meaning is context-sensitive. They pick out different things (people, times, places) depending on the circumstances of use (Chapter 2, pp. 60f.).

knowledge
Non-accidental possession of beliefs that are true (Chapter 4, pp. 91f.).

logos/pathos
A distinction between our faculties of logical deductive thought and our sensibilities, for example our faculty of aesthetic appreciation (Chapter 1, p. 31).

perspectival
A perspectival conception of the world is one that characterises the world from the point of view of a particular kind of creature; contrast **absolute conception** (Introduction, pp. 10f.).

perspectival thinking
Those thoughts that provide us with a sense of position in the world and perspective upon it; thoughts expressed with **indexical** expressions (Chapter 2, pp. 60f.).

primary/secondary qualities
A distinction between qualities that figure in descriptions of the world independently of the effects the world has on us (primary) and descriptions that characterise the world in terms of its effects on us (secondary). It is sometimes claimed that the former are more objective or real than the latter, although this point is denied in Chapter 5 (Chapter 1, p. 41).

representative theory
Of perception, the theory that in perception the primary object of perception is an idea or sense datum caused by the external object. On this theory, such intermediary objects are the only objects we can directly experience; external objects are only perceived indirectly (Chapter 5, p. 117).

sensory qualities
Qualities that are employed in describing the way in which a given kind of creature experiences the world, qualities that characterise their point of view upon the world (Chapter 2, p. 57).

simple truth
The concept of truth that is entailed by acceptance of the **basic constraint**; the notion of things being thus and so independently of whether or not we think that they are thus

and so (Chapter 5, pp. 107f.).

transcendental argument
An argument that shows the conditions necessary for something to be possible, for example an argument that shows that acceptance of the concept of **simple truth** is a condition for the possibility of making any kind of judgements (Chapter 5, p. 110).

transparent language
A language whose meaning is fully encoded in the symbols contained in the language so that there is no scope for misinterpreting the meaning of the language. It is unclear that there could be such a language; it serves as an ideal and model for the notion of the **world's own story** (Chapter 1, p. 47).

world's own story
The language or conceptual scheme suited for capturing the world as it is in itself (Chapter 1, p. 14f.).

Notes

INTRODUCTION

1 *The Gay Science*, Book V, in *The Portable Nietzsche*, ed. and trans. by W. Kaufman (London: Chatto & Windus, 1971), p. 447.

2 Quoted in David Wiggins, *Needs, Values, Truth: Essays in the Philosophy of Value* (Oxford: Blackwell, 1987), p. 89.

3 For a useful discussion of Marx's views on the status of morality, and of whether he thought all morality was ideological, see S. Lukes, *Marxism and Morality* (Oxford: Oxford University Press, 1985).

4 For an account of modern theories of meaning and the continuing influence that the idea of a pure language of thought still plays, plus also discussion of Wittgenstein and Derrida, see my *Contemporary Philosophy of Thought and Language* (Oxford: Blackwell, forthcoming).

5 See J. Habermas, *The Philosophical Discourse of Modernity* (Cambridge: Polity Press, 1987).

6 See C. Taylor, *Sources of the Self* (Cambridge: Cambridge University Press, 1989), esp. ch. 24, 'Epiphanies of modernism'.

7 See R. Rorty, *Objectivity, Relativism and Truth: Philosophical Papers*, vol. I, and *Contingency, Irony and Solidarity: Philosophical Papers*, vol. II (Cambridge: Cambridge University Press, 1989 and 1991).

8 J. Lyotard, *The Post-modern Condition: A Report on Knowledge* (Manchester: Manchester University Press, 1984).

9 Cf. M. Levenson, *A Genealogy of Modernism: A Study of English Literary Doctrine 1908–1922* (Cambridge: Cambridge University Press, 1984).

10 A. Camus, *The Myth of Sisyphus* (London: Hamish Hamilton, 1955).

11 The pervasiveness of the postmodernist threat is evidenced in its hold upon a number of academic disciplines, although it is a hold that is more developed in the US than the UK. For a defence of the practice of historians against postmodernism with which I have some sympathy, see Joyce Appleby, Lynn Hunt and Margaret Jacob, *Telling the Truth about History* (London: W. W. Norton & Co, 1994).

1 THE COSMIC REGISTER

1 The argument from interpretation owes a great deal to the work of Davidson. See his articles collected in D. Davidson, *Inquiries into Truth and Interpretation* (Oxford: Clarendon Press, 1980). Also, see the account of truth given in D. R. P. Wiggins, *Needs, Values, Truth: Essays in the Philosophy of Value* (Oxford: Blackwell, 1987) and his idea of the marks of truth. The above argument is of a kind with Wiggins's investigation of the marks of truth, which is an investigation prompted by asking, 'What properties must truth have if our utterances are to be meaningful?' Put another way, it is an investigation into the properties truth must have for judgement to be possible. For further discussion of these issues and the surrounding topics in the philosophy of language see my forthcoming work, *Contemporary Philosophy of Thought and Language* (Oxford: Blackwell).

2 The idea that reasoning in morals is more properly an act of the imagination and the passions than of reason is an idea that is sometimes called 'emotivism'. It is often traced to Hume. See D. Hume, *Enquiry Concerning the Principles of Morals.* However, as with most matters of Hume scholarship, the ascription of this position to Hume is highly contentious. For example, Wiggins in *Needs, Values, Truth* (op. cit.) offers an account of valuation that, although accommodating Hume's insistence on the role the passions play in understanding morals, is also not an emotivist account. It tries to be an account that acknowledges the role our sensibility plays in the formulation of moral ideas, but also accommodates the role of reason and truth-seeking in morality. Another author who has explored the scope for non-emotivist accounts of our sensibility is Annette Baier in *A Progress of Sentiments* (Cambridge, Mass.: Harvard University Press, 1991). For a very different account of morals that stresses the role of sentiment see R. Rorty, *Contingency, Irony and Solidarity* (Cambridge: Cambridge University Press, 1989). Rorty's description of his position as 'ironist' is employed, in part, to capture the idea that moral discourse is not subject to norms of truth. It is more an exercise in imagination in which we offer and commend different options to one another.

3 The account that I refer to in the text as the traditional account of Bacon was overturned with the publication of P. Urbach, *Francis Bacon's Philosophy of Science* (La Salle: Open Court, 1987). This book not only gives a total revision of the traditional reading of Bacon, but provides many examples of how Bacon thought his method worked. A discussion of Bacon's example of his method in the theory of heat, referred to in the text, can be found in Urbach's book, pp. 160–85.

4 For a useful selection of Karl Popper's views see D. Miller (ed.), *A Pocket Popper* (London: Fontana, 1983). For a more general survey of contemporary philosophy of science including Popper's position, see A. F. Chalmers, *What is this Thing called Science?* (Milton Keynes: Open University Press, 1982).

5 On the use of the primary/secondary quality distinction in formulating the notion of the absolute conception of the world, see B. Williams, *Descartes* (London: Penguin, 1978); also, C. McGinn, *The Subjective View* (Oxford: Clarendon Press, 1983) and H. Putnam, *Reason, Truth and History* (Cambridge: Cambridge University Press, 1981).

2 MIND – THE FINAL MYSTERY?

1 There are a number of excellent texts that cover in more depth the issues just sketched and those to come. Paul Churchland, *Matter and Consciousness* (Cambridge, Mass.: MIT Press, revised edition 1988) is an excellent introduction. It is written from the point of view of someone who is much more optimistic than I about the possibility of a scientific account of the mind. See also C. McGinn, *The Character of Mind* (Oxford: Oxford University Press, 1982). A book with a broader scope than either of these, but still written at a very elementary level, is Gordon Graham, *Philosophy of Mind: An Introduction* (Oxford: Blackwell, 1993).

2 The following example is taken from a seminal paper by T. Nagel, 'What is it like to be bat?', published in his collection *Mortal Questions* (Cambridge: Cambridge University Press, 1979). See also his *What Does it All Mean? A Very Brief Introduction to Philosophy* (Oxford: Oxford University Press, 1989). The issues raised by this kind of example concern what are normally referred to as *qualia* – the qualitative character of the way in which we experience the world. There is an enormous philosophical literature on the nature of the problems, if any, that *qualia* pose for physicalist accounts of consciousness. For a view that dissents from that taken in the text, start with the Churchland book (op. cit.), Chapter 2.

3 The assumption just noted is contentious. The support I gave for it consists in thinking through a thought experiment. Not all philosophers would accept the point made, nor the method for making it. For the contrasting view that meaning is fully encodable see Churchland, *Matter and Consciousness* (op. cit.) and, much more advanced, S. Stich, *From Folk Psychology to Cognitive Science* (Cambridge, Mass.: MIT Press, 1983). The issue here is central to the question of whether a formal symbolic model of our cognitive skills is possible. Writers such as Churchland and Stich think that it is. I disagree. Note that accepting the reality of our conscious experiences as something to be plotted and described is not the same as accepting a familiar Cartesian model of conscious experience. If we accept that conscious experience is real, we accept that there is such a thing as phenomenology – the study and description of our subjective point of view. However, it is quite different to think of that point of view as adequately modelled as some kind of private inner display in a hidden inner theatre to which the subject has an infallible introspective access. Accepting the possibility of phenomenology is compatible with accepting the thought that our subjective reports on our own

experiences can be fallible and opaque. Inveighing against the Cartesian private theatre model of subjectivity is compatible with accepting that there is such a thing as subjectivity.

4 The importance of indexical thoughts in our conception of what it is to be a conscious subject has become a topic of considerable recent interest. See C. McGinn, *The Subjective View* (op. cit.) and T. Nagel, *What Does it All Mean?* (op. cit.). The semantics of indexical thoughts has produced a lot of work in contemporary philosophy of thought and language. See my forthcoming *Contemporary Philosophy of Thought and Language* (Oxford: Blackwell) and Q. Cassam (ed.), *Self-Knowledge* (Oxford: Oxford University Press, 1994).

5 See Churchland (op. cit.) for an account which treats it not only as credible, but the best option! Also, in general, any naturalistic account of mind must be committed to accommodating the reality of our mental lives within a natural, scientific framework. There are many different versions of naturalism, some of which, like Churchland's, deny the reality of our ordinary talk of the mental. Others accept the reality of our ordinary talk of the mental but then proceed to offer scientific accounts of it; for example J. Fodor, *Psychosemantics* (Cambridge, Mass.: MIT Press, 1987). Dennett's position is a subtle blend of instrumentalist and realist views about our mental life: see D. Dennett, *The Intentional Stance* (Cambridge, Mass.: MIT Press, 1987) and *Consciousness Explained* (Harmondsworth: Penguin, 1992).

6 For an advanced discussion of this idea as it applies to a variety of phenomena studied in fields such as moral and mental philosophy, psychology, biology and social science, see the essays in D. Charles and K. Lennon (eds), *Reduction, Explanation and Realism* (Oxford: Clarendon Press, 1992).

3 NO ARCHIMEDEAN POINT

1 See Rorty, *Contingency, Irony and Solidarity* (Cambridge: Cambridge University Press, 1989). Although Rorty allows for the possibility of knowledge (e.g. he speaks of and offers an opinion about the relative merit of different literary canons in a way that would appear to acknowledge the existence of knowledge) he denies that knowledge is possession of truth. In part, I suspect that this is because of his very restrictive notion of what an account of truth must look like. In Chapter 1 of *Contingency, Irony and Solidarity* he repeatedly inveighs against the idea that truth is 'out there'. This, however, is either a straw man or nothing other than the cosmic register image of absolute truth. Rorty says that truth is not 'out there', for truth is a property of sentences and sentences are not 'out there'. The simplest way of understanding these claims is to see them as making the point that there is no world's own language – there are no sentences 'out there' that human sentences must try to mirror in order for knowledge to be possible. However, to accept that there are no sentences out there because there is no such thing as the world's own language, still

leaves everything to play for in the matter of determining a rigorous concept of truth that underpins the idea that possession of knowledge equals possession of the truth. The starting point of this book is the critique of the cosmic register, but it is a starting point that, if the argument of this book is correct, leaves truth, reason, knowledge and the self as legitimate concepts.

2 This issue has received an enormous amount of attention from philosophers. An early classic collection of articles concerned with the problems of cross-cultural understanding is B. Wilson (ed.), *Rationality* (Oxford: Blackwell, 1967). A later update on the debate is S. Lukes and M. Hollis, *Rationality and Relativism* (Oxford: Blackwell, 1978).

3 Rorty denies the charge of relativism, and with good reason. As noted in the introduction, relativism is a self-defeating position. In addition, Rorty cannot be a relativist who holds that truth is relative to culture, community or whatever, for he claims that there is no truth. That is why I think it is more helpful if we describe the extreme postmodernist threat as anti-rationalist. This helps to keep a focus on the requirement that we legitimise our notion of rationality. The requirement to produce such a legitimation arises if we agree with the postmodernist critique of the idea of rationality as an ahistorical faculty. For a contrasting approach to these problems and one that sees Rorty as simply a relativist, see R. Trigg, *Rationality and Science* (Oxford: Blackwell, 1994). Trigg's arguments, for the main part, criticise Rorty and others for their relativism and for making plain that the position Rorty adopts threatens what Trigg calls realism. However, I am not convinced that Trigg takes sufficiently seriously the need to legitimise the kind of realism he rightly thinks is threatened by postmodernism.

4 The Copernican revolution was a key stage in the history of science. For more on this, and on the general topic of the distinction between theory and observation, see A. F. Chalmers, *What is This Thing Called Science?* (Milton Keynes: Open University Press, 1982).

5 The point here that experience cannot force us to accept one theory or another is generally accepted. However, it does not mean that there are no decision methods for evaluating theories on the basis of experience. Many contemporary researchers in the philosophy of science are engaged in the attempt to specify the procedures that should be employed in providing support for theoretical claims on the basis of empirical results. For an accessible survey of issues involved in the attempt to map out a scientific method, see W. H. Newton-Smith, *The Rationality of Science* (London and Boston: Routledge, 1981, esp. ch. 9), or B. Skyrms, *Choice and Chance* (Belmont, Calif.: Wadsworth, 2nd edn, 1986). If any account of scientific method is successful, it will be an approach that assumes that the search for objective knowledge is possible. The current enterprise is concerned with legitimating that assumption. If the legitimation is successful, it is another matter what account, if any, we decide gives the best decision procedure for evaluating theories on the basis of experience.

6 The source for the voluminous debates about the Azande is E. Evans-Pritchard's book, *Witchcraft and Magic among the Azande* (Oxford: Clarendon Press, 1934). His work was brought to the attention of philosophers in a seminal article by P. Winch, 'Understanding primitive societies', in Wilson (ed.), *Rationality* (op. cit.).

7 The example of the chicken oracle I use in the text is taken from film of the Azande oracle used in the Channel 4 series, *The Real Thing*, broadcast in August 1992.

4 NOTHING IS CERTAIN, NOTHING IS KNOWN?

1 Popper built his whole epistemology on the idea of our fallibility. The fact that Popper took the acknowledgement of our fallibility as the heart of the knowledge-gathering process only shows that we will beg too many issues if we think that deep sceptical problems arise from the lack of foundations where that amounts to no more than an acceptance of our fallibility. Something more must be at stake for the lack-of-foundations issues to amount to anything serious. For a good introduction to Popper's views see D. Miller (ed.), *A Pocket Popper* (London: Fontana, 1983).

2 The definition of knowledge employed in the text, as a true belief that we hold because it corresponds with the facts, is only intended as a rough guide. There has been a considerable philosophical industry of attempts to provide a definition of knowledge that is not subject to counter-example. None of the definitions so far offered succeeds. For a good summary of different approaches see J. Dancy, *An Introduction to Contemporary Epistemology* (Oxford: Blackwell, 1985). Furthermore, there is an approach to the theory of knowledge which is quite different from that taken in the text. Naturalistic theories of knowledge treat human knowledge and belief formation as natural phenomena. As such, knowledge is to be studied in a manner that is continuous with the naturalistic scientific study of human beings and their relationships with the environment. On a naturalistic theory of knowledge, knowledge is a scientifically describable relationship that we bear to the world. Clearly, even if such a naturalistic account were right, an appeal to it here would miss the whole point of the postmodernist critique of the fragmentation of truth, rationality and self. Again, for details on such approaches see Dancy, op. cit., and also K. Lehrer, *Theory of Knowledge* (London and Boston: Routledge, 1990).

5 A WEB OF OUR OWN CONCEIT?

1 As previously argued, I suspect that Rorty's hostility to the concept of truth is no more than a hostility to the idea of the cosmic register and that is something that can be separated from what we say about truth. See the discussion in note 1, Chapter 3, for Rorty's views on truth as expressed in *Contingency, Irony and Solidarity*.

2 The sort of transcendental argument that I sketch in the text is becoming familiar in very recent work in the philosophy of thought and language. I believe that the more recent work by Donald Davidson can be represented in this way, even if he does not do so himself. Another source for such arguments is work done by philosophers within a tradition of theorising about thought that goes back to the German philosopher and mathematician Gottlob Frege. Very recent work in the neo-Fregean tradition by writers such as Gareth Evans, John McDowell and Christopher Peacocke offers examples of the kind of transcendental argument I offer. All this material is difficult and inaccessible. One way into such fields is via my *Contemporary Philosophy of Thought and Language* (Oxford: Blackwell, forthcoming).

3 Note that the argument in the text is an argument to legitimise simple truth. It is not intended to legitimise anything so contentious as metaphysical realism. The argument is derived from the work of Donald Davidson and David Wiggins, in particular Wiggins's work on the marks of truth (*Needs, Values, Truth: Essays in the Philosophy of Value*, Oxford: Blackwell, 1987). The minimalism of Wiggins's account of truth has been challenged by, among others, Crispin Wright (*Truth and Objectivity*, Cambridge, Mass.: Harvard University Press, 2nd edn, 1994). Wright complains that the sort of minimalist concept of truth that Wiggins defends does not support the realist view of true judgements latching on to a reality fixed independently of our thought and concepts. Just so, but I would not want simple truth to provide grounds for such a contentious notion. I suspect that Wright's concerns with simple truth are concerns premissed on the idea that truth must be that which fixes upon the world's own categories. But, if we have rejected the cosmic register imagery of the world's own story, we have no reason to suppose that the categories of the world are fixed independently of the way that we come to conceptualise our experience. However, to say this is not to say that the central concepts of object, space and time are ours in an idealistic sense. To think so is to work with a contrast between the world's own categories and human categories that presupposes the possibility of a metaphysical realism committed to the notion of the world's own story. In short, Wright's complaints amount, I suspect, to the presumption that without imagery of something like the cosmic register truth is not worth having. I think this begs the question.

4 For discussion of Descartes's attempt to find knowledge independent of a human perspective, see B. Williams, *Descartes* (London: Penguin, 1978). Williams's discussion of Descartes is not easy reading, but it is one of the most influential and important accounts of the Cartesian project in recent times. On certain key aspects I disagree with Williams's reconstruction of what Descartes was up to, but even so, anyone wanting to make a serious attempt to understand Descartes has to understand Williams.

5 It is significant that Locke appeared to have held a representative theory of experience. It is no surprise then that he also held that

colours were not real. The real properties of the tomato are, according to Locke, exhausted by its powers, including its power to produce red sense-data in us. However, Locke thought that the tomato's powers could be fully characterised with the primary qualities of shape, size, motion, etc. If this is right, then it is not Locke's distinction between primary and secondary qualities as such that delivers his view that colours are not real. That metaphysical claim flows from his theory of perception. I have discussed the ambiguities that plague so much discussion of these matters in my 'On the way the world is independently of the way we take it to be', *Inquiry*, 1989, vol. 32, pp. 177–94. The idea that it is Locke's theory of perception that does all the metaphysical work in stripping colour off the world has been acknowledged by, amongst others, B. Stroud in his John Locke lectures at Oxford in 1987.

6 The representative theory of experience is one of the key ideas that Rorty sees as problematic in much epistemology, in *Philosophy and the Mirror of Nature* (Oxford: Blackwell, 1980). I agree with him. However, he does not do justice to the scope for a direct theory of experience. I think there is a good explanation for this. Most philosophers who adopt a representative theory of experience do so because they think it is required in order to give an account of false and illusory experiences. For example, if I hallucinate a ripe tomato, something looks red, but there is no tomato there. Therefore, do I not need a red sense-datum in order to account for the hallucinatory experience? And then the simplest explanation will invoke the same intermediary item in the veridical experience too. However, the idea that representative intermediaries are required to make sense of illusions is simply an invalid claim. The phenomena of illusions and false perceptions do not entail the need for representative items like sense-data. To think that the phenomena do entail sense-data is to think that an account of experience must be an account of something that is common between veridical and illusory experiences. Many philosophers assume this, but it is unclear why we should make the assumption. If we also assume that we have infallible access to the character of our experiences so that they are transparent, then we will have a reason to assume that an account of experience is invariant between the veridical and illusory. However, it is now becoming common to question why we should assume that the character of our experiences should be thought transparent to us. And that then takes away the central assumption which is normally taken to force a representative theory of perception. These matters are contentious and still poorly understood. On the general issue of the reality of non-transparent descriptions of objects, colours, etc., see the essays in D. Charles and K. Lennon (eds), *Reduction, Explanation and Realism* (Oxford: Clarendon Press, 1992).

7 In places Rorty comes close to the sort of position I have described. For example, he does not want us to abandon doing science and he extols its virtues in *Contingency, Irony and Solidarity*. However, he never sees these virtues in cognitive terms rather than political

terms. He does not allow the sort of appeal to truth and knowledge for which I have argued.

6 WHOSE GAME IS IT ANYWAY?

1 Note the importance of the argument of Chapter 4: we do not require certainty in order to have knowledge. Contrariwise, if the demand for certainty is reinstated at this point in order to support an anti-rationalist version of postmodernism, then the threat has lost whatever force it might have had. If anti-rationalism can only be argued for on the basis of highly contentious speculative demands that certainty is a requirement of knowledge, it is far from clear that such an argument deserves serious consideration.

2 This is certainly the point of Rorty's version of liberalism and his promotion of the values of tolerance in *Contingency, Irony and Solidarity* (Cambridge: Cambridge University Press, 1989). However, Rorty's tolerance is not guided by any cognitive regulation in the name of truth. This means that although Rorty might applaud the apparently disinterested research in science and wish that we might transfer similar attitudes to other domains of enquiry, his liberalism can amount to no more than an invitation to experiment and develop theories and knowledge claims unfettered by the demands of truth and rationality. His liberalism must become an 'anything goes' methodology, for, at the end of the day, none of the forms of human enquiry can be, for Rorty, enquiries after truth. Lyotard's approval of the methodological tolerance of the scientific attitude surfaces in *The Postmodern Condition: A Report on Knowledge* (Manchester: Manchester University Press, 1984), section 16.

3 For a striking attempt to apply a strong form of sociological reductionism to science see B. Latour, *Laboratory Life: The Construction of Scientific Facts* (Princeton: Princeton University Press, 1986).

7 THE FRAGILITY OF KNOWLEDGE

1 In so far as I accept that the label 'analytic philosophy' designates a clearly identifiable tradition, I think it fair to say that analytic philosophers have been learning to live with Theses I–IV for quite some time now. Precisely because analytic philosophy has rarely conceded to a pretence to speculative general theories of everything, it has not particularly sought to speak the world's own story, nor been much fussed by the recognition that no such thing was available. Speculative metaphysics has not been so much the fashion in the Anglo-American tradition, and so neither has the deep sense of despair at its loss been keenly felt. In part, but only in part, this explains why the very label, let alone the options, of postmodernism has been addressed more earnestly by those working in what is sometimes dubbed the 'continental' tradition of philosophy: Lyotard, Baudrillard, Rorty. However, the labels are crude and divert attention from the real and

49

important points of crossover between writers who naturally refer to a different set of key texts. It would not be outlandish to think of Peter Strawson's advocacy of 'descriptive metaphysics' in *Individuals* (London: Methuen, 1959) as an Anglo-Saxon version of a Nietzschean 'God is Dead' position, in the sense that Strawson was there offering a description of the metaphysics we make do with (and the only one we can have) in the absence of the speculative pretence to read the cosmic register.

2 The case of Chinese herbal therapy is different again. Although it offers a good example of a rival system of diagnosis to western medicine, it also appears to offer a rival methodology to even critical empiricism. This is because traditional Chinese herbal therapy claims to treat patients as individuals and not as instances of a common type. The significance of this point is contentious, and there is insufficient evidence at present to support the thesis that such practices genuinely diverge from the methodology of repeatable testability of phenomena by their classification into repeatable types of events.

3 There is one case of knowledge-gathering that provides a counter-example to the idea that truth and knowledge should in principle be available to all. The case concerns the possibility of knowledge revealed to a chosen few by divine revelation. However, I am reluctant to concede much to the supposed existence of such cases. Suppose someone claims that he or some other person or group of persons has a privileged position because of being granted revelation of the truth. As a claim about the means by which someone accesses truth I can see no a priori objection to the possibility of revelation. However, if it is truth that has been revealed to this subject or group of subjects, they still have to acknowledge that the truth that they thereby access is a truth independent of judgement. The claimed existence of revelatory states is a claim about the epistemological access someone has to something that is still, like all truth, something that can obtain independently of judgement. That is to say, the advocate of revelation as a source of knowledge must still acknowledge the basic constraint of Chapter 1 – the truth/judgement distinction. Now, if the supposed possessor of revelatory knowledge is to acknowledge that the truth is independent of judgement, but is also to claim that he has a privileged access to truth that is unavailable to others, it is unclear that he can put any substance into the notion of the truth/judgement distinction. He claims that that to which he has revelatory access is truth and, as such, it is something that is independent of judgement. However, just because he and only he has access to it, there is no ready model to hand to say in what this distinction between truth and judgement consists. This means that the onus must lie on the advocate of revelation to show that he has succeeded in giving content to the truth/judgement distinction. It is this that I suspect is deeply problematic for such a position and it is for this reason that I remain sceptical of the possibility of knowledge by revelation.

8 WHO ARE WE?

1 The idea that gender is a contingent feature of self is perhaps surprising, but follows immediately from one popular way of trying to define the essence of a human, the method of defining the essence of an individual by its origin. Suppose that what makes me the person that I am is that I originate from one particular fertilised ovum rather than another. Then, given that the sex of the foetus is not determined until approximately the twelfth week of pregnancy, it must make sense to say that I might have been a woman.

2 The use of the analogy between colour concepts and evaluative concepts was employed to much effect by J. L. Mackie in his anti-objectivist tract *Ethics: Inventing Right and Wrong* (London: Penguin, 1977). The debate about the analogy both as a tool against objectivist theories of value and in favour of objectivist theories has flourished ever since. Two recent books cover much of the relevant ground: D. McNaughton, *Moral Vision* (Oxford: Blackwell, 1988) and J. Dancy, *Moral Realism* (Oxford: Blackwell, 1994). See also the papers in the collection *Explanation, Reduction and Realism*, ed. D. Charles and K. Lennon (Oxford: Clarendon Press, 1992).

3 It is claimed that the ancient Greeks would not have recognised a rigid distinction between logos (the way of truth) and pathos (the way of sensibility). This is why ancient accounts of morality have become fashionable in recent years in the attempt to construct a theory of morality which accommodates the idea that our sensibilities can be subject to truth. More of this in the next chapter, but see Alasdair MacIntyre's *After Virtue* (London: Duckworth, 1981) for a classic recent statement of the pervasive emotivism in modern moral philosophy and how this replaced an older, more unified conception of the moral subject combining both logos and pathos.

4 It was Hume who said that, in consideration of the claim that murder is a vice, we will not find the viciousness of the murder by looking at the facts in the world: 'There is no ... matter of fact in the case. The vice entirely escapes you, as long as you consider the object. You never can find it, till you turn your reflexion into your own breast, and find a sentiment of disapprobation, which arises in you, towards this action' (*Treatise of Human Nature*, book III, part 1, section 1). The interpretation of Hume has undergone some modification in recent years and it is possible that the position he describes is compatible with a form of cognitivism. However, on the traditional reading of Hume he is a non-cognitivist emotivist.

5 The whole issue of disagreement and the role of taste is complex. Even Hume seemed to allow that matters of aesthetic taste were subject to assessment and correction ('On the Standards of Taste', in his *Essays Moral, Political and Literary*). One should not then slip too easily into assuming a clear distinction between taste and cognition that fails to recognise the possibility of knowledge regarding matters of taste.

6 The repackaging of Rawls's theory began with an important article,

'Justice as fairness: political not metaphysical' (*Philosophy and Public Affairs*, 1985, vol. 14, no. 3), and has continued into *Political Liberalism* (New York: Columbia University Press, 1993). For further discussion of Rawls, A. Brown, *Modern Political Philosophy* (London: Penguin, 1986) is a good introductory level discussion of Rawls and other theories of justice. More advanced is S. Mulhall and A. Swift, *Liberals and Communitarians* (Oxford: Blackwell, 1992) which also covers material I shall address in the next chapter.

9 CITIZENS OF THE HERE AND NOW

1 For many postmodernist writers the dissolution of the self is a key feature of postmodernity, especially amongst French theorists. Here, as elsewhere, there is little coherence in the offerings made about the self. For example, J. Lyotard, in *The Postmodern Condition* (Manchester: Manchester University Press, 1984, p. 15), refers to J. Baudrillard's claim of the 'disintegration of social aggregates into a mass of individual atoms thrown into the absurdity of Brownian motion'. The Baudrillard claim still has individual entities, but they are no more than Brownian atoms. To this Lyotard responds: 'A self does not amount to much, but no self is an island; each exists in a fabric of relations that is now more complex and mobile than ever before. Young or old, man or woman, rich or poor, a person is always located at "nodal points" of specific communication circuits, however tiny these may be. Or better, one is always located at a post through which various kinds of messages pass' (ibid., p. 15). However, Lyotard's concept of a 'nodal point' fails to address the key question of whether there is anything worth calling a self that has an identity that survives through the passing of different messages. Indeed, on the very next page (p. 16), Lyotard develops the cybernetic image of selves as nodal points in nets of information transmissions and claims that the selves are 'displaced by the messages that traverse them' and that each node, on receiving a message, 'undergoes a "displacement", an alteration of some kind that not only affects him in his capacity as address and referent, but also as sender [of messages]'. It is not clear what we are supposed to make of this imagery, but the suspicion must be that, in place of the Brownian motion of atomic particles, Lyotard offers not a self as a nodal point, but the flexing of an informational web in which, at any point in time, nodes may be identified, but these nodes have no identity that survives the passing and referral of the messages that cross at that point. This then is a dissolution of the self. One or two writers have seen fit to celebrate the cybernetic imagery in the cause of the dissolution of the self, for example N. Land (*The Thirst for Annihilation*, London and Boston: Routledge, 1992), whose work is heavily influenced by G. Deleuze and F. Guartari. However, the position of these writers, although sometimes classified as postmodernists, depends on the prior and unargued-for acceptance of one of the oldest grand narratives of

all, namely, the idea that there is a single currency of description that will capture all that can be said about our world and our place (or non-place) within it. The only difference is that these writers pick on cybernetics as their grand narrative as opposed to the religious narratives of old. Far from being avant-garde, such an approach seems, to me, dated.

2 See A. Brown, *Modern Political Philosophy* (London: Penguin, 1986) for a clear discussion of utilitarianism. For a classic and concise account of the arguments for and against utilitarianism see J. J. C. Smart and B. Williams, *Utilitarianism: For and Against* (Cambridge: Cambridge University Press, 1973).

3 The distinction between prioritising the right over the good or the good over the right creates a classic problem for utilitarians – how to give an adequate account of the concepts of justice and rights if they take the primary measure of moral concern to be the production of the greatest good for the greatest number. Mill devotes Chapter 4 of his *Utilitarianism* to this problem but is generally thought to fail. For a succinct and rigorous statement of why utilitarians have such a problem giving content to our ordinary concerns for justice see A. Sen, *On Economic Inequality* (Oxford: Clarendon Press, 1972, ch. 1, esp. pp. 15–18). For more detail on what Mill's form of liberalism looks like see J. Skorupski, *Mill* (London and New York: Routledge, 1991) and for a defence of individual liberty that continues to demand the respect due to a classic, see Mill's *On Liberty*, available in a number of editions, the most accessible being in the Everyman collection, *Utilitarianism and Other Writings* (London: Dent, 1972).

M. Sandel's book, *Liberalism and the Limits of Justice* (Cambridge: Cambridge University Press, 1982) is the best example of a communitarian position. Other writers to whom the label has been affixed include A. MacIntyre, *After Virtue* (London: Duckworth, 1981) and *Whose Justice? Which Rationality?* (London: Duckworth, 1988); C. Taylor, *Sources of the Self* (Cambridge: Cambridge University Press, 1989); M. Walzer, *Spheres of Justice* (New York: Basic Books, 1983). There are important differences between the writers classed as communitarians and perhaps all that they really have in common is an opposition to the metaphysical individualism in modern liberal theory exemplified in Rawls. Some of the differences will be noted below. For a useful recent study of the debate between liberal and communitarian see S. Mulhall and A. Swift, *Liberals and Communitarians* (Oxford: Blackwell, 1992). For a more general and very accessible background to options in political philosophy try A. Brown, *Modern Political Philosophy* (op. cit.).

4 Sandel, op. cit., p. 179.

5 See Charles Taylor's *Sources of the Self* (op. cit.) for an account of the self that holds that it is a necessary precondition of any tenable account of the self that it conceive of the self as having an 'orientation to the good'. This phrase is ambiguous between the two positions I identify in the text. It is not clear if Taylor means only that a self must have the capacity to orientate to the good or that it must be

so orientated. I suspect that Taylor would favour the latter, in part because of his particular theory of the good. Taylor believes that any credible theory of good must be founded upon a theory of hyper-goods that, by the end of Taylor's book, turn out to be goods with an ineliminable religious component. This I find incredible. For a fine short review of Taylor's rich and suggestive book see J. B. Schnee-wind's review in *The Journal of Philosophy*, 1991, vol. lxxxviii, pp. 422–26.

6 A central problem in the literature on communitarianism is the threat of totalitarianism. This is well expressed in Amy Gutman's essay, 'Communitarian critics of liberalism' (*Philosophy and Public Affairs*, 1985, vol. 14). As she says, 'A great deal of intolerance has come from societies of selves so "confidently situated" that they were sure repression would serve a higher cause. . . . The enforcement of liberal rights, not the absence of settled community, stands between the Moral Majority and the contemporary equivalent of witchhunting.' I prefer to see this particular political threat as an instance of a more general worry addressed in the text. That is to say, it is only because communitarianism threatens the loss of the cognitive control and evaluation of our beliefs that political totalitarianism becomes an option. It is an option because, on the communitarian position, there is, as it were, nowhere to step back to in order to evaluate the beliefs that tradition hands down to us. In that case, we can do no more than acquiesce in those beliefs and will have no recourse to complaint as the traditional beliefs are inculcated in the name of our community's presumed superior vision.

7 Again, see the Gutman article (op. cit.) for observations on the inappropriateness of assimilating our moral and political obligations to the sorts of relationships that obtain in very small social groups like the family. See also Mulhall and Swift (op. cit.).

8 Of course, the whole point of Rorty's version of political liberalism is to advocate a politics of solidarity in which the point of that word is to stress the non-cognitivist nature of our moral and political attachments. Rorty believes that moral and political discourse is not to be understood as engaged in a debate of reasons and knowledge. Rather, he likens such discourse to poetry. We try to influence each other in our moral and political talk, but the influence is not the influence of the giving of reasons; it is the influence of poetic imagery, of getting people to feel like us rather than getting them to believe with us in things that are candidates for objective truth and falsity. The general inadequacy of Rorty's approach in making sense of moral disagreement is, I take it, obvious. On Rorty's account, the Prot-estants and Catholics of Northern Ireland, the Serbs and Muslims of Bosnia, the Hutus and Tutsis of Rwanda are not in disagreement about real issues of right and wrong; they merely suffer from a clash of poetic imaginations! It is no accident that the title of Rorty's *Contingency, Irony and Solidarity* (Cambridge: Cambridge University Press, 1989) carries no terms of cognitive evaluation. On the inad-equacy of poetry as a model for personhood see the essay by Martin

Hollis, 'The poetics of personhood', in A. Malachowski (ed.), *Reading Rorty* (Oxford: Blackwell, 1991). There are a number of excellent essays in this collection, namely those by C. Taylor, D. Fischer and B. Williams. A more general bibliography on postmodernism and the political would include: S. K. White, *Political Theory and Postmodernism* (Cambridge: Cambridge University Press, 1991); Agnes Heller, *Can Modernity Survive?* (Cambridge: Polity Press, 1990); D. Harvey, *The Conditions of PostModernity* (Oxford: Blackwell, 1989); T. Docherty (ed.), *Postmodernism: A Reader* (Brighton: Harvester, 1993), which includes Rorty's essay, 'Postmodernist bourgeois liberalism'.

9 The point accepted in the text, that we need to supply some account of the in-principle detachability of ends, underpins the political argument for pluralism. It is because of our general fallibility that we need to be able to detach our ends. It is because of this fallibility that we need to acknowledge, in principle, a pluralistic approach to the determination of the ends of human life. Pluralism about the ends of human life is the only defendable epistemological position. However, it does not follow from this that we should endorse the sort of metaphysical pluralism about ends that results in relativism. One of the central political imperatives is to cope with pluralism without, at the same time, endorsing the extreme liberalism that refuses to criticise the beliefs of others. Criticism has to be the only viable tool in the evaluation of our beliefs and those of others. Totalitarianism is the institutional enforcement of a uniformity in belief. The kind of pluralism we need in order to confront totalitarianism is not a pluralism that institutionally enforces difference in belief and elevates difference to the status of an institutional defence of the right to believe anything at all about human ends. The pluralism we need is a pluralism that encourages criticism of belief. That much is surely uncontentious and would be in accord with Rawls's political defence of his position based upon the need for pluralism (J. Rawls, *Political Liberalism*, New York: Columbia University Press, 1993). The difference between Rawls's pluralism and mine lies in the repertoire of resources with which we provide people for engaging in the determination of and critique of human ends. Rawls's conception remains extraordinarily thin and does not do justice to the thought that there may be a political dimension to the provision of resources, over and above that determined by the original position, necessary for us to acquire the rational agency that puts us in search of worthwhile conceptions of human ends. This leaves scope for the thought that there may be good reason for not tolerating some belief systems. For example, religious belief systems that withhold from agents or groups of agents the wherewithal to engage in the crique of beliefs should not be tolerated. There is no good reason, in the name of pluralism, to tolerate religious systems that systematically oppress women or other identifiable groups in society.

10 See Iris Marion Young, *Justice and the Politics of Difference* (Princeton: Princeton University Press, 1990) for an account of justice with which I have much sympathy. Like me she wants to acknowledge that

there are issues concerning justice that turn not on the distribution of possessions but on matters of ontology, on what kind of entity we conceive ourselves to be. In addition, she also acknowledges that we should not prioritise the good over the right. In so far as her position is a kind of communitarian position it is distinct from the communitarianism found in Sandel.

11 Heidegger has a long discussion on the nature of belonging. It is, however, suffused with a heady mix of his complex speculative metaphysics. Although there is doubtless a case to be made for the similarities and analogies between the approach that I develop and a Heideggerian position, I have not pursued the point.

12 The simple and melodramatic way in which I present the difficulties faced by the concept of mercantile belonging are characteristic of contractarian arguments in moral and political philosophy in which relationships and duties are grounded in contracts based on self-interest. The general problem is that if our contracts/relationships are grounded in self-interest, we have no reason to honour them once our interest is no longer protected. The most famous example of this difficulty is Hobbes's attempt to base the notion of political obligation to the state/sovereign on the preservation of self-interest. As Hobbes famously concluded (writing just after the English Civil War), our obligation to the sovereign lapses if the sovereign state fails in its duty to offer protection to its citizens. Despite its age, C. B. Macpherson's *Possessive Individualism* (Oxford: Clarendon Press, 1962) is still a rewarding study of this problem in Hobbes and in general.

13 This problem is the problem of legitimation referred to in the previous chapter (section 4) in another guise. It is a problem about how to account for our sense of obligation towards others if the only basis for such notions is the contractual one defined in terms of the satisfaction of our self-interests. Notwithstanding the presentation of this problem in the text, many writers pursue a contractarian approach in ethics. A good example of such an approach is D. Gauthier, *Morals by Agreement* (Oxford: Clarendon Press, 1986).

10 THE MAKING OF OUR SELVES

1 The idea that moral cognitivism is even so much as coherent, let alone a tenable option, may strike some as extraordinarily avant-garde. Although the possibility of moral cognitivism has been a lively matter of debate among professional philosophers for nearly twenty years, outside the profession the influence of the non-cognitivism of much of this century's account of morality stills holds sway. A good recent survey of the prospects of moral cognitivism is David McNaughton, *Moral Vision* (Oxford: Blackwell, 1988). A very important collection of essays with which I have much sympathy is David Wiggins, *Needs, Values, Truth: Essays in the Philosophy of Value* (Oxford: Blackwell, 1987).

In part, the current preparedness of many philosophers to counten-

ance the possibility of moral cognitivism is a function of a more
general turning aside from the limited positivist metaphysics of earlier
generations. The general drift here is the drift away from the restricted physicalist and naturalistic metaphysics that charactised the positivism of the Vienna Circle and A. J. Ayer, and the scientism of
leading American philosophers such as W. van O. Quine. As already
mentioned in the notes to earlier chapters, the collection *Reduction,
Explanation and Realism* (ed. D. Charles and K. Lennon, Oxford:
Clarendon Press, 1992) usefully plots a number of the issues involved
in the proliferation of non-physicalist and non-naturalist explanatory
frameworks.

Note that physicalism and naturalism are separate doctrines. Naturalism is the view that all phenomena can be explained in the methodologies and languages of the natural sciences. Physicalism is the more
restricted view that all explanations of the natural sciences can be
reduced to physical explanations – explanations of physics. Naturalism thus allows that there might be forms of explanation and modes
of description that are peculiar to the special sciences and refuse
regimentation in the mould of physical explanations. For more on
the varieties and forms of explanation, see David-Hillel Ruben,
Explaining Explanation (London: Routledge, 1992).

2 My thinking on these issues owes an enormous debt to the work of
David Wiggins. See especially the essay 'Truth as predicated of moral
judgements' in his *Needs, Values, Truth* (op. cit.). For an extended
discussion on the concept of truth and of its central characteristics,
see my *Contemporary Philosophy of Thought and Language* (Oxford:
Blackwell, forthcoming), especially chapters 2–4.

3 The standard response to this is to say that the explanations provided
by physics possess a generality that explanations that appeal to colour
properties do not. If we explain our judging that tomatoes are red
in terms of the physical structure of the tomato rather than its colour,
then we get an explanation that brings the phenomenon within the
same broad explanatory scheme as most other things that occur in
the world. The explanation by physical properties invokes properties
with 'wide cosmological role'; that is, physical properties crop up in
all kinds of explanation whereas colour properties, at best, occur only
in a very limited range of explanations. But note that this response
depends on the very same assumption that we keep on meeting,
namely, the assumption that there is one uniform explanatory framework capable of subsuming the whole of creation. We have seen
reason to reject this in earlier chapters and so it is wholly unclear
why we should be worried that colour properties lack a wide cosmological role. That fact is obvious and is constitutive of their being non-
absolute properties. They are properties that can only be accessed via
the perspectives of particular kinds of creatures. There is now a lively
debate among philosophers about the viability of the idea of the
proliferation of explanatory frameworks that I have been employing
at key points in my argument. Suffice it to say that the presumption
against proliferation is now more frequently challenged than it ever

used to be. Again, perhaps the most useful collection on these issues is Charles and Lennon (eds), *Reduction, Explanation and Realism* (op. cit.). Taking the matter deeper, there is a large literature on the status of colour, the analogy between colour and values, and on the central issue of what constitutes factual discourse. Crispin Wright has written extensively on all these matters (*Realism, Meaning and Truth*, Oxford: Blackwell, 1987; and *Truth and Objectivity*, Cambridge, Mass.: Harvard University Press, 2nd edn, 1994).

4 The distinction that I mark in the text between the independence of truth and the independence of conception is basic to the whole enterprise of this book. Until recently it was a distinction that went largely unnoticed and many philosophers seemed to assume that the search for truth was *ipso facto* the search for the absolute conception, the conception of the world independent of human concerns. For example, see B. Williams, *Descartes* (London: Penguin, 1978) in which Williams identifies the search for knowledge (truth) with the search for the absolute conception. Williams now acknowledges the distinction between objective truth and absolute conception and the idea that we could have the former without the latter. See my 'On the way the world is independently of the way we take it to be' (*Inquiry*, 1989, vol. 32, pp. 177–94) for a clarification of the different distinctions that can be confused in this area. See also, for example, C. Taylor, *Sources of the Self* (Cambridge: Cambridge University Press, 1989), esp. ch. 3, 'The ethics of inarticulacy', for recognition of the distinction between independence of truth and independence of conception.

5 C. Taylor, *Sources of the Self* (Cambridge: Cambridge University Press), 1989, p. 44.

6 *Needs, Values, Truth: Essays in the Philosophy of Value* (op. cit.), pp. 255–6. I cannot recommend Wiggins's book too highly. It contains some of the most dense and detailed, but also most illuminating, discussions of the nature of our moral life available in contemporary philosophy. It is not an easy read, but it is richly rewarding.

7 Apologies to Alasdair MacIntyre, but the point is precisely that the scenario with which he opened *After Virtue* (London: Duckworth, 1981, ch. 1) fixes on the wrong model of moral knowledge, a propositional model.

8 The issues briefly referred to in the text are complex and contentious. One aspect of the new paradigm that I refer to is the development of connectionist models of cognition. These are models which treat cognitive processes not as symbol manipulation, but as trained skills that are implemented on massively parallel computer systems rather than the linear systems of a digital computer. There are a number of good books about this work. See, for example, W. Bechtel and A. Abrahamsen, *Connectionism and the Mind* (Oxford: Blackwell, 1991). A leading advocate of this approach is Andy Clark, *Associative Engines* (Cambridge, Mass.: MIT Press, 1994). For many researchers connectionism is a heresy – see especially J. Fodor's work, for example *Psychosemantics* (Cambridge, Mass.: MIT Press, 1987).

Another development is the work of Gerald Edelman, *Neural Darwinism* (New York: Basic Books, 1987). Edelman goes further than the connectionist model in advocating a developmental training approach to robotics. Note that none of these developments denies that one day we might be able to build an artificial intelligence, a smart robot. The issue concerns only what has to be done in order to achieve this. The developments referred to emphasise that the task will be achieved not by building a complex symbol cruncher, but by building a system with the ability to experience, explore and develop its sense of being in the environment. Research in what has become known as situated robotics acknowledges that although cognitive functions must be subject to a compositional analysis, the analysis is not of symbol strings but of actions in the world. Some of this work is reported in F. Varella, E. Thompson and E. Rosch (eds), *The Embodied Self* (Cambridge, Mass.: MIT Press, 1993). See the discussion of Brooks at pp. 208–212.

Another line of work pushing in the same direction is that of the philosopher H. Dreyfus (*What Computers Can't Do*, New York: Harper & Row, 1979). Also, very recent work in the neo-Fregean tradition of the philosophy of thought and language emphasises the contextual embedding in the real world of many of the kinds of thoughts that are central to our sense of self. J. Campbell, *Past, Space, Self* (Cambridge, Mass.: MIT Press, 1994) is a fine example of this approach. For more general background on this, see my *Contemporary Philosophy of Thought and Language* (op. cit.).

9 I extrapolate from the idea of using the concept of a feel for the game as deployed by Pierre Bourdieu, *The Logic of Practice* (Stanford: Stanford University Press 1990), to make a similar point. See my critical study of this book, 'Practice makes knowledge?', *Inquiry*, vol. 35, 1992, pp. 447–61.

10 David Sudnow, *Ways of the Hand* (originally published by Routledge, 1978; reprinted Bradford Books, Cambridge, Mass.: MIT Press, 1993), p. 152.

11 For those unfamiliar with the metaphysics of the Australian aborigines, Bruce Chatwin's *The Songlines* (London: Jonathan Cape, 1987) is a stunning guide.

12 Interview broadcast on Channel 4 in April 1994; transcript published by Channel 4 Television, p. 5.

13 For example, the study by Cambridge economist David Dickinson, widely reported in the British press, showed a marked correlation between patterns of young male unemployment and burglary through the 1980s (*Guardian*, 7 January 1994). Studies on the effects of Headstart programmes in the US show that delinquency goes down 25–30 per cent for those young Americans who benefit from such investment. See C. S. Wisdom, 'The intergenerational transmission of violence' in N. Weiner and M. Wolfgang (eds), *Pathways to Criminal Violence* (California: Sage, 1989). These examples are mere pointers and on their own prove little. The point, however, is that on the

model of moral knowledge I have sketched, such studies have much more scope for significance than on propositional models of moral knowledge.

Index of names